COACH

ALSO BY KEITH DUNNAVANT

Time Out!: A Sports Fan's Dream Year (with Edgar Welden)

The Fifty-Year Seduction

COACH

The Life of Paul "Bear" Bryant

Keith Dunnavant

Thomas Dunne Books
St. Martin's Griffin ≈ New York

To my father

Robert Dunnavant, Sr.,

who taught me to dream.

THOMAS DUNNE BOOKS.
An imprint of St. Martin's Press.

COACH. Copyright © 1996, 2005 by Keith Dunnavant. All rights reserved. Printed in the United States of America. No part of this book may be used or reproduced in any manner whatsoever without written permission except in the case of brief quotations embodied in critical articles or reviews. For information, address St. Martin's Press, 175 Fifth Avenue, New York, N.Y. 10010.

Design by Bonni Leon-Berman

www.stmartins.com

Library of Congress Cataloging-in-Publication Data

Dunnavant, Keith.
    Coach : the life of Paul "Bear" Bryant / Keith Dunnavant.
        p. cm.
    Includes index (p. 356)
    ISBN 0-312-34876-2
    EAN 978-0-312-34876-2
    1. Bryant, Paul W. 2. Football coaches—United States—Biography.
3. University of Alabama—Football—History. I. Title.

GV939.B79D86 1996
796.332'092—dc20
[B]

                                    96-28989
                                            CIP

First published in the United States by Simon & Schuster Inc.

First St. Martin's Griffin Edition: September 2005

10 9 8 7 6 5 4 3 2 1

Contents

Acknowledgments

This book, originally published in 1996, probably started growing inside me in the early 1970s, when I was just another devoted young fan of Paul "Bear" Bryant's Crimson Tide. Growing up in the wonderful Tennessee Valley town of Athens, Alabama, I was exposed to the Bryant legend at an early age. Although I didn't know it at the time, the late John Forney, the longtime play-by-play voice of the Crimson Tide, was preparing me for this task during those memorable Wishbone years. So were my favorite sportswriters of the day. I can remember racing home from elementary school to devour the sports pages of *The Huntsville Times*, especially the columns of the paper's gifted sports editor, John Pruett. And I can remember riding my bike uptown just so I could buy the Birmingham papers and see what Alf Van Hoose and Bill Lumpkin had to say on the subject of the Crimson Tide. Those first-rate journalists formed the foundation of my understanding of Bryant and college football.

Not too many years later, I started covering Alabama and Auburn football and other sports as a teenage sportswriter, first for a weekly newspaper in my hometown, *The Journal*, and later for *The Decatur Daily* and *Huntsville News*. At that time, of course, I had no thoughts of writing a book on the man who seemed larger than life to us all. I was more concerned with passing algebra. But that period laid the foundation for this work, and I will forever owe a debt of gratitude to those who helped me during those formative years, especially Helen Stagner, Billy Mitchell, and Lee Woodward.

My early experience led to a full scholarship—first arranged by Bryant and his sports information director—as a student assistant in the Alabama athletic department, which allowed me to work my way through college. It's doubtful that this book would exist if not for the people who believed in me then, giving me the chance to grow as a writer while learning about college athletics from the inside.

No work of this magnitude would be possible without the

cooperation and assistance of a large number of people. Dozens of Bryant's friends, relatives, rivals, former players, and former staff contributed their time, passion, and candor to these pages. Some had never spoken publicly about the man. While they are too numerous to list individually, each has my sincere gratitude.

I would also like to thank my many friends in the University of Alabama athletic department for their help with this project, especially Larry White, Steve Townsend, Tommy Ford, Brenda Burnette, Barry Allen, Barbara Butler, Wayne Atcheson, and Ann Baron. Also, thanks to the staff of the Paul W. Bryant Museum, particularly Taylor Watson, Clem Gryska, and Ken Gaddy. My former agent, Ed Novak, deserves credit for encouraging this project three years before it finally materialized, and my current agent, David Black, has my thanks for his role in helping make this new edition possible.

Two talented and dedicated editors helped me shape this book: Jeff Neuman of Simon & Schuster, which originally published this book in hardcover, and for this subsequent edition, Pete Wolverton of the Thomas Dunne imprint of St. Martin's Press. Both men pushed me to make this book better, and I will always be grateful for their significant contributions.

Bryant's 1974 autobiography—*Bear: The Hard Life and Good Times of Alabama's Coach Bryant*, which he wrote with *Sports Illustrated* veteran John Underwood—was an invaluable resource. And so was *The Legend of Bear Bryant*, an entertaining and informative book written by Bryant friend Mickey Herskowitz.

I would like to take the opportunity to thank my friends and family members, especially my parents and my brothers—Tom, Ron, and Jim—for their unwavering support during the writing of this book. My oldest brother, Bob Jr., died suddenly while I was writing *Coach* in 1995. In addition to his standing as a first-rate journalist in his own right who taught me so much by example, Bob was my most ardent supporter, and I could not have written this book without acknowledging his significant influence on this book and my writing career.

Fordyce

ON THE MORNING OF DECEMBER 29, 1982, Paul "Bear" Bryant leaned back on the sofa in his hotel suite and stared out the fourteenth-floor window overlooking the Mississippi River. For a moment, he seemed lost in the distance. A dozen men clutching notepads and pens waited for him to speak, the silence broken only by the muffled sounds of *The Young and the Restless* emanating from the bedroom television set, which someone had forgotten to turn off. He was dressed in a red sport coat, blue shirt, and gray slacks, and a steady trail of smoke flowed from the unfiltered Chesterfield cigarette dangling from his lips. On the day of the final game of his epic coaching career, Bryant's sixty-nine-year-old face was a sea of wrinkles and sadness, and his usually vibrant, piercing eyes reflected his melancholy mood.

"I remember the first time I came to Memphis," he mumbled to the small group of reporters, launching into a memory nearly sixty years old, of the day when he had hitchhiked from his home in Fordyce, Arkansas, to the banks of the big river. "So long ago . . ."

Two weeks after declaring Alabama's Liberty Bowl date against Illinois as his final game on the sidelines, the winningest coach in college football history arrived in Memphis as an American folk hero who seemed larger than the game, larger than life. Calling him a football coach seemed inadequate, like referring to Frank Sinatra as a pop singer. The Bear's presence demanded adjectives and bold type. In Memphis as in other southern cities and towns, he could not walk down the street without being mobbed. He was like a rock star or a monarch, but he was also a tired old man in failing health, and although he didn't want to quit the game, he knew the time had come.

Several hours after this impromptu gathering, the Bear was late for a pregame meeting with key members of his staff at the team hotel. Sam Bailey, his longtime aide, who knew more than he wanted to know about the details of Bryant's health, started worrying. His boss was a stickler for punctuality. Bailey feared the worst.

After searching throughout the hotel without success, Bailey happened to walk by a darkened ballroom on the first floor. He opened the door just a crack and saw his boss sitting all alone behind the head table, staring past all the empty chairs and into the darkness with a faraway look in his eyes. Football had transformed the Bear from impoverished and insecure to wealthy and beloved. It had been his life. The old man knew more than a career was ending that night. He knew that something inside him was about to die.

Around the turn of the century, Wilson Monroe Bryant migrated from Georgia to rural Arkansas, where he met his future wife, Ida Mae Kilgore, in church. Like many southerners of the time, the Bryants lived a life virtually untouched by the progress experienced in the industrial cities of the North. Much like their ancestors, who had blazed a trail through the American wilderness, Ida and Monroe and their nine children lived off the land and struggled against the elements to survive. They were simple people, sustained by their faith, hard-working, thrifty, and self-reliant. Monroe, a large man with a scrubby mustache and a distant, somewhat melancholy disposition, was the son of poor Georgia farmers. The couple settled on a small patch of land in a sparsely populated area between the hamlets of Fordyce and Kingsland, where the acres were cheap, plentiful, and unforgiving. The area was not marked on any map, but the Bryants and the half-dozen other families scattered among two or three square miles called their community Moro Bottom, for its proximity to Moro Creek.

Their domicile was more a shack than a house. A plank wood structure with a front porch running the length of the house and a wooden swing hanging by chains at one end, it consisted of four rooms: a kitchen with a fireplace used for heating and cooking; the parents' bedroom; a children's bedroom; and a living area called the "big room," where some of the children also slept on pallets. They supported themselves by growing vegetables and raising chickens and hogs; they had no electricity, telephone, or indoor plumbing, but no one ever went to bed hungry or felt deprived of love.

Ida Bryant was a sturdy woman with long, prematurely graying hair. Friends and family members described her as a woman of unusual determination and resourcefulness. "Miss Ida was always a lady, but she was as tough as a sack of nails," said her nephew, Dean Kilgore. In an era when women's suffrage was the most divisive political issue, she was the dominant figure in the Bryant clan. While most of the children were still school age or younger, Monroe fell ill and was rendered a semi-invalid for the rest of his life. Unable to endure the kind of physically taxing work a family farm required, he mostly sat around the house. The illness may not have been purely physical: One night, after a big rain, Ida discovered Monroe missing from their bed, and after an exhaustive search, he was found sitting in a large mud puddle in the middle of the road that ran alongside the house. He couldn't explain why he was sitting in a puddle of water in the middle of the night. Some of the neighbors and townsfolk who didn't know any better believed he was lazy, and that became a burden for his youngest son. After he became ill, Ida took charge of the farm and was, in all but ceremonial functions, the head of the family.

Their faith was a powerful anchor for the Bryants. Before Paul was born, Ida had served for a short time as a lay preacher at Smith's Chapel down the road toward Kingsland. That a woman was allowed to enter the pulpit in such a fundamentalist environment was a testament to the respect she enjoyed from her friends and neighbors. Every night after dinner and chores, the children gathered around their parents in the "big room" and listened, under the glow of a kerosene lamp, as Ida read a passage from the Bible. As far as the children could remember, the Bible was the only book their parents ever kept in the house. The Bryants believed so fervently in the strict teachings of the Church of God that they considered it sinful to seek medical treatment. Monroe's mysterious illness lingered for at least fifteen years without a doctor's care until he died in 1931 at the age of forty-six with what was believed to be a case of pneumonia.

"Mother and Daddy believed if you had enough faith you didn't need a doctor," said Louise Goolsby, the Bryants' tenth child. "Well, Paul just couldn't understand that. He thought his father suffered and died needlessly."

Born on September 11, 1913—the year then-unknown Notre Dame used a new weapon called the forward pass to upset football powerhouse Army—Paul was the eleventh of twelve children. Ida never consulted a doctor during her pregnancies or the ensuing births. After delivering a child in her own bed, she usually returned to the fields within a few days. Three of her children died as infants. From oldest to youngest, the surviving children were Barney, Orie, Harlie, Jack, Ouida, Kathryn, Louise, Paul, and Frances.

The working day on the farm started before dawn, when Ida lit a lamp and walked around the small house waking her children, who slept two and three to a bed. There were cows to be milked, hogs to be slopped, water to be pumped from the well. At first light some headed for the fields to plow or pick, while others trudged off to school. It was grueling, back-breaking work, and as much as he hated it, Paul learned the value of hard work and sacrifice at an early age.

A mama's boy who hung on her every word, Paul was shameless in pursuit of Ida's attention. The special bond between Ida and her youngest son may have been cemented when he was about four years old. After he had misbehaved one night during the Bible reading, Monroe pulled down the boy's pants and started whipping his naked butt with a long wooden paddle with a hole in it. The boy cried and cried, and Monroe kept on whipping him until Ida, who was standing nearby with the other children, thought he had crossed a line; fearing for her son, she pulled Monroe off Paul and told him never to hit another child of hers like that again. The boy's father dropped the paddle and walked away. The challenge to his authority as the man of the house enraged and embarrassed Monroe, and his relationship with his wife and children was never quite the same. From that point on, Ida handled all the discipline. Paul was a mischievous boy who always seemed to be trying his parents' patience—he once created a community scandal by stealing watermelons from a neighbor's garden—and Ida was not one to spare the rod on him or any of their other children; when one of the children misbehaved, she pulled out her plum tree switch and got busy. But her discipline was always tempered by her memories of Monroe's whipping.

By the time he was six or seven, Paul's brothers were mostly grown up and were leaving to make their own homes, so as the only remaining son he was responsible for feeding the mules and hitching them to the family's wagon every morning before breakfast. During the week, he and his sisters would drive the wagon to the one-room schoolhouse three miles down the dirt road in Kingsland, a town of some nine hundred souls that was really just a larger collection of small dirt farms. The trip required crossing Moro Creek, which was no simple task after a big rain. In fact, Jack Bryant, who fancied himself a shrewd businessman, kept a team handy to pull the occasional wagon or automobile out of the drink—for a reasonable price. During the bitterly cold winters, when the creek sometimes froze solid, Paul and his sisters would heat bricks in the fireplace and sit on them during the trip to Kingsland to keep from freezing. On Saturdays throughout the year, Paul and his mother would load the wagon with vegetables, butter, milk, and eggs and head for Fordyce to peddle the homegrown merchandise door-to-door.

Years later, whenever a writer referred to Fordyce as Bryant's hometown, he always made a point of emphasizing that Moro Bottom, which wasn't a town at all, held that distinction. This was his way of saying he never forgot those unhappy Saturdays. Fordyce was a town of about thirty-six hundred people in the early 1920s. Its downtown included two general stores, a movie theater, a train station, a hotel, a dry goods store, and a livery stable, among other points of interests. In those days, the children of Fordyce attended school until noon on Saturday. Invariably, Paul and his mother would wind up in front of the school about the time the boys and girls were dismissed. There was always a group of more prosperous "city" boys and girls waiting to tease the poor boy from the "country." They made fun of his dusty old overalls, his bare feet, the way he talked, that beat-up wagon, and those tired old mules; they ridiculed the fact that he was so poor that he had to go around with his mother scraping for enough pennies to buy those things they couldn't raise on the farm. In time, he and his mother moved on through town and past the hateful voices, but he knew they would be there when he and his mother came through the next Saturday, and the Saturday after that. At a vulnerable, impressionable time in his life, when his self-image was shaped by the way others saw him, those children had the power to make him feel inferior.

"I can pass that school now and hear those voices," Bryant wrote in his 1974 autobiography, *Bear*, with John Underwood. "I still remember the ones that did it."

Years later, when he was the very embodiment of his profession, Bryant often was asked what motivated him to succeed. "I didn't want to have to go back behind that plow . . . or peddling through Fordyce with my mama," he would say. "I was motivated by the fear of having to go back to that more than anything else."

Those Saturday encounters helped shape the insecure boy's evolution as a man. They fostered his feelings of inferiority, which infused him with an intense need for attention and acceptance and, for a while, made him an angry young man. But those encounters also lit a fire inside him. It seems clear that his incredible ambition was driven not merely by the desire to break free from a cycle of poverty, but also by the need to prove something to himself and all those voices of doubt that rang in his head. Like many men with weak fathers, he was driven by a determination to be strong.

"There were people who thought they were better than Paul,

and I don't think you ever get over that," said his sister Louise. "He was never ashamed of where he came from or having been poor, but he never forgot the ones who belittled him and our mother. He was determined to show them he was made of something special."

When Paul and his mother finished their rounds, they drove the wagon over to the Kilgore Brothers general store on Main Street. Ida's brother, who owned the store and a hotel across the street and was considered their rich relative, would buy the rest of her vegetables as a favor and treat her to a good meal. Paul was so bashful and so self-conscious about his table manners, he didn't want to go to the restaurant with his mother, so she let him buy a hunk of cheese and a handful of soda crackers and walk two blocks south to the railroad station to watch the afternoon train rumble through town. There was a water pump at the livery stable next door for when he got thirsty, as he always did after devouring his cheese and crackers. From the top of an old boxcar, he could see the courthouse clock; at four o'clock, he would head back to the wagon to help his mother load the supplies she had bought and head for home. Until then, he could dream about becoming a railroad man and riding one of those trains out of town for good.

When the older boys came of age and started moving away, the Bryants hired a man to help around the farm. Mr. Dukes was a big, strong man in his forties who had his mind set on winning the affections of a teenage farm girl down the road. When he wasn't busy riding past the girl's house and enduring the wrath of her father, Dukes became an uncle of sorts to the youngest Bryant son. Bryant later credited the farmhand with teaching him the facts of life and how to cuss, among other skills. "He would teach me a few words, then he'd go tell Mama and she'd whip me," Bryant said. Though he never said so, it seems clear that Dukes was more of an influence on him than his own father.

As a timid young boy, Bryant believed in the existence of ghosts and goblins. He was extremely fearful of graveyards and tombstones, especially the century-old marker that stood no more than fifty feet from their back door. Whenever he walked on that side of the farm, Paul always cut a wide swath around the grave, as if its inhabitant might rise up out of the ground and drag him under, as in one of his brother Jack's scary stories. One night when Jack was a teenager and Paul was six or seven, Jack told Paul he would give him thirty-five cents to walk up to the grave and slap the tombstone. Naturally, Paul was scared, but thirty-five cents was thirty-five cents; in those days a man would work all day in the fields to make fifty cents, so thirty-five cents was a lot of money for a poor boy with no dependents.

After working up his courage, Paul accepted the challenge and walked slowly toward the grave as Jack watched. He was scared, but he just kept thinking about that thirty-five cents, which bought an awful lot of courage in those days. Just as he reached down to slap the gravestone, he saw something covered in white rise up from behind the stone. With a look of utter terror on his face, Paul started running for the house. He didn't stop to get the ghost's name. He just ran.

On the way back to the house, he slipped. So complete was his fright that instead of taking the time to get up off his knees, he simply crawled the rest of the way home. Later, of course, he learned that the ghost he thought he had seen had really been Mr. Dukes under a white sheet. Jack and the farmhand enjoyed quite a laugh over their little prank. But Paul got the last laugh: When their mother found out about the stunt, she made Jack give him the thirty-five cents.

The old Bryant homestead was demolished decades ago, but the gravestone remains on the edge of the woods near the modern brick home owned by small businessman Ray Bryant, Jack's grandson and Paul's great-nephew. The few people who live in Moro Bottom now mostly work in nearby Fordyce, or twenty miles away in Warren. Moro Creek, once a barrier too deep for some wagons and early cars to traverse, now is crossed by a bridge so small as to go totally unnoticed by most motorists. After inheriting the old farmland from his family, Ray Bryant erected a large wooden sign that proclaims Moro Bottom, "Birthplace of Paul Bear Bryant." Occasionally, a car will stop, and if he has time, Ray will take the tourists to see the grave and recount the infamous story. "When I was a boy and Uncle Paul would come to see us, he liked to tell that story on himself," Ray told a visitor one winter day in 1995.

When Paul was eleven, Ida moved the family to a small house in Fordyce, where she took in boarders. They kept the farm, but they stayed in town during the week so the children could benefit from the better education offered the students of Fordyce. It was a move that would change Paul's life. Had he not moved to Fordyce and attended Fordyce High School, he might never have played football—and he might never have escaped Moro Bottom. The transition to life in what still seemed like the big city sometimes left him bewildered. One time he was walking down the street with classmate Jack Benham. "This car came barreling down the street and he started running from it," Benham said. "It was the first car he'd ever seen, and it scared him half to death."

Soon after the Bryants moved to Fordyce, Paul took a part-time job in his cousin's general store after school and on Saturdays. Typical of the country stores of the day, the Kilgore Brothers store was an odd amalgamation of groceries, meats, vegetables, farm supplies, pharmaceuticals, and sundries. Cooled by ceiling fans in the summer and warmed by a potbellied stove in the winter, the place always smelled of roasted coffee and smoked meats. Always big for his age, Paul was then uncoordinated to the point of clumsiness. "He could mess up faster than I could clean up behind him," said his cousin and boss, Dean Kilgore, who was eight years his senior. "He tried so hard, but he was always spilling sugar or flour or something." Around the same time, Jack became a sharecropper on a patch of land in Moro Bottom, and when school closed for the fall harvest he hired his little brother to chop cotton for fifty cents a day.

Over time, the shy, insecure boy grew into a large young man who cast an intimidating shadow. As an adolescent, Bryant's temperament often got him into trouble; although he was as big as a full-grown man by his early teens, he was immature and often belligerent. The young man who was still struggling with the boy's feelings of inadequacy sometimes went looking for fights. "I guess you could say I had a chip on my shoulder," he once said. At the ripe age of thirteen, when he stood six-foot-one and weighed 180 pounds, Paul got into a fistfight with a grown man who refused to pay him for some groceries he had delivered.

"He was meaner than hell growing up," said Joe Rummel, who was about Paul's age and lived down the road from the Bryants. "He was tough, too. One day we were going to Fordyce in a wagon. We hit a chuckhole and the wheel ran over his head and pushed him down in the mud. Mashed his head to where it looked like a butter bean. We thought it had killed him."

Not long after the family moved to Fordyce, a man rode into town on a wagon trailed by a black bear in a cage. The man was offering a dollar to anyone fool enough to wrestle the bear for a minute on the stage of the Lyric Theater. After convincing old man Smith, who owned the theater, to let his friends in for free (everybody else paid a dime), Bryant stuck out his barrel chest and said he'd do it. Years later he told *People* magazine, "I would have wrestled King Kong for a dollar a minute."

Those were the days of the silent movie. In a world before television, when a radio was still too expensive for most people to own, the nightly parade of stars such as Tom Mix, Douglas Fairbanks, and Gloria Swanson at the Lyric represented the town's only real connection to the outside world. It was a small theater by the standards of the grand picture houses of the day, with no more than two hundred seats arranged on a sloped floor. Hillbilly musicians sometimes performed on the small wooden stage. By the time Bryant walked onstage that night with the man and his bear, the place was packed.

"Half the people in there probably wanted to see him get

torn up by that bear," said his friend Clark Jordan, who sat in the second row, hoping the bear wouldn't kill him.

As soon as the bear reared up to face him, Bryant pulled him to the ground and played a little prevent defense. The animal was muzzled, so Bryant figured all he had to do was to keep the bear from squashing him like a bug. Eventually, though, the bear worked itself free and they rolled around on the stage for a few moments. Sensing the need for a little more drama, the bear's owner walked over to the beast and yanked off its muzzle. They tussled around some more, and then Bryant felt a burning sensation on his right ear. The bear had bitten him and he was dripping blood all over the stage. Having earned his dollar, he didn't feel the need to become permanently maimed, so he jumped from the stage and crash-landed in the front row of seats. The whole bout lasted no more than two or three minutes.

"You should have seen him jump off that stage when he realized that thing had bit him," said his sister Louise, who sat mesmerized in the second row. "He was brave enough to get up there and wrestle that bear, but he wasn't about to let it eat him alive."

The bear and its owner skipped town before Bryant could get his money. "Paul was awful mad about that man cheating him out of his dollar, because a dollar was a lot of money," said his cousin Dean Kilgore. But he acquired a nickname and a reputation that day; henceforth and forever he would be known as Bear Bryant. His participation in the stunt said something powerful about his need to attract attention, and it spoke volumes about the tenacity and self-confidence that would carry him a long way in the world from the Lyric Theater. One day, the fearless kid from the sticks would be a legend, and those few moments of combat with a wild animal would define him for the ages.

When he was in the eighth grade, Bryant happened to walk past the field where the Fordyce High School football team was practicing. Bob Cowan, the head coach, couldn't help noticing such a large physical specimen, so he walked over to him and asked if he wanted to play football.

"Yessir, I guess I do," Bryant said. "But how do you play?"

"Well, you see that fellow catching the ball down there?"

Bryant nodded.

"Well, whenever he catches it, you go down there and try to kill him."

Bryant's basic football philosophy never deviated very far from those simple instructions. From the beginning, he impressed the coach with his aggressive approach to the game. The next Friday, Bryant played in the first football game he had ever seen. His parents thought sports, especially sports involving a certain kind of violence, conflicted with their religious beliefs, but they didn't try very hard to stop him from playing. Neither of them would ever see him play or coach, however. His first week on the team, Bryant took his only pair of shoes to the town cobbler and had him screw cleats to the soles. He wore those black hightops everywhere, and they made a terrible racket.

In those days of two-way football, when the helmets were made of leather light enough to squeeze in your hands, Bryant proved to be only an average pass receiver, but he quickly developed a reputation as a player who would knock the hell out of anyone in his path. His size, strength, and tenacity made him an outstanding blocker on offense and a feared tackler on defense. "He was the most aggressive player I ever saw," said his teammate Jack Benham. "The coach liked to use him as a model: 'Here, watch Bryant show you how to block.' And Bryant would knock a guy five yards off the line."

Even then, he played with a ferocity that suggested he knew it was his ticket out. "All I had was football," he later said. "I hung on as though it were life and death, and it was."

No joy to coach, Bryant often got into fights during games, and in his junior year, the principal suspended him from the team for cutting classes. But his teammates loved him. He connected with them in a way that foreshadowed his success as a coach. Though not the best athlete on the team, he was certainly the meanest, and his tenacity helped him earn All-State acclaim. In his senior year, 1930, when the Redbugs finished undefeated and won the state championship, they were leading in a close game with a team from Hope one night when Fordyce quarterback Clark (Click) Jordan—one-half of the famed Jordan twins who later starred at the University of Arkansas—was tackled late and way out of bounds. Jordan limped back to the huddle with a sprained ankle. It was obviously a cheap shot.

"Don't worry, Click, I'll get that sonofabitch," Bryant said.

In this age before scoreboard clocks, the officials kept the time on a stopwatch. After Jordan was hit out of bounds, Bryant bided his time. He didn't want to do anything to cost his team the game, so after every play, he went up to the official and asked him how much time was left. Finally, when only a few seconds remained and the game appeared in the bag, Bryant lined up opposite the Hope player who had taken the cheap shot on his friend. An instant before the snap, Bryant started swinging. He went right to the Hope player's head and then wrestled him to the ground, and he didn't stop swinging until the officials pulled him off and threw him out of the game.

"You could say Bear had more loyalty than judgment in those days," Jordan said.

Football gave Bryant an identity. For the first time, he wasn't simply that mama's boy or that invalid father's son or that rube from the sticks; he was one of the heroes of Friday nights who rode off to places like Little Rock and Hot Springs on specially chartered trains to represent the folks of Fordyce. His mama always tried to teach him to be proud of himself, but nothing she said could ever instill self-respect quite as well as those people cheering for him and calling his name.

As difficult as this immature and belligerent adolescent must have been to raise, Ida was responsible for instilling in Paul many of the important values that would help him succeed. She was a stickler for manners, and the effects of her teachings can be seen throughout his life. His language could be as crude as a sailor's in private and especially on the field, but from the time he exorcised all his teenage demons, he was always a gentleman in public and especially around women. Nearly a half-century after he left Arkansas, Bryant was leaning against a goalpost of the Louisiana Superdome before the first Sugar Bowl played indoors, when Joe Paterno, the coach of the opposing Penn State Nittany Lions, walked over and asked him why he wasn't wearing his trademark houndstooth hat. Without missing a beat, he said, "My mama always told me to take off my hat inside." Not all of her teachings took, of course; she forbade him to smoke or drink, but he consumed both cigarettes and liquor from an early age. However hypocritical it may have been, his inability to smoke or drink in front of her —till the end of her life—suggested an old-world respect for her wishes. She tried to instill in him a religious fervor to match her own, but while he clearly harbored certain core religious beliefs and became a man of extreme charity who was capable of tremendous kindness, the premature death of his father—who refused medical treatment because he believed it violated the teachings of his church—left Bryant with a lifelong ambivalence toward organized religion. The most valuable lesson she gave him, however, lay in her struggle through the day-after-day hardships of her life without ever giving up. This experience fostered a sense of independence and determination that would form the foundation of his life.

His newfound status as a star athlete gained him plenty of attention from the opposite sex. The once timid boy was growing into a handsome young man with broad shoulders, smoldering eyes, and a charisma that defied description. In affairs of the heart as in the rest of his life, he sometimes pushed too hard. One night when he was staying with his cousin Dean, he came in from a date with his face scratched and bloodied. Bryant's hormones had been raging that night, and he had not wanted to take no for an answer. "That girl fought me off like crazy," he told his cousin, shaking his head.

His background and his reputation as a hell-raiser rendered him off-limits for some girls. Just as the boys and girls had once teased him, no small number of fathers and mothers looked down on him because of his modest origins, branding him a loser in their small-town caste system. "My mother and daddy didn't want me to date him, so we had to sneak around," said Julia Sparks, one of his high-school girlfriends. "Even when he was a big football star, a lot of people—including my parents—looked down on him because he grew up on the wrong side of the tracks."

A poor student who cared little about his studies, Bryant was not the type of young man of whom great things were expected. In fact, he failed to graduate with his high-school classmates in the spring of 1931 after flunking a language class. Ike Murray, his classmate and sometime romantic rival who later would become attorney general of the state of Arkansas, once remarked, "If I had been writing the class prophecy for our senior class, I'd have written this about Paul: 'He'll be lucky to stay out of the penitentiary.' "

But a life can be altered in the blink of an eye. In the spring of 1931, at the depths of the Great Depression, an assistant coach from the University of Alabama arrived in Fordyce to attempt to sign the Jordan twins. After he realized he was going to lose both of them to Arkansas, Hank Crisp asked the high-school coach if he had any more college prospects. Yes, the coach said, I have one who will fight till he drops. That fall, Bryant climbed into the rumble seat of Crisp's car and rode off to his future in Tuscaloosa, Alabama, but he would never shake the dust of rural Arkansas from his soul. The cruel voices of his youth pushed him to get out and achieve, but the family and friends he so treasured always brought him back— first, as an impoverished college student, by hitchhiking or hopping a freight, and then, when the money and fame started to flow, in his own private airplane.

The louder the world cheered for him, the more often he returned to his roots. Sometimes he flew into the tiny airstrip outside Fordyce and stayed just long enough for a double helping of his mama's black-eyed peas and cornbread; as much as he craved the spotlight, he enjoyed the reality check that his visits provided. The man who played golf with the president of the United States also enjoyed going bird hunting with his brother Jack, the farmer; the man who watched the Kentucky Derby as the governor's guest was once so touched by the sudden death of his niece's horse that he took her out and bought her a replacement just to see her face light up. Success afforded him the opportunity to build his mother a nice little white cottage on the road to Fordyce, and she never wanted for anything for the rest of her life.

As much as he craved an escape, he could never completely shake football from his mind, even when he returned to the only place in the world where everyone called him "Paul." The game was never any farther away than the yellow legal pad he kept at his side on such trips, just in case a sudden inspiration presented him with a new way of burning Auburn for six.

BMOC

AS CONFINING AS LIFE IN rural Arkansas must have seemed to a boy of such untrammeled ambition, the outside world was not exactly beckoning Paul Bryant with streets paved with gold when he finished high school. The world was running short of hope in 1931. Two years after the stock market crash, banks were failing in record numbers, unemployment was rampant, and bread lines and soup kitchens provided millions of Americans with their only sustenance. Even the Ford Motor Company, which more than any other institution symbolized the flower of American capitalism, had reluctantly suspended production because the market for automobiles had vanished almost overnight.

But despite the widespread deprivation of the Great Depression, football could still be a lifeline for a young man who could run, pass, catch, block, or tackle. Bryant, who was big and strong and played the game as though his life depended on it, had landed a scholarship to the University of Alabama without bothering to graduate from high school. In this era of less stringent admission standards, his academic deficit was more a nuisance than an impediment. Once he arrived in Tuscaloosa, Bryant enrolled in Tuscaloosa High School for the fall semester; while he worked toward his high-school diploma, the university picked up the tab for his housing and meals and, without violating any of the limited rules of the time, he practiced with the Crimson Tide. He would not see action in a varsity game for two years, but he loved practice because he got to hit people. He liked to hit people. One day late in the year, Frank Thomas, the Crimson Tide's first-year head coach, stopped practice during a blocking drill and implored his team to "watch this high-school boy show you how to do it."

Like many young people who go off to college, Bryant found the adjustment difficult. He felt isolated, homesick, and self-conscious because of his country roots. After word arrived from home of his father's death, he wrote his cousin Collins Kilgore that he was considering leaving Alabama to return to Arkansas or, perhaps, to migrate to Texas and land an oil-rigging job. The letter was written in a moment of weakness.

Collins knew his cousin; he knew what drove him and he knew how to get to him. Collins realized Paul had reached a turning point in his life, and he fired off a telegram fraught with indignation:

GO AHEAD AND QUIT JUST LIKE EVERYBODY PREDICTED YOU WOULD

The wire framed the stakes perfectly. The homesick farm boy knew that all those people who had looked down on him back in Fordyce—the children who had mocked him and the fathers who had forbidden their daughters to date him— would love to see him fail, to see him quit. "I wasn't about to quit after that," Bryant said years later. He never forgot the emotion those words stirred deep inside him. *No! I won't give them the satisfaction!* As a coach, he would often force his players to make that same choice, between giving their all and going home in shame. In Bear Bryant's world of physical and mental strength, quitting became the ultimate act of weakness.

In the South of the early twentieth century, the Civil War was still more of a closely held grudge than a page ripped from the history books. Sixty-five years after General Robert E. Lee surrendered at Appomattox, the American nation remained divided along the Mason-Dixon line in ways both real and philosophical. Innovations such as electricity, radio, and the telephone spread through the South only after they had become commonplace in many parts of the North. Many Yankees looked down on southerners and their agrarian culture, which was in sharp contrast to the industrial society that had developed in and fundamentally transformed the North. The South's educational systems were widely considered inferior, even antiquated. Many southerners, remembering the various indignities of the war and Reconstruction, distrusted Yankees and their institutions as foreign and contrary to the southern way of life. In even the most benign of regional conflicts, many southerners were inclined to hear echoes of the lost cause.

Like many other institutions developed in the North, football arrived late in the South. On November 6, 1869, when Rutgers defeated Princeton, six goals to four, in the first intercollegiate football game, many parts of the old Confederacy were still being subjected to martial law by occupying forces of the United States Army. By the time a large number of southern colleges started fielding teams in the early 1890s, northern pioneers such as Harvard, Yale, and Princeton had already shepherded the game through a generation of rules changes and strategic innovations. Alabama's football program was barely underway when President Theodore Roosevelt, appalled at the rash of serious injuries being inflicted on the playing field, threatened to ban the game, which led to the formation of the National Collegiate Athletic Association and the adoption of a series of rules with the intent of tempering the sport's brutal tendencies.

For decades, southern football was considered inferior, and it probably was. Innovations such as the forward pass and the single wing slowly trickled down from the North. As late as 1923, Alabama was coached on a part-time basis by a sportswriter named Xen C. Scott. After every football season, Scott moved back to Cleveland, where he covered horse racing throughout the spring and summer for *The Plain Dealer*, returning to Tuscaloosa in time for preseason practice. The school offered no scholarships, relying mostly on tryouts from among the student body.

But southern football took a giant leap forward on New Year's Day 1926. Alabama, the first southern team to be invited to the Rose Bowl, stunned heavily favored Washington, 20–19, taking with the improbable victory the mythical national championship of the day. In addition to transforming the Crimson Tide into a national power alongside Notre Dame, Southern Cal, and Michigan, the upset victory resounded throughout the South as a triumph for the region over its back-water reputation. It gave southerners the rare opportunity to claim national superiority in something other than historical angst.

"We were the South's baby," said Hoyt Winslett, an All-America end on Alabama's 1926 Rose Bowl team. "We felt like the Rose Bowl was more than just another football game."

Despite being a late addition to southern culture, football quickly assumed a greater importance in the region than in other parts of the country. In this largely rural region, with few outlets for organized recreation, college football teams provided a powerful unifying force for a physically scattered population. In Tuscaloosa, the entire front page of the local Sunday newspaper was often devoted to coverage of the Crimson Tide. Before radios were affordable for the common man, fans in far-flung parts of the state would gather outside Western Union offices to listen for the ticker-taped reports of 'Bama games. Wallace Wade, the Tennessee-born architect of that seminal victory over Washington, proved his success was no fluke by taking the Crimson Tide to two more Rose Bowls: In addition to tying Stanford 7–7 in 1927, 'Bama knocked off Washington State 24–0 on New Year's Day 1931. In eight years, Wade won three national championships, won four Southern Conference titles, and had an enviable 61–13–3 record that served as the down payment on his plaque in the College Football Hall of Fame.

Nine months before Bryant arrived in Tuscaloosa, Wade, a stern man who was too thin-skinned for his own good, left 'Bama for Duke in a dispute with the administration. Frank Thomas, who replaced Wade after serving as a line coach under Harry Mehre at Georgia, had played quarterback for Knute Rockne at Notre Dame and was considered one of the nation's foremost practitioners of the Notre Dame box offense, which he brought to Alabama. Thirty-one years old when he arrived in Tuscaloosa, Thomas looked more like a butcher than a football coach, with a squat, chubby body and a round face. The son of an Indiana steelworker, he would lead Alabama to an impressive 115–24–7 record, the 1934 national championship, four titles in the newly formed Southeastern Conference, and six bowl bids before being forced into a premature retirement with a heart condition in 1947.

Of his coach, Bryant letter said, "We all respected him, but we weren't particularly crazy about him." Nonetheless, as many would later confide about him, Bryant grew to idolize his coach. No slave driver, in many ways Thomas was the antithesis of the coach Bryant would become. He could be extremely aloof, but Bryant absorbed many parts of Thomas's coaching style into his own, especially his emphasis on fundamentals and defense.

Like many of the Alabama players, Bryant felt closer to Hank Crisp, Thomas's top assistant, a crusty old cuss with leathery skin and a stub for a right hand who could have been a stand-in for the Marlboro man. Crisp was much more of a motivator than Thomas. "You could win him over just by trying like hell, by fighting as hard as you could," Bryant said. "He could get me to play. Some people have that and some don't." There was a genuine affection between the two men for the rest of Crisp's life; years later, when Bryant was being courted to return to Alabama as head coach and athletic director when Crisp was the AD, he refused to take the job until Coach Hank personally bestowed his blessing on the deal.

In addition to handling all the discipline—which mostly consisted of running steps at Denny Stadium for offenses such as missing curfew or being seen drinking a beer—Crisp tried to solve all the players' petty problems, such as having enough money for dates. The rules defining amateurism were still rather loose and unenforced, and Crisp always carried a roll of dollar bills for his boys in need. After a big win, he was known to walk around the locker room from player to player, handing out ten-dollar bills. During practice the week of Ala-

bama's 1935 Rose Bowl game against Stanford, Crisp was so
frustrated at the huge media horde on the field that he leaned
into a huddle and said, "The first man who runs over one of
those suckers gets two dollars from me." Dixie Howell called
a pass and threw deep to Bryant, who barreled into an unsuspecting newsman and then sought out his coach to collect his
prize money. Later, Howell made him split the two dollars.

On the outstanding Alabama teams of the mid-1930s—the
Crimson Tide compiled a 23–3–2 record with two Southeastern Conference championships during Bryant's three varsity
years—Bryant and Don Hutson represented opposite ends of
the spectrum.

Hutson, the Tide's left end, was all skill and grace. No small
number of football historians credit Hutson and Howell with
inventing many of the modern pass patterns. In an age when
the passing game was still rudimentary and often haphazard,
scouts from the Green Bay Packers were dazzled by Hutson's
four-catch, two-touchdown performance in the Crimson Tide's
29–13 Rose Bowl victory over Stanford—and they signed him
on the spot. On his first play in the pros, the Alabama Antelope
dashed eighty-three yards for a touchdown. He set NFL records that stood for decades. A splinter of a man at six-one and
175 pounds, he possessed speed and hands and a knack for
getting open.

Bryant, the Tide's right end, was a street fighter. Known as
"the other end," his pass-receiving abilities seemed awkward
and clumsy compared to Hutson's. He wasn't especially fast or
creative at getting open, but Bryant, who by then had blos-
somed into a six-foot-four, 210-pound hunk of immovable
force, could knock your head off. "When he walked onto that
field, he was a man at war," said Joe Riley, an All-SEC halfback
for the Crimson Tide in 1934–35. When Alabama ran, it typically ran right because Frank Thomas knew Bryant would take
out the end and the tackle. He was selected second team All-
SEC in 1934, and he played defense with equal ferocity.

"Bryant only knew one speed—full speed," said his 'Bama teammate and lifelong friend Young Boozer. "He was the hardest-working, hustlingest guy I've ever been around. There was no finesse to him. He was just hell-bent for action."

Bryant knew he wasn't talented like Hutson or some of the other athletes on the Alabama team. He compensated by fighting for everything. "You always knew Paul was giving it every ounce he had," Hutson said. If he had been a great talent like Hutson, Bryant might have evolved differently as a coach; he might have placed more emphasis on strategy and skill, might have coddled his players instead of pushing them. But football was never anything less than a test of wills to Bear Bryant. The game meant everything to him, and he learned he could give more than he thought he could.

No one practiced harder. Many days, he would return to his dorm room all beaten up and bloodied and unable to sleep. "He would be in such pain he couldn't even lie down and get some rest," said Boozer, who roomed with Bryant in his senior year. "One time he dislocated some cartilage in his chest and he'd practice and be in such pain. He'd come in, sit on the foot of his bed, and then I'd pick his legs up and put him in his bed."

In those days of flimsy pads, small squads, and strict substitution rules, everyone played with little and big hurts, and often with injuries. There were no mouthpieces, and the field was often strewn with teeth and blood. There were no bars on the primitive leather helmets, so a wicked forearm could inflict serious damage. A player who left the field for any reason could not return for a quarter. The dedicated football player learned to persevere under difficult circumstances—like the excruciating pain of a broken rib or a pulled hamstring.

Three years after Wallace Wade took over the Alabama program and charted a course to national prominence, Robert Neyland arrived at the University of Tennessee and started building the Volunteers into a powerhouse. For most of the next two decades, Alabama and Tennessee dominated southern football. Their annual meeting on the third Saturday in

October became the South's most heated rivalry—a clash of Neyland's single wing and Thomas's Notre Dame box, for bragging rights and, more often than not, the SEC championship. Between 1923 and 1946, the two programs won or shared fourteen conference titles. Five times during that period, one team handed the other its only loss of the season.

The week before the Tennessee game in Knoxville in his senior year, 1935, Bryant broke the fibula in his right leg during a loss to Mississippi State. He spent the next week in a cast hobbling around on crutches. No one expected him to play against the Volunteers; not even Bryant could play on a broken leg. He dressed for the game and was going to stand with the aid of crutches on the sideline while backup Ben McLeod started at right end, but in an emotional locker room before the game, Crisp, dangling a cigarette, walked down the row of players and looked each one in the eye.

"I'll tell you gentlemen one thing," Crisp said, walking from man to man. "I don't know about the rest of you . . . but I know one damn thing. Old 34 will be after 'em, he'll be after their asses."

Bear was stunned. He had to check his jersey number to make sure his coach was actually talking about him. What could he do? How could he let his team down? Against Tennessee? He played. And, incredibly, he played what may have been the game of his career. That afternoon, Bryant scored on a long touchdown pass, lateraled to quarterback Riley Smith on another scoring play, and contributed some decisive defensive stops as Alabama crushed Tennessee, 25–0.

"It hurt like hell," he later conceded, "but it was just one little bone."

The story seemed too good for many to swallow. Georgia was hosting Alabama the next week, so the Monday after the Tennessee game, *Atlanta Constitution* columnist Ralph McGill arrived in Tuscaloosa full of skepticism and demanded to see the x-rays of Bryant's leg. McGill, who would win a Pulitzer Prize a quarter-century later for his coverage of the bombing of a Jewish temple in the early days of the civil rights movement, confirmed the broken bone to his readers. "As far as this seasoson is concerned," McGill wrote, "Paul Bryant is in first place in the courage league."

The trip to Pasadena during his junior year was an eye-opening experience for the country boy from Arkansas. In addition to traveling in luxury cross-country on a specially chartered train and getting to tour a movie studio, the Crimson Tide took the field against Stanford before a then-record Rose bowl crowd of 84,474, which was 72,474 larger than the seating capacity of Denny Stadium in Tuscaloosa. More people saw the Rose Bowl than had watched all five of the Tide's home games that season—combined. In the fourth quarter, with 'Bama leading 29–13, Bryant looked down from the huddle and saw a number of silver coins strewn across the field. He didn't know where they came from and he didn't stop to count them; they must have totaled two or three dollars altogether, which was several days' wages chopping cotton back home, so he reached down and scooped them up in his hands. He thought he'd take them to the sideline between plays and have one of the other players keep them for him, but on the very next play, before he could figure out what to do with the money, one of the Stanford backs ran his way. Underscoring his commitment to winning in a rather unique fashion, he dropped his loot and administered a thunderous hit on the Stanford runner. The money scattered and he never got it back.

Bryant's determination to win knew no bounds. At once the most aggressive and most uncoordinated athlete on the team, he once attempted to pitch in a team baseball outing. Determined to win, he reared back and threw the ball as hard as he could possibly throw it—and the ball landed with a thud on guard-turned-catcher Charlie Marr's bare forehead. "I swear you could read Spalding on his forehead," recalled Boozer, unable to contain his amusement more than a half-century later. The impact knocked Marr to the ground, where he lay, unconscious, until the trainer brought the smelling salts. Bryant was never allowed to pitch again.

"Even if he was playing a supposedly friendly game of cards, he was bound and determined to win," said his friend and classmate C. E. Hornsby, who often played gin rummy with him at the Alpha Gam sorority house. "One time he got really mad at me because he thought I wasn't taking the game seriously. He wasn't there for chit-chat; he wanted to win."

No longer the immature adolescent who went searching for fights, Bryant nevertheless was not the kind of man you wanted to cross. One summer, he and teammate Joe Riley spent six weeks as counselors at a camp for young boys in Wisconsin. After putting the boys to bed one night, they rode off in the camp owner's dilapidated Model T to locate an open bar and, if they were lucky, to find a couple of girls interested in a little carnal activity. But the pair wound up getting into a fight with two local smartasses who had pushed their car off the road and had declined, in a manner of speaking, to apologize. After Riley's sparring partner had run off into the night, Bryant was still using his for a human punching bag. Every time his blood-dripping victim fell down after a thunderous punch, Bryant helped him up…and started pounding on him again.

After a few minutes, Riley started yelling at Bryant, "Hey, Paul, let me have a whack at him…mine's run off…I don't have anybody to hit."

Bryant just kept punching.

Somewhat less competitive in the classroom, he earned a degree in physical education but was no academic star. Melvin Israel befriended him as sports editor of The Crimson White, the student newspaper, and later, while working toward his law degree, taught a speech class in which Bryant was enrolled. "As a student, he was a hell of a football coach," said Israel, who later changed his name to Mel Allen and gained fame as the longtime voice of the New York Yankees. "Clearly, he was a very bright guy, but I don't think he put much into his studies."

With each passing year, Bryant placed more and more distance between himself and that timid, insecure country boy. The new environment allowed him to start fresh, to reinvent himself, and to shed the chip from his shoulder. Confident without seeming arrogant, charming without seeming phony, tough but a gentleman, he appeared comfortable for the first time with who he was. He developed a way of walking, talking, and interacting with people that exuded a charisma that, even then, made him stand out in a crowd. People liked him. Everyone wanted to be his friend.

"He was a real man's man," said his friend C. E. Hornsby. "You just couldn't help liking him."

With his effortless charm, imposing stature, and rugged good looks, Bryant also became extremely popular along sorority row. Like most of the athletes on campus, he never had much money and didn't own a car. The sorority girls, in contrast, represented the state's gentry who could afford college despite the Depression. Yet Bryant moved with ease into their world. In addition to his personal attributes, he was a football star for the Crimson Tide, which was an aristocracy in itself.

Mary Harmon Black came from money. Not filthy rich, she was, in the parlance of the Old South, "well-to-do." Born in the small southeastern Alabama town of Troy, her father, a prominent businessman, died during the influenza epidemic of 1918, when she was three. Five years later, her mother married attorney Martin Folmar, who moved the family to Birmingham. Like all well-to-do children of the day, she lived a relatively carefree life, playing with her dogs and her extensive doll collection. Her mother, grandmother, and stepfather smothered her with love and material things.

"Manie was the kind of child that the grown people thought could do no wrong," said her first cousin Mary Parks, who grew up with her in Troy. "She never got in trouble, even when she was right in there messing up or misbehaving with the rest of us."

A dark-haired beauty with a movie star's features, she exuded class, even elegance. One day in the fall of 1934, she saw Bryant walking out of the university's supply store. They struck up a conversation about football, and after a few minutes he worked up his courage to ask her for a date. One of the most popular girls on campus, she took out her black book and started thumbing through it, finally suggesting a date several weeks later.

Bryant stiffened. "Shoot, honey, I'm talking about tonight," he snapped, and then he walked off.

Later in the day, Bryant received a call on the community telephone in the dusty old gym where he and his teammates lived. Mary Harmon Black had rearranged her schedule, and she could see him that night after all. Soon, they began dating seriously and it was clear to all the girls on sorority row where the relationship was heading. One well-heeled and particularly smitten young lady, devastated when Bryant stopped calling her, begged Mary Harmon to give up her football star.

"How much will you take for him?" she asked, sobbing.

Mary Harmon didn't hesitate. "He's not for sale."

Eight months after that fateful meeting on the quad, on June 2, 1935, Paul and Mary Harmon were secretly married by a justice of the peace in Ozark, Alabama. When, much later, her parents read about the nuptials in the newspaper, they were shocked. They had expected their daughter to have her pick of any of those handsome boys from fine Alabama families with promising futures. Bryant, whose upbringing was the flipside of hers, was not what they had in mind, and at first they refused to accept the union.

Bryant had married Mary Harmon without knowing how he would support his wife and the children who would surely follow. For some time, he had thought about becoming a coach, but he had no coaching offers. He was also intrigued by the notion of playing professional football, although he knew he was not good enough to warrant the kind of money his friend Hutson was earning with the Packers.

"In those days, most of us didn't have the luxury of thinking about careers," said Boozer. "It was the middle of the Depression, and we were just concerned about how we were going to eat. Your career was secondary."

One day toward the end of the 1935 season, Bryant was pacing around his dorm room while Boozer was lying in his bunk. Bryant was lamenting his predicament—no job, no prospects, and a wife to support. He let the word wife slip out without thinking.

"You're not married!" Boozer said.

"The hell I'm not. I've got the deed to her!"

Bryant told his friend to jump down from his bunk and open the trunk at the foot of his bed. Sensing his roommate wasn't teasing, Boozer hopped down from the bed and opened the lid. There, underneath some clothes, he found a marriage license dated more than five months earlier. He was married! Because Frank Thomas forbade his players to marry while they were in school, Bryant had feared losing his scholarship, so he and Mary Harmon kept their marriage under wraps until after his senior season. For those five months, Bear had managed to keep the union secret from his teammates and his coaches. But by then Mary Harmon was pregnant—she would give birth to Mae Martin the following March—and the expectant Papa was getting nervous. His scholarship would be running out soon, and jobs were hard to find.

"Boozer," Bryant said after a while, "I'm gonna try to coach. I don't know where, but I'm gonna try to get a job coaching. How 'bout giving me your playbook? Mine's not worth a damn, the way I keep things, but I know you've kept everything Coach's given us in yours. Would you mind? You don't need it anymore, but I could sure use it."

So Boozer, who was heading for a job in a bank back home

in Dothan, Alabama, walked over to his trunk and retrieved his playbook, with its plays drawn out with the precision befitting an accounting major. He handed it to his friend, who thanked him and rushed out the door to make a class.

Coach

SOMETIMES, GREATNESS BEGINS WITH a gift; a man is born with some talent and he feels the need to follow it, like an invisible voice in the night. Sometimes, greatness begins with a void; a man is born into circumstances that, for any of a number of reasons, force him to feel that he has something to prove to the world and to himself, so, instead of being impelled in a specific direction by some mysterious gift, he follows his naked ambition down the first path that opens for him. Paul Bryant was propelled by such a force; he desperately needed to become *somebody* long before he wanted to become a football coach.

Frank Thomas deserves enormous credit for recognizing Bryant's potential as a coach and for encouraging his pupil to cast his lot with a very unpredictable profession. The Alabama head coach often took his intense, hard-nosed end along to coaching clinics, and he saw how the players and coaches reacted to him, how they listened and paid attention to him. Part of this was his size, for a man standing six-foot-three and weighing 210 pounds commands a certain respect, but it was also the way he carried himself, at once intimidating and char-ismatic. This magical talent to lead came second in the evolu-tion of Bear Bryant, after the raw ambition, and the observant and analytical Thomas was the first man to exploit it.

After the Bear completed his playing eligibility in the fall of 1935, Thomas arranged a temporary job for him at tiny Union College in Jackson, Tennessee. The small college's head coach was looking for someone to install Alabama's variation of the Notre Dame box offense, and Bryant, with a wife to support, a baby on the way, and no prospects, jumped at the chance. The job paid $170 per month.

Bryant knew by then that he wanted to make a career out of coaching, but he was tempted by some feelers he had received from several professional teams. The National Football League was nowhere near as popular as the college game in those days, and the kind of money journeymen players earned—from seventy-five dollars to one hundred dollars a game—required many to secure off-season jobs just to make ends meet. Bryant needed something stable, and fate intervened when Thomas called him back from Union College to coach the Alabama guards for $1,250 a year.

In his six years as an assistant coach before World War II, at Alabama (1936–39) and Vanderbilt (1940–41), Bryant developed a reputation as a hands-on coach who loved to get down in a three-point stance and take on all comers. He taught by doing, and often by bleeding, and any young man who could block him or tackle him was destined to be a football player.

His views about strategy and tactics were born of his experiences on the field; from his earliest days as an assistant coach, he believed games were won with hard-nosed defense and special teams. As a recruiter, he used his immense charm to win over players and their parents, who saw in him the kind of young man they wanted their sons to become.

No one taught Bryant how to coach. He was born with the ability to make young men strive, and this talent to lead began to blossom during his days as an assistant coach. He could spend a small amount of time with a player and know how to make him play his guts out. Duffy Daughtery, the live wire who coached Michigan State to two national championships, once paid his friend the ultimate compliment, and it stuck like glue: "He could take his 'n beat yours, then take yours 'n beat his."

At the core, this was a gift, but Bryant also was a man of uncommon intelligence about human relations, and he used what he learned through the years to interact with his players to great effect. He had that chiseled face that bespoke toughness, the imposing frame that imparted an air of strength, and the gravelly voice with the heavy southern drawl that enunciated authority. As a young coach, he developed a manner of walking and talking slowly and deliberately, which suggested self-confidence. His speech could be at once soft and authoritative, forcing his audience to listen closely and hang on every word. He filled his talks with perfectly timed stops, starts, and pregnant pauses. As a head coach, he learned to carefully limit the amount of time he spent with his teams and with individual players, which gave every syllable out of his mouth the weight of a message from on high.

As a young coach, he made many mistakes in handling his players and in sideline tactics, but blessed with almost total recall, he was able to learn from his errors. Unlike many coaches, who spend their careers reinventing the wheel, he embraced change at every juncture of his coaching life, and this became the foundation of his longevity. No great strategic innovator, he was a man who was defined, from his first team to his last, by the intangibles of leadership.

Young men wanted to follow him. Some players loved him and were determined to do whatever was necessary to please him, so they gave him everything, which often was more than they thought they had to give. Others hated him for the way he pushed them, and they were equally determined to prove that he couldn't run them off, so they reached deep inside and found the will to show him. Either way, he won. "He had this incredible ability to manipulate how you felt about him to his advantage," said Harry Bonk, who played under him at the University of Maryland.

In his first few years on the sidelines, however, Bryant appeared to be hedging his bet. The gift and the naked ambition were struggling for control of a young man who wanted to coach but was not content to be an assistant. In 1937, with a family to support on the meager earnings of an assistant coach, he borrowed enough money to buy a Tuscaloosa dry cleaner's with his buddy Don Hutson, who was redefining the role of the receiver in professional football as a star for the Green Bay Packers. For more than two years, Bryant divided his time between his coaching duties and managing Captain Kidd cleaners, which was located in a big white house three blocks west of campus.

Using his position and his closeness to Hank Crisp, Bryant won the contract to clean 'Bama's football uniforms in 1938. But someone at Captain Kidd bungled the order the very first week, after a season-opening victory over Southern Cal, and the uniforms shrank like doll clothes. Coach Hank was furious, but after an explosion of anger resembling a mushroom cloud in the desert, he ordered new uniforms and covered for his boy. Bear never asked for any more business from the athletic department, and within a year, he and Hutson sold the cleaners.

"Bear had a gruff way about him," said Charles P. Hayes, who worked the register and solicited cleaning business from the fraternities and sororities while he pursued a degree in education. "He wasn't the kind of man to sit around and chit-chat. He was all business all of the time. But he was fair. The people who worked for him at the cleaners had a lot of loyalty toward him."

During a trip to the Rose Bowl in 1938—when Alabama lost for the only time in six appearances, 13–0 to California—someone finagled a Hollywood screen test for the handsome young coach. If only for a fleeting moment or two, he had visions of becoming the next Johnny Mack Brown, the former Tide star who had parlayed his trip to the 1926 Rose Bowl into stardom as a cowboy movie idol. The studio didn't sign Bryant, but some fast-talking agent offered to double his 'Bama salary if he would stay in California and give the movies a shot. "I knew that they were trying to make a silk purse out of a sow's ear," said Bryant, who probably realized by then where and how he was going to make his mark.

On the same trip, Bryant befriended a young newspaperman from Nashville named Fred Russell. "I could see he was going places," Russell said. "He had that aura about him." More than two years later, when Bryant was growing restless in his role as the lowest-ranking coach on the Alabama staff, Russell told his former classmate Red Sanders, who was putting together a staff at Vanderbilt, about the young coach. Tough as nails, he said. Had something special, he said. Never heard of him, Sanders said.

Sanders, who would later build a powerhouse at UCLA, told his old friend that he planned to offer the job to Mississippi

State assistant Murray Warmath, who would lead Minnesota to a national title two decades later. But Warmath turned him down, and remembering Russell's enthusiasm for the guy from Alabama, Sanders drove to Tuscaloosa and offered the job to Bryant, who was eager for the pay raise and additional responsibilities the position offered. Several days later, Russell answered his telephone at the *Nashville Banner*.

"Hello, Fred," Sanders said. "I want you to say hello to my new assistant coach."

"Well, hello, Murray. I'm sure you'll really enjoy—"

"Murray, hell!" the gruff voice on the other end of the line interrupted. "This is Bear!"

(Shortly before Bryant was offered the Vanderbilt job in 1940, he applied for an opening on Frank Howard's staff at Clemson. Even then, Howard could see that Bryant was not a man who worked easily for someone else. His zeal to be a head coach gave him an arrogant, ruthless quality that his peers could see a mile away. Years later, Howard told a coaching colleague, "There was no way I was about to hire Bear. In no time, he'd have slit my throat, drank my blood, and had my job.")

As the top assistant on Sanders's Vanderbilt staff, Bryant spread his wings by developing game plans, supervising discipline, and playing a large role in the program's recruiting efforts. He even took charge of the team for a week in 1940 when Sanders collapsed with appendicitis, leading the Commodores to a rather unremarkable 7–7 tie with Kentucky. But friends of Bryant's say Sanders felt overshadowed by his assistant, and according to some accounts, Sanders fired him at the end of the 1941 season.

Of all the lessons assistant coaching taught Bryant, the most important was that he was not cut out to be an assistant coach. He was too headstrong, too driven, too much of a leader to be anyone's follower. What happened at Vanderbilt was bound to happen eventually, the inevitable result of a pressure cooker left too long on the stovetop. After the University of Arkansas fired mild-mannered Fred Thomsen at the end of his thirteenth season in 1941, some prominent alumni started pushing their school to hire the twenty-eight-year-old firebrand with Arkansas ties. In his interview with the president and the athletic officials on campus in Fayetteville, Bryant filled their heads with talk of championships and bowl games, and on the drive back to Nashville, he knew the job was his. But then he heard the news on the car radio: It was Sunday, December 7, 1941, and the Japanese had bombed Pearl Harbor.

The impact shook the entire ship with the force of an earthquake. Lieutenant Commander Paul Bryant, who was playing poker below deck, grabbed his canteen and his gun and rushed to the deck of the USS *Uruguay*, which started listing and taking on water through the stern. Moments later, the captain ordered "abandon ship," and by the time he realized the ship wasn't going to sink and reversed the order, more than two hundred crewmen had drowned. Bryant and most of the rest of the crew stayed onboard and survived the accidental ramming by another American ship. For three days in the spring of 1942, the *Uruguay* lay dead in the water, a virtual sitting duck for a German U-boat loaded down with torpedoes. But the *Uruguay* went undetected, and on the third day, a rescue ship arrived to transport the crew to a base in Bermuda. Several weeks later, Bryant made his way across to North Africa on another ship without incident.

Like millions of able-bodied American men, Bryant kissed his family good-bye and enlisted in the Navy the week after Pearl Harbor. The war cost him his first head coaching job, but his naval service would ultimately lead him back to the sidelines with his success all but guaranteed.

After basic training and officers' training school, he spent most of the war as a physical training specialist for a naval air squadron at Port Lyautey, French Morocco. Even in a world of leaders, Bryant stood out, said his commanding officer. "Bryant knew how to handle men and how to keep their respect," said Rear Admiral Magruder H. Tuttle. "Sometimes I wondered who was working for whom."

In a letter dated April 3, 1943, he wrote to his grandmother:

> Dear Grandma:
> Received your letter of Feb. 8. It was certainly sweet and thoughtful of you to write and I enjoyed and appreciated it very much.
> We are not allowed to write anything about what's happening over here. The country is about like North Fla and most of the Natives are Arabs. They don't shave, dress in robes and ride little donkeys and camels.
> Our food is not good but aside from that it is not bad. I like it fine and would be alright if it weren't for being away from Mary Harmon and the Baby. I miss them more than words can express and am living for the day when I can return to them.
> Hope I am lucky enough to bring you a German scalp. In any event I shall give every effort to get the job done.
> Please remember me to all the family and write when you can.
>
> > With Love,
> > Paul

In the summer of 1944, when the Allies were struggling to fight their way off the beaches of Normandy, the Navy reassigned Bryant to the naval preflight training school at the University of North Carolina in Chapel Hill. Like dozens of public colleges throughout the country, UNC was abuzz with potential aviators and airmen being educated at the taxpayers' expense in courses ranging from physics to geography. The cadets also were required to take a certain amount of physical fitness training every day, so football became a logical extension of campus life. Because of the dearth of available athletes, most college teams suspended play in 1943, but many returned to action the following year with squads composed largely of freshmen and young men who were classified 4-F by the military for medical reasons. Military teams from hastily arranged units, including Randolph Field, Iowa Pre-Flight, and El Toro Marines became overnight powers in college football by mixing former college and professional players. Bryant recognized the opportunity to build his first football team, and he seized it.

With all the charm at his disposal, Bryant convinced his old commander to use his influence to have any available trainee in the East with a football background assigned to North Carolina. "He walked into my office carrying a ten-pound ham and said he needed a favor," Admiral Tuttle said. "But he didn't need the ham. I would have done it just because I liked him. Bryant had the gift of making people want to please him, even his superiors."

Over the next few months, a rather talented team took shape in Chapel Hill. In addition to a large number of teenagers right out of high school, the unit included former college players such as Frankie Alberts, the All-America quarterback from Stanford, and former pros such as Ray Bray of the Chicago Bears and Bill Leckebe of the Brooklyn Dodgers. The team of volunteers played a full slate of games—even knocking off nearby Duke, coached by former Alabama coach Wallace Wade —and endured grueling, year-round practices that foreshadowed the day when Bryant's harsh methods would be the subject of intense national scrutiny.

"It was so tough, so unrelenting, that I thought about quitting. We all thought about quitting," said Joe Drach, a seventeen-year-old lineman on the team. "I mean, we just got beaten bloody every day, and no one said you had to play football to stay in preflight training."

Reunited after Paul's two years in North Africa, the Bryants lived together in North Carolina and had their second child, Paul Junior, in December 1944.

Even after VE Day in May 1945, the war in the Pacific continued to rage with no end in sight. A full-scale invasion of Japan was expected in the fall, and casualties were likely to be high, so the air cadets in Chapel Hill continued their training under the assumption that they would wind up fighting the Japanese. But then came Hiroshima and Nagasaki, and suddenly, everybody started thinking about getting back to the real world. College recruiters started buzzing around Chapel Hill like flies drawn to honey, but Lieutenant Commander Bryant had devised a way to keep the team intact and parlay his wartime efforts into a boon to his postwar career.

He called a meeting and offered a hand-picked group of seventeen players a deal. "I've had three coaching jobs offered to me," he said. "I could go to Alabama as assistant coach or Georgia Tech as assistant coach, or I could go to Maryland as the head coach. Why don't you fellas decide? You choose the place you'd like to go and we'll all go as a package deal."

As their coach no doubt expected, the players chose Maryland, where he would be his own boss for the first time. George Preston Marshall, the gregarious owner of the Washington Redskins, brokered the deal between Bryant, who had scouted for him before the war, and his good friend Curly Byrd, the willful, ironfisted president of the University of Maryland. Byrd and Bryant were, however, too much alike. They were on a collision course from the moment they met.

On September 18, 1945—two weeks after the Japanese surrendered to end World War II—Camp Shelton was awash in sweaty uniforms and impatience. Vic Turyn kept looking at his watch. Like every one of the hundreds of officers and candidates who had converged on the base outside Norfolk, Virginia, Turyn, a tall lanky Ohioan, endured the heat and the long lines so he could receive his discharge and get on with the rest of his life. He was already late for football practice.

One by one throughout the afternoon, the aviator trainees from Chapel Hill walked out the camp's front gate and stepped into a bus parked across the street. Like millions of Americans who had sacrificed nearly four years to the war effort, they were anxious to get about the business of peacetime. And time was of the essence; classes and football practice had already started in College Park, and the first game was less than a week away. Not one of them had even so much as visited the University of Maryland, but they trusted their coach's instincts. Because of a paperwork snafu, the Navy had been unable to provide the men with their one-hundred-dollar mustering-out pay, so every one of them, including Bryant, was dead broke. They had no civilian clothes, so after a long, bumpy bus ride that lasted until the small hours of the morning, they arrived at Maryland wearing the smelly training uniforms that would constitute their entire wardrobe for the next several weeks.

Practice the next day was a collision of two worlds, and there was never any doubt which side would win. The largely 4-F contingent that made up the existing Maryland team resented the arrival of the preflight players, because they knew they were about to lose their jobs. Only one of the holdovers won a starting position—tackle Larry Cooper.

"We were probably pretty arrogant about the whole thing," conceded tackle Joe Drach. "We'd all been together for a good while and we weren't about to let any of those guys beat us."

Bryant moved into a tiny motel room for the duration of the season. With the large number of veterans attending colleges under the GI Bill, housing shortages were common, so Mary Harmon and the children stayed with her parents in Birmingham for a few months. Mae Martin turned nine that year, and Paul Junior turned two. Bryant spent most of his time with his four assistant coaches, especially right-hand man Carney Laslie, a silver-haired sage who would remain at his side for more than twenty years.

The players he brought from North Carolina had already been through numerous "gut checks," but Bryant's hard-nosed brand of football came as a surprise to the Maryland holdovers. The Washington Redskins practiced on the adjacent field, so Maryland scrimmaged against Sammy Baugh and company two or three times a week. "Those pros just kind of lolligagged around most of the time compared to what we were doing," said Joe Drach.

"You had to have something inside you to play for Coach Bryant," said Vic Turyn, who became the Bear's first starting quarterback and went on to earn a high post with the Federal Bureau of Investigation. "He wasn't interested in how much talent you had. He wanted to know if you were willing to throw everything you had on that practice field every day. He was going to push you until you either became a player or you quit."

Bryant was a nervous wreck before the opener at home against tiny Guilford College from North Carolina. "I spent the entire night before throwing up," he said. His fears were unfounded; in the opening moments, Turyn threw a short screen pass to receiver Sammy Behr for the first touchdown of Bryant's coaching career, and the rout was on. Maryland's victory was even more lopsided than the 60–6 score indicated, and everyone on the roster played.

Like many Bryant teams to follow, the Terps were outweighed at many positions, but they were better conditioned than most of their opponents. Turyn, the ringleader, had been too small to play high-school football, but by the time he reached preflight, he had matured into six-feet-one and 180 pounds of pure determination. Bryant, who was his first coach, loved his cockiness. "He had this way about him that made you feel like you could whip anybody, any time," said Turyn, who ran Maryland's Notre Dame box with a linebacker's mentality. Added Harry Bonk: "Quitting became a dirty word. Coach Bryant taught you not to quit, no matter what."

The man who had once played against Tennessee with a broken leg expected his men to overcome minor injuries. "Minor," of course, was a matter of interpretation. During the first half of a game that the Terrapins tied with West Virginia in Morgantown, Joe Drach broke a bone in his right hand, and it was throbbing with unbearable pain. Bryant took one look at the tangled limb, which looked more like a question mark, and told one of the coaches to tape it up.

"Tape it up?" Drach replied incredulously.

Bryant grabbed his player by the arm and pressed the hand against the wall of the locker room until the bone popped back into place. Drach passed out, but once he came to, he played the entire second half.

Bryant was learning, even as a thirty-two-year-old rookie head coach, how to motivate. "The real brilliance of him was his tremendous knowledge of psychology," said Harry Bonk, a fullback on the first Maryland team. "He knew what to say and when to say it to make you reach for that extra ounce of potential."

Beneath his tough exterior, some saw a tender side. After playing a game at Griffith Stadium in Washington, the ancient home of the Washington Senators baseball team, two of his players were standing on the sidewalk window shopping outside a men's clothing store. As they had every day up to that point, they were wearing their Navy uniforms because they didn't have enough money to buy civvies. "Bet you'd like some of those clothes," a booming voice behind them said, and they turned around to see their coach, who had just happened to be walking down the same street. He told the players he had just gotten a loan from George Preston Marshall to tide him over, but, "You fellas need some clothes as bad as I do," so he pulled a wad of bills from his pocket and gave the players one hundred dollars each, which was more than twice the average man's weekly salary. This gesture, of course, violated even the broad principles of amateurism of the day, though it would be nearly a decade before the NCAA got around to strictly defining the parameters of the athletic grant-in-aid and creating a division to enforce such rules. Bryant felt an obligation to help his players, although such small gestures would later become taboo, and he would adjust to the new realities.

In a 6–2–1 season of highs and lows in which Bryant committed innumerable rookie mistakes, his first team displayed a trait that connected it to every team he coached: the 1945 Terrapins hit people. *Hard.* Offenses and defenses would come and go like women's hemlines, but the kind of knock-you-on-your-ass football Maryland played that season would become the hallmark of his coaching career. And even then, it created controversy.

After Maryland upset undefeated Virginia 19–13—which cost the Cavaliers a trip to the Orange Bowl—Virginia coach Frank Murray collared Bryant on the sideline. "I want to congratulate you for playing the dirtiest game I've ever seen," Murray said with a sneer.

Bryant stiffened and glared at his counterpart. "If you weren't such an old man, I'd knock your ass on the ground."

"Coach Bryant taught us to hit with everything we had," said Harry Bonk. "In fact, he used to take a lot of time talking about how he believed the only way you could get hurt on the football field was if you weren't going full speed. But he never taught us to play dirty. We just hit them so hard they thought we were playing dirty."

Three days before the Virginia game, campus police informed Bryant that one of his players, tackle Larry Cooper, had been drinking at a roadhouse a few blocks off campus. Although Bryant had few strict rules, drinking was forbidden during the season. He suspended Cooper, who was big and tough and the only one of the original Maryland players to crack the starting lineup. Rules were rules to Bryant, and he didn't make exceptions. His players sometimes thought his rules were too restrictive, but they respected the fact that he applied them consistently.

After the Christmas holidays, Bryant returned from visiting his family in Birmingham to discover that Curly Byrd had been playing in his sandbox. Byrd, who was a former football coach himself, had reinstated Larry Cooper. He had also fired one of his assistants, Herman Ball. Bryant was incensed. The football team was going to be his football team, and he would not tolerate interference from anyone, not even the president of the university. He knew he couldn't tolerate such a public undermining of his authority and still do his job properly. "I knew I had to quit," Bryant later said. "It broke my heart, but I knew . . . if Curly was going to pull things like that, I couldn't work for him."

While he was away from campus, Bryant's mail and telephone messages had started to pile up, so he grabbed a large stack and took them to his new house, the house no one knew he had bought, and started thinking about finding another job. As he went through his correspondence, he came across a four-day-old telegram:

WOULD YOU BE INTERESTED IN POSITION AS HEAD COACH UNIVERSITY OF KY STOP IF SO PLEASE TELEPHONE ME REVERSING CHARGE STOP WOULD LIKE FOR YOU TO COME FOR INTERVIEW SATURDAY JANUARY 12 CONFIDENTIAL

H L DONOVAN PRESIDENT

Two days later, Bryant clandestinely traveled to Lexington, Kentucky, and won the job as the University of Kentucky's head football coach. Then he went back to College Park and told Curly Byrd what he thought of him. Even though Bryant was working without a contract—which was another point of contention between the two large egos—Byrd tried to tell him he couldn't go. They argued for more than an hour, and Bryant finally just walked out. Earlier in the afternoon, the coach had broken the news to his team, which felt deserted. Somehow, word leaked out about the reasons for Bryant's departure, and a large group of students staged a student strike. They blocked the entrances to various academic buildings and picketed outside the administration building, shouting, "Bear stays! Curly goes!" Some students even burned classroom furniture. It went on for three days, and the resulting national headlines gave Bryant his first taste of fame, albeit under circumstances he never expected. On the third day, Bryant climbed the steps of the administration building and thanked the students for their support but told them they should go back to class. "I'm leaving . . . there's nothing that can be done," he said.

If the incident demonstrated Bryant's need for absolute control, it also demonstrated his determination to cling to his principles. His style of leadership was based on discipline, and he realized that he couldn't maintain discipline if Curly Byrd could overrule his decisions. Most of his players understood,

but they still felt betrayed. "It was a matter of principle for
Coach Bryant and I respected that," Drach said. "But all of
us had cast our lot with him and then he abandoned us. We
understood why, but that didn't make it any easier to accept."

After falling to a 3–6 record in 1946, Maryland hired Jim
Tatum, who led the Terrapins to their greatest glory over the
ensuing decade—including the 1953 national championship.
By that time, Bryant had performed some heroics of his own
in Lexington, where he faced a major rebuilding job at a school
where even the Bear could not make football king.

Kentucky

ADOLPH RUPP CAST A SHADOW as large as the state of Kentucky. At night, when ambitious little boys all across the Commonwealth laid head to pillow, they dreamed about sinking a perfect set shot at the buzzer for the Baron. An autocratic, temperamental little man who owned Southeastern Conference basketball like no coach before or since, Rupp easily could have been elected governor—or king. At a time when college basketball was, in most of the country, a minor sport with a limited fan base, it flourished to the point of obsession in Kentucky.

The football Wildcats attracted mostly yawns. With neither a winning tradition nor a well-developed feeder system at the high-school level—the better athletes preferred being fouled on the basketball court to getting more seriously roughed up on the football field—the program had languished in Rupp's shadow for more than two decades. Between 1936 and 1945, the Wildcats won a total of five conference games. For most UK partisans, the parade of autumn losses served as little more than a buffer between basketball seasons. Every few years, Kentucky changed coaches, but the program never got any closer to a bowl game or a championship.

Paul "Bear" Bryant was a young man so full of brass that he believed he could win anywhere. When he took over the Anywhere program in January 1946, Kentucky, like many other universities, was being flooded with ex-servicemen. Many wanted to play football. At the same time, the school could sign an unlimited number of high-school players, so in addition to trawling the state of Kentucky for the odd athlete who had somehow bucked the tide and chosen football, Bryant and his coaches hit the road in pursuit of the best talent in the neighboring states of West Virginia, Ohio, and Pennsylvania. The combination of high-school signees, tryouts, and ex-GIs swelled the Kentucky roster to more than two hundred players in the years immediately after the war, which allowed the coach to make practices as difficult as he wanted.

Practice? It was more like war. The Wildcats worked themselves to a bloody pulp the year round. By some estimates, the attrition rate topped 75 percent. The security of not having to worry about losing some talented stud in those heady days—there were always a dozen more ready to step up and play—reinforced Bryant's Darwinist approach to the game while he was still learning how to coach.

"He worked us like we were getting ready to fight the Japanese all over again," said Walt Yaworski, who made the Kentucky squad as a freshman lineman in 1947. "It was his will against ours for four years."

Bryant didn't invent the militaristic approach to football coaching, but he certainly perfected it. Like the military, he used a combination of fear and discipline to mold his football teams. He seized control of his players' lives down to the smallest detail—he forbade his players to keep cars on campus, for instance, and required that they always wear a coat and tie before and after games.

Off the field, he demanded that his players act like gentlemen—which was, for some rough-hewn youngsters fresh from the farm or the coal mine, an accomplishment. On the field, he expected his players to attack like animals. Although he made sure they understood that he always wanted them to play within the rules—"the surest way to lose a ballgame is to get a bunch of penalties," he often said, reflecting the disciplined, ordered world that he created—Bryant wanted his athletes to take the field with a certain recklessness.

In practice, he pushed them to their physical and mental limits in drills that resembled Marine boot camp. He believed in the survival-of-the-fittest approach, and the fittest were not always the most talented, the strongest, the biggest, or the fastest. He probably ran off more great players than any coach in the history of football—many, he would later concede, for reasons having less to do with good sense than his own unrestrained zeal to transform even the supremely talented into overachievers.

Never known as a great strategic innovator, Bryant nevertheless was far ahead of his peers in organization on the practice field. Each period of drills was strictly timed and planned.

There was very little standing around during his profanity-laced practices. A player was either hitting someone or preparing to hit someone, which both toughened his will and, as with any other kind of teaching, proved the value of repetition. A player who loafed was liable to be punched or kicked. Whether a player was going from one side of the field to the other or all the way to the fieldhouse, he ran. If he got caught walking, the coaches would tell him to turn in his uniform. There were no water breaks—Bryant didn't know about the dangers of dehydration; needing liquids was thought a sign of weakness —and considering the conditions they endured, Bryant was lucky to have never cost a player his life. Often, at the end of practice, Bryant would call out for the players to pair off and go one-on-one in blocking and tackling drills until one partner dropped from sheer exhaustion.

"All right, men," Bryant would sometimes say as he walked among the nonstop hitting, "today we're gonna separate the champions from the turds!"

The sign that hung on the locker-room wall needed no explanation:

BE GOOD OR BE GONE

During his first few summers in Lexington, he bused the team to an isolated military academy twenty-five miles north of campus in Millersburg, where they rose before dawn, practiced three times a day on the side of a hill, and "separated the chaff from the wheat," in the words of one of the survivors, Howard Schnellenberger. Of the 132 freshmen who made the trip in 1951, 40 returned with the team to campus. "At night, we'd be lying in bed, and you could hear the sound of guys sliding down drainpipes from our two-story dormitory . . . sliding down so they could escape," recalled Schnellenberger, who became an All-America end for the Wildcats and a celebrated coach who led the University of Miami to the 1983 national championship. "It was a demanding time for all of us. Coach

Bryant always made it so difficult that a certain amount would leave, and the ones who stayed had a tremendous amount of commitment to him and the team."

Of his particular brand of Social Darwinism, Bryant often said, "I'd rather have a young man quit in practice than in the fourth quarter."

The game meant something powerful to those who survived his grueling conditioning, and he knew, when those players were dog-tired, dripping with sweat and blood, and trailing in the fourth quarter, they would reach deep inside and perform for two very fundamental reasons: Winning was important to them; and after surviving his numerous "gut checks" in practice, they knew that they could always play a little harder.

In explaining his philosophy, he once said: "If you ask me what makes a young man suck his guts up, I'll tell you I don't know. . . . But if my 75 percent boy plays 15 percent over his ability and your 100 percent boy slogs around and plays 15 percent under his, then we'll beat you every time."

Some players from those early days believe his methods were motivated by insecurity. "He didn't feel comfortable just getting a bunch of good players and putting them on the field," observed Joe Drach, who helped launch the legendary career as a tackle at Maryland and stayed close to his coach for a lifetime. "He was determined to work his players so incredibly hard that no one could ever accuse him of not doing his job. If they lost, then the only conclusion you could draw was that the players weren't tough enough to take what he was dishing out."

Walt Yaworski, who would figure prominently in the Bear's Kentucky era, was bitter for many years at the way Bryant pushed him. "I respected him as a coach, but I didn't like him much as a human being," said Yaworski, who continues to scout college players for the Dallas Cowboys. "He was so young and full of himself. But did he help me rise to a different level as a ballplayer? Sure. He helped make me a better player."

On the way to the airport after an upset loss to Ole Miss in 1948, Bryant, burning mad, ordered his three buses to stop on the side of the road. It was already dark, and the players were exhausted and anxious to get home. "Carney," he yelled out to his top assistant, Carney Laslie, loud enough for his players to hear, "run out there to that field and see if there's a bunch of logs or stuff out there. If there's not, we're gonna have us a practice right here."

A few moments later, Laslie returned to the bus and told his boss that the field simply wouldn't work for practice. "OK. That's fine," Bryant said, returning to his seat. "We'll just wait till we get home."

It was well past midnight when the plane arrived back in Lexington, and true to his word, Bryant took his team to the practice field and went to work. It wasn't the loss that infuriated the coach as much as the way his team had dragged around without, in his estimation, hitting anybody. So he turned on the lights and they scrimmaged until four o'clock in the morning.

"You know when football's brutal?" he yelled out to them at one point. "When one side's hittin' and the other side ain't. Remember that."

Some players loved him. Some hated him. Some thought he was crazy. But the ones who survived felt in awe of him and wanted to please him. Upon meeting him for the first time, George Blanda, who became his first quarterback at Kentucky, remarked, "This must be what God looks like."

His process of separation sifted out the ones who would not bend to his will. "He didn't have to motivate me," said Dude Hennessey, who played as a five-eight, 165-pound end. "I was scared to death he was going to find out I couldn't play a lick, so I went full speed all the time." When lineman Charley Bradshaw arrived home for dinner one evening spitting blood and holding two of his front teeth in his hand, his exasperated wife asked what the dentist had told him. "I haven't seen the dentist," he mumbled. "Had to finish practice."

"In those days, the coach was like God," observed former Wildcat Harry Jones, now a member of the UK board of trustees. "You didn't argue. You didn't question. You just did whatever he told you to do. We had been taught to have respect for authority figures, and that went even further with Coach Bryant because he was such an intimidating presence."

Thirty-two and as strong as a horse when he arrived in Lexington, Bryant liked to teach with his forearms and elbows. The players loved the chance to go one-on-one with the man responsible for all their pain, but they rarely got the best of him. Only a few years older than some of the ex-GIs on his team, he could still deliver a jarring blow without pads.

"Coach Bryant was the smartest coach I was ever around," said Charley McClendon, who played at Kentucky and later coached at LSU. "He knew just how far he could push you. I don't know how he knew where that line was, but he knew."

One day, the coach lined up and prepared to demonstrate a blocking technique on McClendon, who was a frequent target of his hands-on teaching. But after being on the receiving end of all those thunderous licks, McClendon was fired up, and Bryant could see it in his eyes. "He could see I had a little fire in my belly," McClendon said. So Bryant raised up, dusted off his khaki pants, and looked Charley Mac squarely in the eyes. "Aw, hell, you get the idea!"

One of his favorite demonstration dummies was a mountain of a man named Bob Gain, who stood six-four and weighed 235 pounds and was destined to become one of Kentucky's all-time greatest players. Like his coach, Gain had grown up tough; not long after losing his father when he was eleven, he started work in the coal mines of West Virginia to help the family make ends meet. But in the test of wills between himself and Bryant, Gain, like the rest of the Wildcats, was destined to lose. Bryant pushed him harder than the rest because he was talented, but Gain was too young and impetuous to understand the reasoning behind his coach's brand of teaching. So one day after being knocked around by his coach on the practice field, a frustrated and enraged Gain told his teammates he was going to go over to Bryant's house to whip his ass.

As competitive athletes are wont to do, several of his teammates decided to put a little wager down on the impending bout. One of the guys started talking about establishing a line, but no one wanted to bet on Gain. Said Hennessey: "Everybody thought as I did that if they fought three times a day for a year, Bob would never whip Coach Bryant."

As several players watched from the bushes later that evening, Gain gathered up his courage and knocked on the front door of Bryant's beautiful four-bedroom brick home on Cherokee Pike. The coach answered the door and gave him a steely look. "What the hell do you want, Gain?"

Gain hesitated for a few seconds before finally blurting out, "Coach . . . I just wanted to know if I could go home for Christmas."

Gain, who became the standard by which all of Bryant's future linemen would be judged, clashed with his coach throughout their time together. "I wish I could've played for him after he got Kentucky and Texas A&M out of his system," he said. "Coach Bryant was so determined to prove himself in those days that he made a lot of mistakes with his players."

A short time after he finished college, when Gain was an Army draftee awaiting shipment to the front in Korea, he wrote his coach and told him, "I love you now for the things I used to hate you for." This simple testimonial could have come from almost any of the players who survived Bryant's formative, overly aggressive early years as a head coach.

"He was the most impressive human being I have ever been around," said Harry Jones, a lineman on the Kentucky teams of 1950, 1951, and 1952. "He was just everything you wanted to be."

To those who could see past the constant feelings of exhaustion and the frustration of having their lives controlled with such force, Bryant was teaching more than football. "I believe there are certain things you can't learn in school, in church, or at home," he said. "Football teaches a boy to work and instills him with many of the attributes he needs to compete in life." His players generally were the first members of their families to attend college, and his influence on them was profound.

"Coach taught me that hard work and sacrifice could get

you somewhere in this world," said Schnellenberger. "He set
the tone for my whole life."

In his eight seasons at Kentucky, Bryant proved that his kind
of football could transform even the lowliest program into a
powerhouse. He guided the Wildcats to an impressive 60–23–
5 record (.710), their first four bowl games, and the 1950 Southeastern Conference championship that still stands, more than
four decades later, as the pinnacle of the program's achievement. Considering the conspicuous lack of facilities, tradition,
and in-state material—and the constant specter of Adolph
Rupp—no man in the history of the SEC ever achieved so
much with so many handicaps.

But Bryant's days in Lexington also revealed that his intense
desire to win could blow up in his face.

The winning came quickly at Kentucky. Their 7–3 mark in
1946, accomplished mostly on the arm of quarterback George
Blanda and a defense full of no-names, was the school's best
since 1912, the year before the head coach was born. Seven
more wins in 1947 earned the Wildcats a bid to the short-lived
Great Lakes Bowl in Cleveland, where they knocked off Villanova 24–14 in the first of what would become an NCAA
record twenty-nine postseason appearances for Bryant-
coached teams. But even as he started to experience a measure of success, the brash young coach continued to work
through his own growing pains. He was so obsessed with the
task at hand that he sometimes kept his coaches in staff meetings until the wee hours of the morning and still expected
them to be fresh the next day. He was so intent on his psychological battles that, in 1948, he left the entire starting backfield
at home when the 'Cats played (and beat) Marquette.

Although he could seem arrogant to his players, Bryant
could also act humbly. Even as a young coach, he was given to
bouts of false modesty that would become a large part of his
persona. Southerners call this "poor-mouthing," and the coach

made it an art form, always with an implied wink. In assessing his team's chances in 1951 after capturing the previous season's SEC championship, which established him as one of the nation's top young coaches, he told reporters, "We're about six years behind the other teams from a coaching standpoint. The only way we can compensate for such poor coaching is working hard." In another instance: "I'm not the brightest coach in the world, but I've been lucky. We'd had some awfully good players to make up for my poor coaching." The players knew damn well that their coach didn't believe a word of such nonsense, but they appreciated the gesture.

No event symbolizes the way Bryant approached the business of creating a winning football program in Lexington quite as well as the case of Don "Dopey" Phelps. Phelps, a veteran who had grown up in nearby Danville, Kentucky, earned his way onto the squad in 1946 and saw action at linebacker for the next two seasons. Then, during preseason drills in 1948, he failed to show up for practice and Bryant dropped him from the squad. Like all the other players, Phelps, who was then a junior, knew the cardinal rule of football practice under the Bear: If you're not at practice, you'd better be in the hospital.

Phelps pleaded for a second chance; he said his baby daughter had been sick and had kept him up several nights in a row. Bryant wouldn't budge. From the moment he arrived in Lexington, the coach had been bombarded with stories about how Kentucky's football players had been coddled, and he was certain that this was one of the foremost reasons why they had not won. The Phelps case gave him an opportunity to teach his team a lesson in discipline, so he seized it. The local newspapers got wind of the story and portrayed the coach as a callous tyrant. Bryant remained firm, no doubt proving his point to the football team. Phelps, who said he understood, lost his scholarship and was forced to move out of the football dorm. But even after such a public humiliation, Phelps still wanted to play for Bryant, a fact that reinforced the coach's aura of dominance and discipline more forcefully than the suspension itself. He kept bugging his coach until, in the spring of 1949, the Bear gave him a second chance, allowing the prodigal son to return to the team.

In the years after World War II, the process of recruiting high-school athletes started to reflect the increasing pressure on coaches to win. In the middle of the Depression, Bryant had wound up at Alabama as little more than a consolation prize; none of the 'Bama coaches had seen him play, and he didn't set foot on the campus until the day he enrolled. But Bryant the coach stood at the forefront of the new era. His assistants traveled to watch hundreds of high-school players in action, practically camped out in the homes of the most promising prospects, and brought those interested in signing with Kentucky to campus, where they were wined and dined like movie stars. With few rules governing recruiting conduct —and no such thing as NCAA probation—the high-stakes game started to mirror the anarchy of the Old West. Under-the-table inducements were common, as wealthy boosters played an increasingly important role in the process of acquiring talent.

Bryant gained a reputation as a ruthless recruiter who used all the cunning and guile at his disposal to win the prize. Howard Schnellenberger, who was big and strong and dripping with the kind of toughness Bryant craved, had already verbally committed himself to Indiana University when the man from Kentucky decided to apply the full-court press. Verbal commitments were nonbinding then as now, and Bryant wanted Schnellenberger, who was considered the state's best lineman. When he walked in to the Schnellenbergers' modest Louisville home with the governor of the state, Lawrence Wetherby, Howard and his father were sufficiently impressed. After a long sales pitch from the great charmer and a few words from the governor about how it was Howard's duty to stay home and play for his state university, the young man was prepared to change his mind and go to Kentucky. But his mother held back.

"Now, Howard," she insisted, "you know that wouldn't be

the right thing to do. You've given your word to Indiana. Your word has to mean something."

So Bryant politely retreated. And several days later, he showed up with the archbishop of the Lousiville diocese of the Catholic Church, who took Howard's mother for a walk in the backyard. A devout Catholic, she seemed more mesmerized by the priest than the coach or his friend the governor, which was exactly what Bryant was banking on. A few minutes later, they strolled back into the living room.

"Now, Howard," she announced, "the archbishop has convinced me that God will understand if you change your mind."

"When Coach Bryant goes to war, he doesn't just bring the rifles," Schnellenberger said. "He brings the howitzers. That's the lesson I learned that day."

Some of the best athletes in Kentucky were just beyond Bryant's grasp: Not even the Bear could whip Jim Crow. Soon after he arrived in Lexington, Bryant tried to convince the university president to allow him to integrate the football team, motivated, it seems clear, by the lure of all those fine athletes rather than the pangs of an awakening social conscience. But Donovan refused. The members of the Southeastern Conference observed a gentlemen's agreement forbidding the recruitment of black athletes, and though Kentucky integrated its student body in 1948, the university's administration feared losing its membership in the conference if it broke the color line. On Friday nights, many of the Kentucky players liked to go across town to watch all-black Dunbar High; the best of those hometown products invariably wound up playing on integrated teams in the Big Ten or for Notre Dame. It would be another two decades before Kentucky's Nat Northington broke the SEC color barrier.

In the months after the Phelps affair, the ascension of Vito "Babe" Parilli to the starting quarterback position lifted the Kentucky program to another level. Growing up the son of Italian immigrants in the small blue-collar town of Rochester, Pennsylvania, Parilli had seemed destined for a life in the local steel mills, a rather typical path for first-generation immigrants during the great postwar industrial expansion. But football became his ticket out.

Before the NCAA established rules limiting the amount of time coaches could spend recruiting high-school players, it was common for assistant coaches to virtually kidnap prospects before signing day, thereby keeping them from being lured away by a rival coach. When Kentucky assistant coach Carney Laslie showed up at Parilli's house in Pennsylvania, he told the promising young player that they were going to a baseball game in Pittsburgh. Laslie failed to mention that Coach Bryant had instructed him to bring the young man to Lexington afterward, a seventeen-hour drive away. Parilli didn't even have a change of clothes.

A single-wing halfback in high school, Parilli was being recruited by dozens of major schools, primarily for his running skills. But on the day of his visit to Lexington, when he worked out with some of the Kentucky players, Bryant saw something in the prospect that screamed quarterback. It was more than his arm, which was strong if undeveloped. The coach saw the combination of athletic ability and leadership that he demanded of his representative on the field. Parilli became a quarterback that day, and over the next four years, Bryant molded him into the finest quarterback in the land.

Despite his unimposing six-two, 170-pound frame, Sweet Kentucky Babe, as the newspapers called him, quickly broke away from the pack with his smooth release and heady play. In addition to incredible passing skills—he could throw a strike in the face of an oncoming blitz in the mold of Kenny Stabler—Parilli developed what Bryant demanded of all his quarterbacks: a confidence bordering on arrogance. In 1949, the Wildcats ditched the Notre Dame box and installed the T-formation to better take advantage of Babe's skills.

Every day after practice for the next four years, Parilli and some of the other quarterbacks gathered in Bryant's office to play a mind game. Bryant would describe a situation in detail, including down, field position, weather, and the kind of defense the opposition was showing. The quarterbacks were expected to call the right play for the situation, and Bryant acted as the opposition as he worked on his quarterbacks' confidence as well as their play-calling ability.

"In his performance, he utilized the combined talents of Bryant the coach, Bryant the teacher, Bryant the psychologist, and Bryant the salesman," said Parilli. "Gradually I became part of the Bryant philosophy of football. His quarterbacks were always to be the boss in the huddle, the coach on the field, responsible only to him. And, by inference, he kept demanding that we seek answers within ourselves: Is that what we wanted?"

Parilli "was the best fake-and-throw passer I have ever seen," Bryant said. "So quick and strong with his hands he could jump three times before he threw. We adjusted to Babe. We built [our offense] around him."

Bryant also admired his quarterback's toughness. After undergoing surgery to repair a groin injury that caused internal bleeding, Parilli was lying in a hospital bed, still groggy from the medication. His coach walked into the room and tossed a playbook on his bed. "Learn them," he mumbled. "This is the ballgame."

The Wildcats faced LSU that week in the conference opener of Parilli's junior season in 1950, and while no one expected him to take the field, he started, just one day after he was discharged from the hospital, because his coach expected him to. Knowing it would be foolish to let his quarterback run the conventional offense and risk being mauled on the run, Bryant devised a spread formation that bore a resemblance to the modern shotgun. Minutes before the game, the coach put his arm around his quarterback, who was still sore from the surgery, and whispered a line befitting a Hollywood tearjerker: "Bigness is in the heart, Babe." It was his way of saying that if Parilli believed strongly enough, he could overcome the pain and the fear.

The spread formation kept the LSU defense at bay, and Parilli led the Wildcats to a 14–0 victory that launched a season for the ages.

"Coach had this incredible knack for instilling confidence," said Harry Jones. "He knew what to say and when to say it to make you believe in yourself."

The program had turned a corner the previous season, in 1949. In addition to the sophomore Parilli, who would mature into the nation's best quarterback by his senior year, and tackle Bob Gain, who played both ways and would become only the second All-America in Kentucky history that season, the Wildcats were loaded with talent on both sides of the ball. Starting to play with the kind of ferocity Bryant wanted, the 'Cats' defense recorded five shutouts and allowed more than one touchdown only once, in a 20–7 loss to a good Southern Methodist team. The swarming Kentucky defense returned six interceptions for an NCAA-record 240 yards in a 47–0 blistering of Ole Miss. Eight-and-two after a narrow 6–0 loss to General Robert Neyland's Tennessee Volunteers, the eleventh-ranked Wildcats earned the school's first bid to the Orange Bowl against lightly regarded Santa Clara.

But the young, brash, overzealous Bryant wanted his first big-time bowl victory too much. Two weeks before the game, he took his team to a camp in Cocoa Beach, three hours north of Miami, and turned the reward for a good season into another extended "gut check" session. For two weeks, the Wildcats practiced three times a day in unbearable heat, missing Christmas with their families. Most of the players grew up on farms or in coal-mining towns; many had never been south of Lexington. Florida was like paradise to them, yet Bryant refused to let them go to the beach or see any of the sights. Several players collapsed from the heat.

"Coach just plain overworked us," said Charley McClendon, who was then starting at defensive back. "He saw the trip as a way to get a jump on spring practice without seeing how ridiculous that was. By the time the game rolled around, we weren't fired up. We just wanted to get it over with so we could go home."

That Kentucky lost to Santa Clara 21–13—after leading 13–6 at the half—shouldn't have surprised Bryant, but it did.

In addition to being physically exhausted while facing a fresh Santa Clara team, many of the Wildcats resented the way their coach had become a prisoner of his own determination to win. He never admitted his mistake to his players—"That wasn't his style in those days," said Dude Hennessey—but many years later, he finally conceded the point.

With most of the key components back the next year, Kentucky rolled through the season unbeaten through nine games and captured the school's first Southeastern Conference championship. Bryant's coaching was masterful, epitomized by the way he adjusted to Parilli's injury with the spread formation; Sweet Kentucky Babe's passing was practically unstoppable (his twenty-three touchdown passes remains a UK record); and the defense allowed just sixty-one points the whole year.

For the first time in school history, Kentucky entered the season finale against Tennessee unbeaten and with a shot at the national championship. But during a freak snowstorm in Knoxville, the Volunteers escaped with a 7–0 victory. Although the nation's second-ranked defense played admirably, Parilli was virtually shut down. Three times in the second half, Bryant tried one of his favorite gadget plays, the tackle eligible, but each time it was called back by the officials, although it was a legal, if obscure, play. For years, he believed the officials had cost him the game and an undefeated season.

The pivotal moment of the day, however, occurred in the locker room after the heartbreaking loss, when Bryant walked in and tried to console his team with a bowl bid.

"How many of y'all want to go to the Orange Bowl? Let's see a show of hands."

The players looked around at each other and, with thoughts of last year's bowl outing fresh in their minds, not a single hand was raised.

The Bear looked as if he'd seen a ghost.

Gain, one of the team's captains and the winner of the 1950 Outland Trophy as the nation's outstanding lineman, asked his coach if the players could have a few minutes to discuss the situation alone. Fine, Bryant said. So the seniors, sensing they had the old man right where they wanted him, devised a series of demands. When they called him back in and Gain told him that they would go to the bowl *if* they practiced no more than once a day, and *if* they scrimmaged no more than once a week, and *if* they got to fly home for Christmas, the man looked, for a moment, like big Bob had lost his mind.

"And one more thing," Gain said, milking the moment for all it was worth. "We have to play Oklahoma."

Bryant was flabbergasted, but he knew he couldn't go to a bowl without the twenty-four seniors who formed the core of his team. So he consented to their demands. He left the room for a few minutes and, after several telephone calls, came back in and told the team he had set up a game with number-one-ranked Oklahoma in the Sugar Bowl. The team didn't know he had guaranteed a victory to the bowl people, which probably seemed as outrageous to the people in New Orleans as Joe Namath's boastful vow that his AFL Jets would beat the mighty Baltimore Colts in Super Bowl III. No one could have known it at the time, but the matchup and the way it came about represented a turning point in Bryant's coaching career. In addition to learning a lesson about overworking his teams, which had fomented the locker-room revolt, Bryant never again allowed himself to be placed at the mercy of his players.

The Oklahoma Sooners seemed invincible. In the decade between 1948 and 1957, Bud Wilkinson's powerhouse dominated college football more completely than any other program in modern history, with the possible exception of Bryant's own Alabama dynasty of the 1970s. Alabama's incredible stranglehold on the Southeastern Conference in the 1970s was accomplished against much tougher competition, but the Sooners of the 1950s created an invincible aura by compiling winning streaks of thirty-one and forty-seven games, which remain the two longest in modern history. No other team in the Big Seven was even visible on Oklahoma's radar screen as the Sooners captured twelve straight conference championships during the era of bobby socks and tail fins.

But on New Year's Day 1951, Bryant's Kentucky Wildcats proved the great Sooners were not, as most experts and oddsmakers believed, unbeatable.

Already crowned the 1950 national champion—the final wire service polls would be conducted before the bowls for another fifteen years—Oklahoma entered the game as a heavy favorite over seventh-ranked Kentucky. (It was the first time the Wildcats had ever finished in the nation's top ten.) Over nearly three complete seasons, no opponent had been able to stop the Sooners' version of the Split-T offense, which featured the running tandem of fullback Leon Heath and halfback Billy Vessels, a hard-charging, tough-to-topple Okie who won the Heisman Trophy two years later.

In the preparation for the matchup, while Bryant fretted over devising a way to stop the Split-T, his players spent hour upon hour watching film, and they began to notice a disturbing trend. "We saw Oklahoma players kicking and punching other players, lots of dirty stuff," said Charley McClendon. "Real flagrant stuff." The coach saw the same extracurricular activity, and he warned his players against going to New Orleans with a brawl on their minds.

"I want you to knock 'em on their ass, but we're not going down there to fight," the coach reminded. "We're going down there to win a football game."

Although he himself was never a strategic innovator, Bryant was a master at taking what others created and making it work for him. He could use his team's strengths and negate his team's weaknesses as well as any coach who ever lived. Like every coach who had faced Oklahoma, he was stumped at first by the Split-T, which was power football at its best. But after several sleepless nights, he devised a way of defending the Sooners that may have been the most original, inventive strategy of his career.

Instead of sticking with his traditional three-man front—

which had led the nation in scoring defense—Bryant decided to go with five tackles and bring his cornerbacks and linebackers up close to the line in a scheme that created, in effect, a nine-man line. His team was bigger and stronger on defense than any of the Big Seven teams Oklahoma had faced, and the special scheme was Bryant's way of accentuating that strength.

"Bud was used to playing against all those children in the [Big Seven] and I wanted him to see some men," Bryant later joked.

The strategy was risky because it left the Wildcats vulnerable to the pass. But it worked. Oklahoma had never seen such pressure at the line of scrimmage; the Sooners committed four fumbles, including one deep in their own territory that set up Kentucky's first touchdown. On a chilly, windy day before a sellout crowd of eighty two thousand at mammoth Tulane Stadium—and a national radio audience—Kentucky's defense held the Sooners to 189 yards rushing, half their average, and Sweet Kentucky Babe connected with Shorty Jamerson for two touchdowns as the Wildcats staged a 13–7 upset of monumental proportions. Suddenly, Paul Bryant had become college football's answer to Jim Bagby, Jr., the Cleveland pitcher who stopped Joe DiMaggio's record fifty-six-game hitting streak. The mighty Bud had struck out.

"That game demonstrated what a great defensive coach Paul was," said Wilkinson, who was 145–29–4 in seventeen seasons (.826) as the Oklahoma coach, but 0–2 against Bryant. "He knew how to turn what you thought was your strength into your weakness, and that's what he did to us in that Sugar Bowl. He was the kind of guy who was going to find a way to win."

There was no greater testament to Bryant's genius than the most-valuable-player award that was presented to Walt Yaworski that day. If Kentucky had played in its regular defensive scheme, the feisty substitute linebacker would have stayed on the sidelines for most of the game. But the special alignment placed him as the starter at right tackle, and he became the Sooners' worst nightmare. Using his strength and quickness to overpower the Oklahoma linemen, Yaworski's constant pressure resulted in two fumble recoveries and more than a dozen tackles as he became the embodiment of his coach's game plan.

In contrast to the regular-season films that had so enraged the Kentucky players, the teams played a relatively clean game, but it was a typical hard-hitting affair of the time, with casualties on both sides. Cornerback Charley McClendon lunged for the celebrated Billy Vessels in the second quarter, slipped to the ground, and watched helplessly as Vessels reversed his field and, on his way downfield, slammed a cleat through Charley Mac's right eye. Players didn't wear facemasks in those days, and the completely legal stomp cut a huge gash in McClendon's eye.

"They took me to the hospital and sewed that thing up and I couldn't see a thing for weeks," McClendon said. "But, hey, that's football. It's a rough game."

After the game, Wilkinson shocked Bryant when he walked into the Kentucky locker room and made a little speech congratulating the Wildcats, shaking as many hands as he could and teaching the victorious coach a lesson about sportsmanship. Bryant, who sometimes pouted after losses, had never seen a losing coach make such a magnanimous gesture. Still maturing as a coach and as a man, the Bear gradually realized that he could retain his untrammeled zeal to be the best without wearing it on his sleeve. In later years, he would repeat Wilkinson's gesture many times, which symbolized a certain class even in defeat that became a large part of the Bryant persona. The change to this kinder, gentler Bear came gradually, like the graying of his hair, and it started, ironically, on the day of one of his biggest victories.

Even as a young head coach, Bryant embraced innovation; if he heard of a coach trying some new kind of formation or technique that he thought might work for his Kentucky program, he would call him up and pick his brain, or invite him for a coaching clinic or a round of golf. Most coaches were

land, probably because he could never beat him. I firmly believe that one of the main reasons I was hired was so Coach Bryant could find out more about the general's philosophy."

The Kentucky days gave the Bryants their first taste of the good life. The coach's position and his upper-middle-income salary (which reached twelve thousand dollars by the early 1950s, when the average worker earned about five thousand dollars) afforded them a comfortable, four-bedroom home, two new automobiles, vacations to California and abroad, and entrance into Lexington's old-money social elite. In an Old South culture based less on money than class, the one-time farm boy and his beautiful wife blended easily, socializing with the governor and other prominent political and business leaders. The ultimate man's man and the dark-haired beauty cut a dashing figure, like the elegant Audrey Hepburn on the arm of Cary Grant. Especially after the Wildcats started going to big bowl games, the Bryants moved up on everyone's short list for dinner and parties, and he enjoyed the attention and the other trappings of success.

Mary Harmon, like most women of the time, built her life around her husband. Devoted to him and to her children, she kept the home and took most of the responsibility for raising Mae Martin and Paul Junior while he earned the living. Like so many others who came of age during the middle of the American century, the Bryant children enjoyed all the benefits that had eluded their father. Mae Martin was a high-strung girl who began her turbulent teenage years in the bluegrass. Paul Junior, who started school the same year his father won his first SEC championship, was smart and shy. Their father left home for work by five-thirty in the morning and sometimes returned after they had gone to bed, so they did not spend much time with him.

Whenever he was away on recruiting or other business trips, he always took the time to send his children postcards or letters; one such missive to twelve-year-old Mae Martin closed with a gentle line that belied his gruff image: "You are still my baby and the sweetest little girl in the world and I love you very much." But he was not the kind of man to show up at all the piano recitals and Little League games, and they were taught to understand why. While both their father and mother made certain that they felt loved, they did not always feel close to their papa, as they called him.

"They were brought up to think that their father was a busy man," said Martha Gibbs, who became one of Mary Harmon's lifelong friends during their days at Kentucky, where her husband, Charley Bradshaw, played for Bryant. "They were taught that they shouldn't bother Papa unless it was absolutely necessary."

Their father could be loving—or moody. The children learned to read his temperament. Sometimes, when they heard his car drive up, the children would run upstairs and climb into their beds rather than waiting to test his mood. Like many busy, powerful men of his generation, Bryant later confided that he regretted not having spent more time with his children during their formative years.

If Mary Harmon felt neglected, she grew to understand her role. Bryant's sister Louise remembers a visit to Lexington in which Mary Harmon lamented her lack of time with her husband. "Sometimes, I wish I was married to a ditch digger," she joked. But Gibbs, who often traveled with her to visit family and friends in Birmingham and Troy, said, "I think she understood that that was just the ways things were. She knew his work was important to him."

Her husband could be charming or distant. "They certainly loved each other very much, but their relationship was not the kind of close relationship that made your life carefree and happy," Gibbs said.

In addition to making a good home for her husband, Mary Harmon became a den mother of sorts to his football teams. On the airplanes and buses traveling to and from games, when he was concentrating on the impending battle, she would play cards and joke with the players. Through the years, she made

a habit of staying on the bus for an hour or so once it reached
the stadium. She liked to visit with former players and hear all
about their babies and their lives, and the boys always knew
where to find her.

The victory over Oklahoma catapulted Bryant to national
fame, and he received numerous feelers from other colleges
over the next three years, as the Wildcats continued their newfound winning ways with records of 8–4 (including a Cotton
Bowl victory over TCU), 5–4–2, and 7–2–1. In addition to
spurning offers from Southern Cal and Arkansas, he was approached about replacing Red Drew, one of his old coaches, at
Alabama. From the time he decided to pursue a career in
coaching he started daydreaming about returning to Tuscaloosa someday to continue the legacy of Wallace Wade and
Frank Thomas, but friends convinced him the time wasn't
right. So he milked Kentucky for a raise and a twelve-year
contract extension instead.

"Shucks, son," he drawled to a reporter during the wooing
process, "I'm gonna live and die in old Kentucky."

As much as he loved Kentucky, Bryant never adjusted to
playing second fiddle to Adolph Rupp. Everywhere he went,
he bumped up against some reminder that the state's heart
belonged to Rupp and basketball. He usually smiled and pre-
tended not to be steamed, but the jealousy festered. In later
years, he liked to joke about the all-sports banquet when the
university presented Rupp with a Cadillac and gave him a
cigarette lighter. If he was searching for a symbol of the over-
whelming odds he faced, it was never any farther away than
his coat pocket.

(The Bear and the Baron were rivals, but they never ex-
changed a cross word. It was more of a cold war of egos, and
in the years after Bryant left Kentucky, they actually became
friends. In fact, in the mid-1970s, when Rupp was dying of
cancer, Bryant sent his private airplane to bring the retired

legend to Tuscaloosa for a basketball game, where he was treated like royalty.)

As if it wasn't bad enough for Bryant when the basketball team was riding high, he soon found his program overshadowed by an infamous event in Kentucky's hoops history. In 1951, five members of the Wildcats team that had captured consecutive national championships in 1948 and 1949—including Olympic team stars Alex Groza and Ralph Beard—were convicted of conspiring to fix games during their Kentucky playing days. Several players were also named as receiving illegal inducements by representatives of the school. As punishment for the improprieties, the NCAA and the Southeastern Conference jointly suspended the Kentucky basketball program for the 1952–53 season in a ruling that effectively created the modern NCAA enforcement process.

UK President Herman L. Donovan promised his football coach that he would force Rupp to retire in the near future; it wasn't in writing, of course, but to a man like Bryant, Donovan's word was sufficient. Donovan had also made a commitment to update the football program's antiquated facilities, a promise he never carried out. While the basketball Wildcats lived and worked in relative luxury, the football team practiced and lived in dilapidated facilities that looked like Stone Age relics. So when Bryant picked up a newspaper in February 1954 and read that the university had rewarded Rupp with a new long-term contract, he blew his stack.

In a fit of rage just three weeks before the scheduled start of spring practice, he decided to quit. Just like that. The administration tried to prevent him from leaving, triggering a bitter public fight. Bryant lashed out in the press: "I don't know [what I'll be doing next year], maybe I'll drive a truck, but I won't be coaching at Kentucky." Donovan was enraged, and released the coach from the twelve years remaining on his contract only after being threatened by the governor, who put the squeeze on the president and the board of regents as a favor to his friend the coach. That night, Bryant and two of his closest friends in

Lexington, Bull Hancock and Louis Hagen, huddled around his brand-new air-conditioner—one of the first of those modern marvels in the entire city—and downed a fifth of whiskey in celebration.

The Wildcats haven't won a championship or played in a major bowl game since.

As Kentucky football began its slow descent into mediocrity, Texas A&M welcomed Bryant as a savior. Under different circumstances, the ambitious young man never would have taken an offer from Texas A&M seriously. He had been approached by such prestigious schools with winning traditions as Southern Cal and Alabama, but all the big jobs were filled by the time he threw his very public temper tantrum. He didn't want to wait another year, so he accepted the best offer on the table, which was from the all-male military school that had been mired in the second division of the Southwest Conference for a decade. A&M made pre-Bryant Kentucky look like Notre Dame.

To land the brash firebrand who had revived Kentucky's program, the A&M board of trustees broke many of its long-standing rules. Bryant demanded the job of athletic director to solidify his control over the football program, and he got it. He demanded the then-incredible sum of twenty-five thousand dollars per year in salary, and with the help of a rich alumnus who put him on the company payroll, he got it. He demanded 1 percent of the football gate, which was unprecedented, and a six-year contract—which violated the school's principle of one-year contracts in the wake of the alumni having to pay off former coach Homer Norton—but after some wrangling, he got those, too. He also demanded and won without any discussion the rights to the game films for use in a weekly television program, which probably was the most prescient request of all.

The day after Kentucky grudgingly granted him his release, Bryant flew down to College Station, Texas, while Mary Harmon stayed in Lexington to start making arrangements for the move. She wasn't thrilled. The one-time Alabama socialite felt at home in the genteel, Old South circles to which they had gained admittance, and in her mind Texas was like another country—which, of course, it was. Later, she told friends that when she first arrived in College Station and encountered the desolate, barren landscape, she almost fainted. But Mary Harmon didn't argue when Paul told her they were moving, because wives didn't question their husbands in those days. She just started packing.

Not without his own crosses to bear, the coach was bumped off his flight to Texas and was forced to wait several hours for the next one. He tried to convince a Houston newspaperman to give up his seat, but Jack Gallagher, a veteran sportswriter from the *Houston Post* who had been dispatched to cover Bryant's hasty retreat from Kentucky and his widely anticipated arrival at Texas A&M, took no small amount of glee in refusing the frustrated coach. "You don't think I'm going to stay behind and let all the other writers from Texas greet you when you land?"

When he arrived on campus well past dark that night, the new A&M coach was taken to an outdoor theater called The Grove, where the sky was ablaze with a bonfire stretching two stories into the sky. More than five thousand students showed up at a yell practice to catch a glimpse of the man who would try to reignite the once-proud A&M football program. Without a word, he stepped onto the stage and tossed his hat to the floor, then mashed it like a cigarette butt. Then he threw off his coat and ripped off his tie, rolled up his sleeves and pulled the microphone to his mouth as the place roared with a thunderous ovation.

"I'm Paul Bryant," he said, "and I'm rolling up my sleeves so we can get to work!"

Bryant's presence and his flair for the dramatic captivated a tall, lanky freshman football player in the audience named Gene Stallings. "I'd never seen him or heard of him till that night, but he just made a real impression on me right then," said Stallings, who would later follow in Bryant's footsteps at both Texas A&M and Alabama. "You could look at him and listen to him and know he was gonna be different."

Different was good. The Texas A&M Aggies desperately needed a jolt of something different. Under Homer Norton, A&M had captured three straight Southwest Conference championships immediately before World War II, but for more than a decade the program had been living off the fumes of those glory days. Norton's program was never the same after the war, and the alumni eventually bought out the three years remaining on his contract. The second coach to follow him, Ray George, was an easygoing gentleman who was genuinely liked by most of his players, but his teams were losers. By the time Bryant arrived, the Aggies hadn't posted a winning record in conference play in eleven years, and A&M was hungry for a winner.

Like Kentucky, Texas A&M presented a unique challenge. In addition to playing in the shadow of the University of Texas and the other more successful Southwest Conference teams, A&M was a male-only military school in those days. Phrases like "no girls" and "daily marching" were enough to scare off many of the best recruits in the state of Texas. If the military regimen and the lack of female companionship failed to send a potential recruit fleeing into the arms of the Longhorns, the drab, dismal look of the place often did. "At first glance," Bryant once remarked, "A&M looked like a penitentiary." The cadets mockingly referred to their school as "Sing Sing on the Brazos."

Two years later, when the Aggies were already well on their way to overturning the old order in the SWC, a teary-eyed recruit named Don Meredith told Bryant, "Coach, if you were anywhere else in the world except A&M . . ."

During secret contract negotiations at a Dallas hotel before he agreed to accept the A&M job, Bryant asked a prominent alumnus, Jack Finney, how many of the twenty best prospects in the state he might be able to sign in head-to-head competition with the University of Texas. Finney said ten, which impressed Bryant. He knew he could win if he could land half of the top twenty players in Texas.

But the coach failed to understand the Aggie mentality. Aggies were outsiders who always felt like outsiders, no matter how much power and wealth they accumulated. They were more likely to belong to the Rotary Club than the country club. After all those years of being on the bottom, of being mocked, ridiculed, and taken for granted, the Aggies were prone to a cockiness and a tendency toward Texas-sized exaggeration tinged with a healthy dose of self-delusion—a dangerous combination. Bryant took the job believing what Finney told him, when even Finney deep down knew he was big-dogging it.

"I didn't know the Aggies then like I know them now," Bryant later said. "Old Jack was exaggerating. You couldn't get ten. You would be lucky to get one. The chances were you wouldn't get any. Not then."

Less than two weeks after his coming-out party at The Grove in early March 1954, Bryant commenced spring practice with a group he considered soft, uninspired, and desperately short on athletic ability. The first spring practice under Bryant was so grueling that end Lloyd Taylor made up his mind to quit, which meant going back to an oilfield town in West Texas. "It took me a long time to work up the courage to call my dad and tell him I was coming home," Taylor said. "He said they'd love to have me home for a visit. He didn't understand. I said, 'No, Dad, I'm coming home . . . for good.' He said, 'Boy, if you quit down there, you don't have any home to come home to.' So I stayed."

Spring practice merely confirmed Bryant's worst fears. He had left behind enough material at Kentucky to contend for the conference championship, in order to take over a program saddled with rejects, something that became more painfully obvious with each passing day. While the players were away for the summer, he started looking for a place far away from all the distractions of campus—especially the meddling alumni—

where he could take the team for a boot camp to start fall practice. He wanted to find out who really wanted to play football, who really wanted to make a commitment to his way of life.

Someone suggested a place called Junction.

Junction

DENNIS GOEHRING WAS BORN ON a cattle ranch near San Marcos in the hill country of West Texas. He was always small for his age, with short limbs and a rather slight frame, but he was a fighter, and he had heart. So after the drought arrived like a plague in the early 1950s, and the family lost the ranch, and his daddy took a job in town as a butcher to keep food on the table, Dennis packed up his belongings and hitchhiked off to Texas A&M, where, for some reason—destiny, most probably—he had landed a football scholarship.

"Football wasn't just football to me," he would remark more than four decades later. "It was survival."

On the first day of September in 1954—the typical start of fall practice in those days—Paul Bryant presented his varsity football players with a set of rather cryptic instructions: Pack a toothbrush and a change of clothes and report to one of the two buses parked in front of the dormitory. He didn't say any more. He didn't have to. Bryant's Aggies, like other branches of the military, worked on a need-to-know basis, and all the Aggies needed to know was that they were headed off campus for the start of preseason practice so they could get away from all the distractions and try to build on the work they had started during spring drills. They did not need to know that they were headed for the history books.

Bryant had spent much of the two months of spring drills questioning his own sanity. He had left a solid program in place for Blanton Collier back in Lexington, to start over at a place where the talent level was sorely lacking, and even worse, the halfhearted effort he saw from many of the players he had inherited gave him pause about the future. He had won immediately at Maryland and at Kentucky, but he soon realized that A&M was going to be a different story.

Early in the summer, Bryant started scouting around for a camp of some fashion where he could take the players for preseason practice. It had to be isolated and spartan. One of the assistant coaches suggested a place where some departments of the university often conducted freshmen orientation. Little more than a campground with screened Quonset huts for sleeping quarters, the Texas A&M Adjunct, as it was officially known, was located about 250 miles west of College Station on the outskirts of a town whose name would forever be linked to the legend of Bear Bryant.

The bus ride to Junction, which took the better part of the day, was filled with laughter and storytelling. It was the height of the blistering Texas summer, and the sun beat down on those old buses like an open flame licking a tin can. Everyone wondered where they were going, but no one asked. The exact number of Aggies who made the trip is lost to history, but somewhere between 90 and 115 piled into the buses that day. Ten days later, they needed just one bus as 29 returned.

After five years of horrific drought—annual rainfall had trickled to about one-third of what was considered normal—the landscape was almost completely barren. The soil was dusty and laden with rocks to begin with, and the drought fried any clump of grass that threatened to take root. Today, the place is lush with grass and trees, but in 1954 it looked more like the moon.

"When we drove in that front gate," Bryant later told reporters, "I wanted to puke."

At Junction, the coach expected to separate the quitters from the keepers. The team he inherited included its share of runts, fat bellies, and underachievers, and he was determined to find out whom he could count on, who would lay it on the line and win for him. The Bear never believed in ability so much as performance. At Maryland and Kentucky, he coached many players with outstanding ability, of course; Babe Parilli and Bob Gain were huge talents, among others. But he didn't care how fast you ran the forty if you weren't willing to stretch for every last ounce of potential on every play. "Paying the price," he called it. There was always, in his fear-based motivation, a certain "my way or the highway" principle, but it was not a result of arrogance; he was determined to demand, push, prod, and cajole with such a force and relentlessness that a certain number of players would quit. Those who remained were bound to emerge tougher and more determined. He wanted players who were prepared to make a commitment to him and the team to throw every last ounce of blood, sweat, and fury into the fray on every single down.

Bryant and his staff expected Dennis Goehring to quit. They *wanted* him to quit. He was small, slow, and, compared to many of the Aggies, untalented. Several days into the camp, Smokey Harper, the crusty, cigar-chomping trainer whom Bryant had brought with him from Kentucky, pulled the rancher's son to the side. He'd been watching Goehring, who was all of five-ten and 180 pounds, work at several different positions going up against guys with much more natural ability and thirty pounds on him. He arrived as the seventh-team right guard, and he was getting beaten to a pulp, but he showed no sign of quitting.

"Why don't you give it up? You're never gonna make it," Harper pleaded.

Exhausted but determined, Goehring looked Harper square in the eye and flashed a devilish grin. "I'll be here when you and Bryant are both gone," he said, and stomped back to practice.

The boss couldn't help smiling when the trainer relayed his conversation. The feisty kid, he thought to himself, might make a football player yet.

"What they didn't know was that I didn't have anything to go back to," Goehring said. "I had to stay on that team to keep my scholarship, and I had to keep my scholarship to be able to get an education. Quit? Hell, I couldn't quit. And I wasn't going to give them the satisfaction of seeing me quit."

On the day the Aggies made camp, a delegation from the local chamber of commerce drove out to the Adjunct and offered to throw the team a barbeque, which seemed like the neighborly, Texas thing to do. Bryant was curt: "We didn't come out here to eat," he said. "We came out here to play football."

"That first night we got there, before we started practice, we were all playing cards and joking, and Coach Bryant came around and said, 'I won't have to tell y'all this from now on, but there won't be any more card playing after tonight,' " said Gene Stallings, then a sophomore end from Paris, Texas. "He was right. After that night, we were so tired that if we had a spare minute we were in that bunk trying to get some rest."

The living conditions were primitive. The players slept eight to a barracks in the small Quonset huts stacked from floor to ceiling with Army-style bunks. The floor was a slab of concrete. The ceiling was corrugated tin. The screen walls provided a panoramic view of the camp and the other huts. The upper third of the walls were covered by canvas flaps, and the players quickly learned to push the flaps open to allow any stray breezes to navigate the opening. "There weren't very many stray breezes," noted Goehring.

"In the daytime, you'd try to get a little rest between practices, but they'd put the younger players on the top bunks and that made it murder," Stallings said. "That top bunk wasn't more than a few inches from the tin roof, and that made it like an oven up there."

It was so hot, even in the middle of the night, that most of the players had trouble sleeping, so after a grueling day of practice in the sizzling Texas sun, they played a cynical little game with each other: Every time they heard the gate rattle in the dark, they tried to identify the defector, who was forced to hitchhike or walk into town to wait for the morning bus.

The real torture began a few minutes before daybreak, when the manager ran through the huts blowing his whistle. "We'd try to kick him and shut him up, 'cause [his arrival] meant the start of another day," Stallings said. The Aggies practiced beginning at dawn for about three hours, and then again in the afternoon, with position meetings scattered throughout the day. (Elmer Smith, one of the A&M assistant coaches, kept telling his boss, "Any time you practice before breakfast you're gonna have a losing season." Turns out he was right.) They practiced on a field littered with more rocks and sand spurs than grass. One day late in the boot camp, Bryant loaded the team in the buses and took them to the local fairgrounds, where they found a more suitable field for scrimmaging.

The combination of the intense heat—which routinely topped one hundred degrees—the poor facilities, the torrid pace that Bryant demanded of his players, and the feeling of complete isolation forced many to quit. Bryant later admitted that he hadn't thought he would lose so many players. He certainly took the Aggies to Junction to separate the winners from the quitters, but he never thought so many players—so many talented athletes—would be unable to withstand the punishment.

"It became a test of your physical and mental endurance," said fullback Jack Pardee, the future Houston Oilers coach, who dropped twenty pounds during the camp. "It was hot as hell and it was demanding as hell . . . and some guys just couldn't take it."

"Looking back on Junction," Bryant once said, "there were times when, if you hadn't been so well raised, you would have wished you were dead."

Not all of the defectors sneaked off into the night. Some gathered enough courage to walk into the coaches' cabin and announce their decision to Bryant. As humiliating as such an encounter must have been, it was the only way the quitting player could get out of town without hitchhiking; Bryant showed no emotion during such scenes, but at least he bought the former Aggie a bus ticket home and instructed the managers to drive him into town to catch the next bus.

"You could always tell who was gonna quit by watching this water fountain outside the coaches' cabin," Stallings said. "It would always happen in the afternoon, after lunch. Everybody else would be trying to get some rest, and if you saw somebody go up to that water fountain and just stand around, you knew they were working up the courage to go see Coach Bryant."

Among the defectors was senior quarterback David Smith, who later became an assistant coach at SMU. He said his decision to leave always haunted him. "I don't like to think of

Coach

myself as a quitter, but to a certain degree I was," he said. "It hurt me then and it's still hard on me. I shed a few tears on the way home."

Junction native Rob Roy Spiller, who would enroll at A&M that very fall, estimated that he sold bus tickets to as many as fifty Aggies at the Texaco station on the town's main drag. "They were usually exhausted and kind of down," and Spiller, who graduated from A&M and returned to become president of Junction National Bank. "They seemed embarrassed. None of them wanted to quit."

An untold number of Aggies dropped from exhaustion and sought medical treatment from local physician J. E. Wiedeman, who at one point told Bryant, "I have more players than you do."

Amid all the heat and stress, Bryant didn't allow water breaks, which in light of today's medical knowledge about the dangers of dehydration seems almost barbaric, but was common in 1954. Luckily, no one succumbed to the most severe forms of heat stroke. When tackle Bill Schroeder collapsed in the middle of a scrimmage, the doctor pulled him off to the side and started his treatment by giving him water.

"We were all kind of jealous of him because he got to have a drink," Pardee said.

The purpose of Junction, like any other preseason camp, was ostensibly to get the team ready to play. In truth, Bryant was looking well beyond the 1954 season. One player Bryant was determined to make better was center Fred Broussard, who had earned all–Southwest Conference acclaim the previous year but was a loafer in the view of his new coach. Bryant spent much of the summer watching film of the 1953 season, and he was enraged by what he saw as a lack of effort from the center, who was one of the most talented athletes on the team. At Junction he probably pushed Broussard harder than anyone else.

One afternoon during a scrimmage at the fairgrounds toward the end of camp, Broussard threw his helmet to the ground and walked off the field. Bryant stopped the scrimmage and yelled after him. "Now, Fred, if you don't come back you'll regret it the rest of your life."

Broussard just kept walking.

The next day, after Broussard experienced a change of heart, several of his teammates interceded with their coach, but he wouldn't budge. Bryant told reporters, "He wanted to come back. He told me he had thought it over and that he was sorry, but I told him mine wasn't a hasty decision, either. I told him 'no' because I thought it was best for the team."

The reality was that banishing Broussard was the absolute worst decision for the football team, in terms of its immediate needs, because the Aggies were fresh out of centers. The season was less than two weeks away, and Bryant had allowed one of his best football players to slip away. A lesser coach might have taken him back, maybe punished him in some way, but Bryant would not let the big picture be obscured by short-term needs. It wasn't the first time Broussard had quit and begged for forgiveness; he had done so two or three times with the previous coach, Ray George. As much as he wanted to win immediately, as badly as he needed an experienced center to snap the ball in the Aggies' season opener, Bryant realized that taking Broussard back at that particular moment would have conveyed the wrong message about discipline and commitment to his football team.

To pour salt in the quitting player's wound—and to have someone to snap the ball to his quarterback—Bryant promoted five-eight, 155-pound Troy Summerlin from head manager to center. The media loved that; the coach was giving up a mere seventy-five pounds, not to mention all that ability and experience. Even before Broussard's departure, the daily defections were being updated in the Texas newspapers like casualties from a war. Bryant was being portrayed, even before he coached his first game, as an ogre who was determined to run off any player who wouldn't bend to his will. Which was about right.

Although the Southwest Conference press tour came through for a memorable stop, the only sportswriter in atten-

dance throughout the entire boot camp was Mickey Herskowitz, who as on his first big assignment for the *Houston Post*.
His dispatches included references to "mangled bodies" and
"crunching bones" that disturbed the Bear, although they later
became good friends.

"The one thing everyone in that camp seemed to have in
common that summer was fear. Fear of Bryant," Herskowitz
wrote in his memoir of the coach, *The Legend of Bear Bryant*.
"The players were motivated to get through each day without
screwing up, without forcing Coach Bryant to look right at
them."

As the numbers dwindled, many lesser players moved up
the depth chart, including Dennis Goehring, who worked at
half a dozen different positions. "All those guys leaving in the
night didn't bother me a bit," he said. "'Cause I figured the
more they ran off the better chance I had."

"We'd hear that gate rattle and we'd think, hey, that's one
less we've got to beat out," said tackle Lloyd Hale. "You're
talking about a game of survival and endurance. That's what
Junction was all about."

Ten days after they arrived, Bryant loaded the survivors into
one bus and returned to campus with barely enough players to
scrimmage.

"A lot has been made about the ones who stuck it out being
stronger or whatever," noted Bobby Drake Keith, a back who
returned among the legendary twenty-nine. "But I think most
of us survived because football was important to us for whatever reason, and it was in our nature to do whatever we had
to do to stay on that team and stay in school. Our instinct was
survival."

During a road trip to Georgia in the third week of the season,
two Atlanta sportswriters approached Bryant with the A&M
roster, with its puny list of twenty-nine names.

"You mean this is all the players you got?" one of the scribes
asked.

"These are the ones that want to play," Bryant replied.

On an autumn Saturday afternoon, when the Texas A&M football team runs onto the playing surface at Kyle Field, there is no place quite like it in the world. Although the program has had various zeniths and nadirs through the years, the tradition of unwavering support by the student body and the corps of cadets is unsurpassed in college football. The unique bond is symbolized by the lore of The Twelfth Man, in whose spirit the entire student body stands for the entire game. The sense of togetherness was especially strong during the days when A&M was an all-male military school, up until the 1970s, but even though the dynamic has changed through the years, the fierce link between the team and the student body remains rooted in history.

In the 1920s, during a bruising contest against Centre College in Dallas, Coach Dana X. Bible's Aggies were dropping like flies. Bible started to fear that he would run out of players, so he sent a manager into the stands to fetch a former player named King Gill, who had paid his own way into the game and was wearing street clothes. Gill changed into a uniform and ran out to the sideline, and though it turned out that he was not needed, he was ready and willing to help his old team. Thus, The Twelfth Man was born. In the early 1980s, when Jackie Sherrill arrived to revive the moribund program, he took the legend one step further by holding open auditions for the kickoff team, and manned it entirely with walk-ons from the student body.

Two weeks after the team returned from Junction in 1954, Kyle Field was awash in maroon and optimism. For more than six months, the cadets had been anxiously awaiting the debut of their savior, the man who had brought new life into the Kentucky program, the man who surely would lead A&M back to the promised land. Then Texas Tech drilled the Aggies, 41–9; it was ugly, and it was the most lopsided loss of his career. In his debut, Bryant's team committed six turnovers and looked hopelessly outmanned.

Judged with an eye toward getting the Aggies ready to play for the 1954 season, Junction was a failure. The team was headed for a disastrous 1–9 season, the only losing campaign of Bryant's career, and it was forced to play several unproven performers in the place of returning starters who quit at Junction.

"I don't think Coach thought in his wildest dreams he'd lose as many [at Junction] as he did," said Gene Stallings. "We were awful thin that year, and if we'd had some of those players who quit, who knows."

The lone victory of his loneliest season came in week three against Georgia. During the week of the game, one of Bryant's assistants, Elmer Smith, noticed something interesting in the Bulldogs' game films: Smith could tell by watching the quarterback's feet as he called the signals whether he was going to pass or run. If his feet were parallel to the line, it was a handoff; if one was behind the other, he was going to pass.

Linebacker Jack Pardee, who called the defensive signals, was able to watch the quarterback's feet and check off enough to keep the 'Dogs off-balance. He also caught a short touchdown pass that was the difference in A&M's 6–0 victory.

As poorly as the Aggies played in the opener, they improved gradually and were in every other game they played. Six of the losses were decided by a touchdown or less, which was more frustrating in some ways than being blown out every week. Bryant made a conscious decision early in the year to start building for the future, so he played a large number of sophomores and juniors at the expense of some of the seniors.

Late in the year against SMU, which was one of the conference powers at the time, Dennis Goehring got the shot he had been waiting for. He had played off and on throughout the year along the line—which averaged a ridiculously small 185 pounds per man—but in those days, the substitution rules were so strict that coaches were not able to shuffle backups into the game at will. After one of the defensive tackles was forced out of the game with an injury in the third quarter, Goehring stepped in and faced the prospect of being blocked by Forrest Gregg, the six-three, 225-pound mountain who was destined for All-Pro stardom with Vince Lombardi's Green Bay Packers. Gregg against Goehring was a mismatch of Muhammad Ali–Chuck Wepner proportions. When they lined up, Goehring intentionally jumped offsides and shoved a forearm straight toward Gregg's mouth, beating him to the first punch. The big man staggered around for a few moments, and after they brought out the smelling salts, the game continued.

Bryant was hopping mad about the offsides penalty, but while he was never known to condone cheap shots, he had to admire the kid's ingenuity. Goehring was going to find a way to win, and the little man who was supposed to be a casualty of Junction started every game for the rest of his college career. As a senior guard, he earned All–Southwest Conference honors.

Although Junction failed to help A&M win immediately, it undoubtedly laid the foundation for future success. The Aggies turned the corner the next year with a 7–2–1 mark, and in 1956, the Great Rehabilitator brought the school its first Southwest Conference championship since World War II, with a team anchored by Junction survivors such as Gene Stallings, Dennis Goehring, Bobby Drake Keith, and Lloyd Hale. In addition to hardening those players and setting a tone for the kind of hard work and discipline their coach demanded, Junction created a special bond among the players. As any coach will tell you, athletic ability may win games, but unity wins championships.

"Even though we had a losing season, I believe Junction won us the Southwest Conference championship two years later," Bryant said years after.

In the years to follow, Junction became a large part of the Bryant mystique. Unparalleled in college football history, unlikely ever to be repeated again, Junction was the ultimate object lesson in the Bryant school of football and life. Many coaches set high standards, and many others gave lip service to demanding that their players pay the price, but no coach ever set the bar so high that he lost two-thirds of his team in preseason practice. Survival of the fittest was not just a slogan to the Bear; it was his life, and if it cost him some good players who couldn't measure up to his standards, tough. When he and his team came back from that dusty patch of hell, he knew none of those players would ever quit in the fourth quarter.

The young men who rode those buses into history grew up hardened by memories of a world at war, and they straddled the fence of adulthood at a time when America was defined less by a pursuit of rights than a sense of obligations and responsibilities. Theirs was an ordered world, and respect for authority figures was automatic. In addition to being students and football players, they were military cadets at a time when the military and the government were institutions universally held in high esteem. Few of them considered professional football a serious option; most were the first members of their families to attend college, and football provided the means for them to better themselves.

Looking back on Junction and their relationship with Bryant, many see the time as a turning point in their lives.

"At that point in your life, when you're college age, you're finding out who you are and you face a lot of choices," said Bobby Drake Keith. "Junction and the experience of playing for Coach Bryant taught us all a tremendous amount about discipline, sacrifice, perseverance, hard work."

"I think it gave me a sense of toughness and dedication," said Lloyd Hale. "Coach Bryant taught us to give it everything you've got and to never quit, no matter what. That carries over into so many things."

Through the years, the Junction Boys and their coach shared a special bond. They loved him for the way he pushed them and made them better players and better men. He loved them for walking through fire for him, for surviving ten days of torture and then winning him a championship.

After an Air Force career in which he flew B-47s in Vietnam, Dennis Goehring went into private business and eventually formed a consortium to found the Bank of A&M in College Station. (Just as he promised, he stuck around long after both Paul Bryant and Smokey Harper were gone.) In the early 1970s, when he was trying to thwart a takeover bid by a rival bank, he called up his old coach and pitched him on the idea of buying stock in the company.

The Bear listened politely, and then fairly grunted, "Well, Dennis, how many shares do you need me to buy?"

"Well, Coach," he said, "I'd really love it if you bought a hundred shares."

He paused for a second or two, which felt like an eternity to Goehring.

"Hell, Dennis," the gravelly voice broke through the silence. "I don't want a hun'red shares. I got more faith in you than that. I want a thousand shares."

"At that moment," Goehring said, "I probably could've walked to the moon. For that man to show that much confidence in me, whew! that meant everything."

Eight years later, when the investors sold to the First Republic conglomerate, Goehring became a millionaire and Bryant turned a six-figure profit.

On the twenty-fifth anniversary of the camp in 1979, twenty-two of the twenty-nine Junction Boys returned to walk among the memories, like war veterans returning to the scene of a pivotal battle. The once-barren landscape had grown lush and green, but if they concentrated and closed their eyes, they could still hear the rattling of that old gate, which meant one fewer man they would have to beat. As they finally took the chamber of commerce up on its barbecue idea, the Junction Boys took turns at the microphone talking about what the camp had meant to their lives and what they had been up to in the ensuing quarter-century.

The place was brimming with millionaires and successful men in various fields, particularly coaching. Jack Pardee was coaching the University of Houston Cougars. Gene Stallings was Tom Landry's defensive secondary coach and was destined to follow his mentor at Alabama. Bobby Drake Keith was president of Arkansas Power. Joe Schero was one of the founders of the Church's Fried Chicken chain. Dennis Goehring was the majority stockholder in the Bank of A&M. There were lawyers, businessmen, engineers. And not a slacker in the bunch. Junction didn't make any of those men successful, of course, but it played a role in shaping them, as surely as the hardships of poverty in rural Arkansas had shaped their coach.

Bryant, who was on the verge of his sixth and final national championship this season, took his turn at the microphone and talked about how proud he was of all his boys and how well they have turned out. "I kinda feel like an underachiever in this group," he said with a smile.

Later in the afternoon, Lloyd Hale visited with his old coach for a few minutes. "Coach," he said, "how in the world did you think you were going to be able to field a team with all those guys leaving?"

"I didn't know and I was scared to death," the old man said.

Before the darkness chased everyone back to their cars and their motel rooms, the Aggies presented the Bear with a diamond ring commemorating their unique place in college football history. It was the only piece of jewelry he was wearing on the day he died.

Aggie

AS A YOUNG COACH, BRYANT attacked recruiting like every other facet of his life: with both barrels blasting. Even as he moaned and groaned about the poor hand he had been dealt with his first team at Texas A&M, he was determined to dominate the Southwest Conference, and soon, so he hit the recruiting trail with a vengeance. He could charm mamas and papas with ease, and to a certain cut of young man—the kind who wanted desperately to get out into the world and make something of himself—the Bear was like a magnet. He recognized and identified with their hunger, and they appreciated not only his toughness as a football coach but also his honesty and fairness as a man.

"Coach Bryant was just the kind of guy you wanted to follow," said lineman Charlie Krueger, a member of the coach's first recruiting class.

During the fall of 1954, as the Junction Boys struggled through their disastrous first season, Bryant and his coaching staff went in search of reinforcements. In addition to the twenty-nine hardened souls who had survived the preseason, the large class of freshmen, who had been recruited mostly by the previous coaching staff, arrived on campus in September, but they could not compete in varsity games. Freshmen would remain ineligible for varsity competition until 1972, but the presence of all those rookies meant that the Aggies could at least scrimmage without resorting to six-man football.

Even in the days before 900-numbers and Internet sites devoted to the procurement of pimply-faced eighteen-year-olds, recruiting could be a whorish process, especially in Texas, where everything—including the egos of wealthy and powerful boosters—was bigger and better. During the dragnet for new talent in 1954–55, several overzealous Aggie boosters made illicit inducements to land prospects, and Bryant privately condoned and approved of the practice. In the spring of 1955, two young men—Yoakum quarterback Bob Manning and Gonzales end Tom Sestak—signed affidavits stating they had been paid two hundred dollars each and promised fifty dollars per month above the value of an athletic scholarship to attend

A&M. Alumni from other Southwest Conference schools helped obtain the sworn statements, and the two players eventually wound up at other SWC programs. The conference and the NCAA moved swiftly to place the Aggies on two years' probation, which included a two-year ban on bowl appearances and the invalidation of more than one hundred letters of intent.

The practice of under-the-table inducements above the standard grant-in-aid—tuition, books, room and board—was hardly new in 1955, but the long arm of the NCAA was. In 1952, in response to many complaints from its membership about excessive "subsidization" in college football and basketball by boosters and other university representatives, the increasingly activist National Collegiate Athletic Association formed an enforcement division to investigate and punish rule breakers. The NCAA's suspension of the University of Kentucky's basketball program for the 1952–53 season was the first test of its new powers. A year later, it was Adolph Rupp's former Kentucky colleague who ran afoul of the new watchdogs.

Several months after the allegations became public, Bryant paid a surprise visit to a meeting of the NCAA's infractions committee, which was charged with adjudicating and meting out punishment in such cases. The committee was chaired, oddly enough, by Ab Kirwan, the faculty representative from the University of Kentucky, whom Bryant knew well. After discussing the specifics of the case with the members of the committee for a few minutes, the coach fell silent.

"You mean to tell me that an alumnus can't give these kids money?" he asked.

"Of course he can't, Paul," Kirwan said. "He can't do that."

"Well," he said, "I guess I don't have anything to argue about." He got up, put on his hat, and walked out of the room.

Writing with unusual candor about the situation in *Sports Illustrated* more than a decade later, Bryant said, "I know now that we should have been put on probation . . . I'm not sure how many of our boys got something. I guess about four or five did. I didn't know what they got, and I didn't want to know, but they got something because they had other offers and I told my alumni to meet the competition."

The magazine article may have been the only time an active coach ever admitted such wrongdoing so publicly. Although he never attempted to deny culpability or shirk responsibility for the probation, Bryant believed he was the victim of an old boys network trying to quash him. There was a certain country club feel to the Southwest Conference in those days, and he was an outsider brought in to shake things up. If Bryant felt as though he was being unfairly singled out, he nevertheless learned a valuable lesson from the experience. The probation left him with a sense of profound failure, and he vowed never to run afoul of the NCAA again. His record for the next twenty-eight years was spotless.

Throughout his days in Texas, the coach enjoyed a sometimes contentious, even caustic, relationship with many of the alumni. They wanted to recruit for him, and he learned to be wary of that; they wanted to tell him how to run his team, and he was determined to do it his way or no way. He was sometimes recklessly arrogant in those days when he still had so much to prove; he was sometimes blunt when the situation called for tact. On one such occasion, he stood up at a booster gathering and said with a sneer, "There can only be one chief and I'm it. The rest of y'all are the Indians and don't you forget it." When he won, of course, nobody held such statements against him.

Despite the NCAA's unprecedented gesture of invalidating all those letters of intent, virtually all of the recruits honored their original commitments to A&M. The probation cast a pall over the program and its coach, but it could not derail the Great Rehabilitator. The long-beleaguered Aggies were heading back to the top of the Southwest Conference.

Even after he became successful, Bryant always found time to return to rural Arkansas to see his friends and family, especially his mother, who shaped his evolution more than any other person. She gave him his strength and determination. He enjoyed buying her a new house and giving her nice things, and she sometimes visited Paul and Mary Harmon for weeks at a time.

Although Bryant loved his mother deeply, he could never understand her clinging to religious teachings that forbade the use of doctors. "My mother believed if you had enough faith, you didn't need doctors," said her daughter Louise. When Bryant was coaching at Texas A&M, Ida developed a growth on her neck that threatened her life, but for months she refused her family's pleas that she seek medical treatment. By the time she agreed to have an operation, the tumor had grown so big that her chances of recovery had fallen to fifty-fifty. Yet when they wheeled her into the operating room, she had a big smile on her face.

Later, after the surgery proved successful, Paul sat at his mother's bedside. "Mother," he asked, "knowing your chances of pulling through that surgery, how could you have gone out of here so happy?"

"Oh," she said sweetly, "I thought I was going to meet the Lord."

About two years later, Ida suffered the stroke that would take her life, just as her son was getting started at Alabama. Paul and Mary Harmon were on vacation in Texas, and they flew to Arkansas as soon as they got the news. When he walked into the hospital room and saw her body covered by an oxygen tent, tears streamed down his face.

"Sweetheart," he said as he took her hand, knowing she could not hear him, "this is the first time I've ever squeezed your hand that you haven't squeezed mine back."

Five years after Bud Wilkinson sent a graduating Oklahoma quarterback named Darrell Royal to Lexington to tutor the Bear on the marvels of the Split-T, his Texas A&M Aggies were trying to work the kinks out of the offense. Like Sweet Kentucky Babe, Roddy Osborne was heavily recruited as a running back, but Bryant appreciated his toughness and headiness—if not his rather unimpressive arm—so he moved the sophomore to quarterback in 1955. Behind him were two men headed for stardom in the NFL: halfback John David Crow and fullback Jack Pardee.

The Aggies were to open against defending national champion UCLA, and the game loomed predictably huge in the coach's mind, considering all the pent-up frustration of the Aggies' season on the edge in 1954. But Red Sanders—Bryant's last boss in football during the latter's days as an assistant coach at Vanderbilt before the war—put one of his better teams on the field at the Coliseum in Los Angeles, and the Bruins crushed A&M, 21–0. The offense sputtered hopelessly, and in practice the following week, the coach was presiding over a quarterbacks and backs drill when center Lloyd Hale said the wrong thing.

It was a routine offensive drill in which the quarterback practiced taking the snap from center, rolling down the line, and either pitching the ball to a trailing halfback or faking on the end. Of course, in Paul Bryant's practices, nothing was half-speed; even though the drill was conducted for the purpose of making the quarterbacks more efficient in running the option, the center's job was to fire off across the line as if he were blocking the noseguard. Bryant stopped the drill at one point and started lecturing his backs on one point in particular, and when he finished, he said, "All right, let's try it again."

Bryant was standing right in front of Hale.

"Coach, " Hale said, "you'd better move, you're gonna get hurt."

"What?"

"Coach, I'm gonna fire off, and . . ."

The giant but completely unpadded Bryant giggled like a schoolgirl.

"OK. Let's just see how good you are," he said as he lined up in a three-point stance across from Hale.

"I'm thinking, 'Oh, boy, here's my chance,' " Hale recalled. "I'm gonna tear that old man's head off."

Then Hale snapped the ball and the next thing he knew, he

was on all fours crawling in the dirt. "I fired off and he grabbed me behind the head with both hands and just shoved me to the ground," Hale said, unable to contain his laughter more than four decades later. "It's incredible how strong he was for a man his age. I'm trying to reach for his legs, but he just keeps backing up . . . and he's just a-laughing . . . and I thought I was gonna hurt *him?*"

Bryant fully understood how much of the game of football is played between the ears. He spent large amounts of time in practice on situation drills that made his players think, and a large component of his mental training was his ability to transfer his confidence to his players, to make them believe that they couldn't be beaten.

"Coach had this uncanny ability to make you believe that no matter how bad the situation was, you could do whatever you had to do to win," said John David Crow, who arrived in College Station as a freshman in the summer of 1954.

On November 12, 1955, the situation wasn't bad, it was hopeless. After tearing through the first eight games of the season with a 6–1–1 record that was the surprise of the Southwest Conference, the Aggies arrived in Houston as a heavy favorite over Jess Neely's Rice Owls. But A&M slopped around for most of the game and trailed 12–0 with just over two minutes to play. Hopeless. The stands were slowly emptying out when the game started to get interesting.

As Rice prepared to kick off after adding a late touchdown that appeared to seal the game, Mr. Confidence gathered his starters on the edge of the field. "There's still time, men," he said with a look of determination. "You can still win, if you believe you can."

What followed was one of the most remarkable rallies in the history of football in Texas, or anywhere.

The Aggies spent most of the day backed up to their own goal line, and with slightly more than two minutes left, their coach made the first of two substitutions that live in Aggie lore: Lloyd Taylor in for Jack Pardee. One of the Junction

Boys, Taylor was a smallish halfback out of New Mexico—one of the few non-Texas players on the roster—and there was something relentless in the way he ran when he got up a good head of steam. Bryant was hoping to see a display of that talent right then, which is exactly what happened: Taylor took his first snap and rambled fifty-five yards down the sideline to the Rice three-yard line. Three plays later, he scored and kicked the extra point. Time was running out, but Rice's lead was down to 12–7.

Substitution number two was Jimmy Wright for Osborne at quarterback. After Gene Stallings recovered an onsides kick near midfield, Wright, who was a better passer than Osborne, threw a flying prayer toward a streaking Taylor near the goal line. The man of the hour gathered it in, scored, and again kicked his own extra point. Fourteen points in forty-six seconds from Lloyd Taylor gave the Aggies an incredible 14–12 lead, and then Jack Pardee intercepted a desperation Rice pass and set up a final touchdown by Don Watson. Amazingly, in the space of slightly more than two minutes, the Aggies had gone from certain defeat to a stunning 20–12 victory.

"A certain amount of football is believing," Hale remarked. "And we believed."

The next week, Texas brought the believers back down to earth with a 21–6 thud, but the Aggies were back. The 7–2–1 mark validated Bryant's hard-nosed, driving approach to the game and established the youthful Aggies as one of the teams to beat in 1956.

Throughout his remarkably successful coaching career, Bryant built his teams around two very different kinds of athletes.

One was the average player who shouldn't have emerged as a winner on a championship team but did, the gutty competitor who invariably played over his head and found a way to win in spite of his relative lack of natural gifts, because football meant something powerful to him. Dennis Goehring was a perfect example. The coaching staff took him to Junction hoping he'd quit, but he had what many of the more talented Aggies didn't: a steely determination that Bryant couldn't run him off. That stubborn mind-set made him a football player.

The second category was the player born with exceptional talent who also summoned the ability and will to withstand Bryant's incredible demands. "Coach had no patience for players with a lot of talent who didn't put it on the line," noted his longtime assistant, Dude Hennessey. "None at all." Rather than coddling gifted players and letting them rise to their own level, as many coaches do, the Bear pushed them harder than the rest. Many great talents refused to bend to his will, and he ran them off or they quit. But he won championships with those who measured up in his critical eyes, such as Joe Namath, Kenny Stabler, and Johnny Musso.

John David Crow was the prototype for the great talents who fit the Bryant mold. As a schoolboy star in tiny Springhill, Louisiana, the six-one, 195-pound Crow rewrote the state's rushing records with a combination of speed and moves, and he arrived at Texas A&M in 1954 as one of the prizes of the freshman class. The halfback even looked like a football player was supposed to look: muscular but lean, with a buzz cut of blond hair and earnest blue eyes. A problem during his birth rendered the left side of his face slightly disfigured, giving him a slight droop of the mouth and eye, but it only served to make him look more like a warrior.

A determined and skillful runner, Crow earned consensus All-America acclaim as a junior and senior and captured the Heisman Trophy in 1957, becoming the only Bryant-coached player ever to garner the most prestigious individual award in college football. His open-field running skills became legendary among Aggies fans, but he also was a strong runner who had a knack for churning for the tough yards. In the game against LSU in his junior season of 1956, Crow took a handoff from Roddy Osborne on a trap and ran right as the two pulling guards in front of him collided; quick on his feet, he reversed his field, broke half a dozen tackles, and rambled eighty-one yards for a touchdown. His coach once called it the greatest single run he had ever seen.

Crow also had the fire in the belly that Bryant loved. Although he was a star from the time he arrived on campus and generated excitement from the moment he joined the freshman team, Crow never stopped feeling that he had to prove himself to his coach every single day.

"Coach Bryant had this way of creating a kind of insecurity," said Crow, who later coached on Bryant's staff and became the Texas A&M athletic director in the 1980s. "No matter who you were, you felt like your job was always in jeopardy. So if you were his type of player, you were going to do whatever it took to please him. No matter what he asked of you . . . if you were his type of player, you weren't even going to think about quitting. Just the word itself created a bitter taste."

Although Crow and his classmates missed out on the unique challenge of Junction, they endured four years of Bryant's psychological and physical warfare. Practice under him was a profanity-laced, nonstop barrage of hitting, a grueling endurance contest in which he pushed, and pushed, and pushed until the players thought they could give no more. Then he pushed harder. "I've heard some of the guys [who went to] Junction say that the only difference between Junction and the [practices in College Station] were the facilities," Crow said. "At least at home we didn't have to sleep on a flimsy cot out in the heat."

The reality of Bryant's methods lent itself to wild rumors. Among the more ridiculous exaggerations was the rumor that he built a giant pit on the practice field; he would supposedly throw two players into the crater, and the one who crawled out would earn a starting role. It wasn't quite that brutal, of course, but his kind of player always felt he was competing not just with his teammates but also against his abilities, his own potential. The result was a team that was in superior condition, rarely committed stupid mistakes, and didn't know the meaning of the word quit.

After all those years of suffering on the bottom of the stack, the Aggies returned to the promised land in 1956. With Crow, Osborne, Pardee, mammoth six-six, 240-pound All-America lineman Charlie Krueger, Gene Stallings, and Dennis Goehring leading the way, A&M finished 9–0–1 and captured the Southwest Conference championship. Only a 14–14 tie with Houston at midseason kept them from a perfect record, and the Aggies' fifth-place ranking in the final Associated Press poll was their best since Homer Norton's team walked off with the national championship in 1939. Toward the end of the season, the Southwest Conference voted to lift the Aggies' probation and allow them to play in the Cotton bowl, but the NCAA, which had the final say on such matters, kept the ban in force because of a violation in the school's basketball program, so A&M stayed home.

In addition to spoiling a perfect season, the Houston game was illustrative of the Bear's sometimes inappropriate bravado as a tactician. In the closing moments of the game, with the score tied at fourteen, the Aggies drove the length of the field to the Cougars' one-yard line. With time only for only final play, Bryant decided against letting Lloyd Taylor attempt a chip-shot field goal. In his mind, if the Aggies couldn't punch it in from the one with the game on the line, they didn't deserve to win. He called a quarterback option, and after a missed block, a Houston defender broke through to throw Osborne for a loss as the horn sounded.

The pivotal game of the season occurred the following week during a furious storm at Kyle Field against fourth-ranked and undefeated TCU. Wind gusts were clocked in excess of seventy miles per hour at the nearby airport, and as the game progressed, the afternoon sky grew as dark as pitch. Although the game was anticipated as a clash of two great runners—Crow against TCU All-America Jim Swink—the Aggies' defense provided most of the excitement, holding on four different goal-line stands. When the sun finally peeked from behind the clouds in the fourth quarter, Crow tossed a halfback pass to Don Watson to provide the winning 7–6 margin.

But the sweetest victory of the best A&M season in nearly two decades came in the finale against archrival Texas. Although TCU, Rice, and Baylor were superior to the Longhorns that season, Texas was, after all, Texas. As soon as Bryant arrived from Kentucky, A&M alumni started asking him how long it would take to beat those hated Longhorns. Sometimes he tired of the attention heaped on the rivalry, but like any other general, he needed an enemy. Tradition-rich Texas would do just fine.

Memorial Stadium in Austin can be an intimidating place for visiting teams, especially just before kickoff when the band cranks up "The Eyes of Texas" and the crowd goes wild. So Bryant, who was always attuned to the psychology of the game, refused to let his team take the field until the band finished playing the Longhorns' traditional anthem. He didn't want his boys to have to feel what Texas wanted them to feel when the band struck up that song and the place erupted. The officials had to delay the kickoff, but Texas finally gave in and played the song, and Bryant waited until the last note was finished before sending his team onto the field.

After building up a 21–0 first-half lead, the Aggies survived a furious rally by the Longhorns for a 34–21 victory. It was A&M's first win ever at Memorial Stadium, which was only slightly less historic for the men and women in maroon than humans landing on the moon—which, as everyone knew in 1956, was impossible. The outcome of the game prompted Texas to hire a man named Darrell Royal, a decision that was worth three national championships amid two decades of SWC dominance. (Bryant recommended his friend for the job, and Royal thanked the Bear by beating him the next November in his final regular-season game as the A&M coach.)

"Men," Bryant said softly in the locker room after the game, "I don't have the vocabulary to tell you how proud I am of you at this moment. I've never had a team with more guts."

Despite all the bad publicity generated by Junction and the probation, the man from Moro Bottom had succeeded once again in achieving what many thought to be impossible. For the second time, he had inherited a team on the bottom of its conference and molded it into a championship outfit virtually overnight. If he never won another game, the rings he owned from Kentucky and A&M proved he was the undisputed Great Rehabilitator. But the Bear was just clearing his throat.

With most of the key performers returning in 1957, Bryant's Aggies were picked to repeat as the Southwest Conference champions. A&M stood at 7–0 when, in the waning moments of a one-point game with Arkansas in Fayetteville, quarterback Roddy Osborne was supposed to run out the clock near the Hogs' goal line, but when he looked up and saw Crow wide open in the end zone, he couldn't resist. He let the ball take flight, but instead of reaching Crow for a touchdown, it fell into the arms of an Arkansas defender, who raced down the sideline for what surely would be the winning touchdown ninety-one yards away. Osborne was the only man with a prayer of stopping Donny Horton, who doubled as an Arkansas track star, and a prayer was about right; Osborne was considered the slowest man on the team.

But somehow, Osborne ran Horton down, tackling him near the thirty. Three plays later, Crow intercepted a pass in the end zone to preserve the 7–6 win.

Several days later, Bryant related the story to his friend Bobby Dodd, the Georgia Tech coach.

"But how in the world could a guy so slow catch a speed demon like that?" Dodd asked.

"The difference," Bryant said, "was that Horton was running for a touchdown. Osborne was running for his *life*."

Although not all the A&M players felt quite so motivated,

the Aggies' defense was superb all year. After a 21–13 victory over defending national champ Maryland in the nationally televised opener, Bryant's team didn't allow more than a single touchdown in any game the entire year. In mid-November, the Aggies were 8–0, ranked number one and seemingly headed to the national championship, having gone eighteen straight games without being beaten. Bryant's revival was the hottest news in college football. Words like "genius" and "master" were being thrown about with increasing frequency. Then word leaked out about the Bear returning to Alabama—long before the deal was consummated—and the Aggies lost their final two: 7–6 to Rice and 9–7 to Texas.

For the rest of his life, the coach wondered whether it was the Alabama rumors that cost him the 1957 national championship. Or was it Kenneth Hall?

In a later time, Kenneth Hall would have been called a "franchise player." As a high-school senior in Sugar Land, Texas, he rushed for more than four thousand yards and scored a state-record fifty-seven touchdowns. Every college in the country wanted him, and the Aggies signed him before Bryant took over in 1954. But, of course, the Bear didn't put much faith in statistics, including the incredible 9.7 the boy ran in the hundred-yard dash. Anyone could see Hall was a gamebreaker with the ball in his hands. By the time his senior season rolled around, he was playing with greater frequency, and when fullback Jack Pardee was sidelined with a leg injury against Baylor, Hall became the starter. With four games remaining and the number-one ranking in hand, the coach believed a backfield tandem of Hall and Crow was unstoppable.

But the Monday before the Arkansas game, when his team was counting on him, Hall failed to show up for practice.

To Bryant, failure to show up for practice was like a middle finger thrust defiantly at him and the team. Only two excuses were acceptable for missing a workout: death and illness requiring hospitalization. Tardiness was equally unforgivable; two years earlier, Gene Stallings and Bobby Drake Keith, Junction Boys both, were walking to the practice field one day when they saw footballs flying around, and they mistakenly thought they were late for practice. "We were scared to death," Keith said. "We were thinking very seriously about heading for the hospital until we walked up a little closer and realized we weren't late after all."

So when Hall missed practice, Bryant assumed he had quit. Naturally, the coach was devastated, although he didn't let anyone realize it. When he arrived home that night and found the boy on his front steps, and the young man begged for another chance, Bryant talked with him for a while and finally agreed. Then Hall failed to show up for practice again the next day, and when he returned to the coach's house the following night crying and begging for yet another chance, Bryant said no and reluctantly dismissed him from the squad. Crow asked for the opportunity to intercede, but his coach refused.

Whether having a gamebreaker like Hall in the backfield for those two big games, decided by a total of three points, would have made any difference is unknowable, of course, but Bryant never stopped blaming himself for the way he handled the situation—not just for losing those games but for losing Kenneth Hall. Years later, when his Alabama teams were dominating college football and the world was brimming with young men who owed a large measure of their success to him, he still talked about the way he mishandled Hall, whom his teammates described as unquestionably the most talented player of their era.

Some coaches spend a lifetime replaying pivotal games in their head, and Bryant certainly was no exception, but he was always defined more by his relationship with his players than by x's and o's, and he believed he had failed Hall, not just as a player but as a troubled young man who needed guidance at a turning point in his life.

With a certain kind of player, of course, Paul Bryant was absolutely unbeatable from his first day as a coach until his last. No one could touch him with the Dennis Goehrings or the John David Crows; such players would have taken a bullet for him and risen from a pool of blood to swallow another. But the Hall case reflected his only significant weakness during those days: He sometimes played the part of Bear Bryant too well. He was torn between his belief about team discipline and his sense of obligation to get the most out of every one of his players. Throughout his coaching career, he would be torn by these two conflicting forces.

"Coach Bryant's weaknesses as a coach were the natural opposites of his strengths," observed Bobby Drake Keith. "He could overdo the gruffness, the rigidity. A certain kind of player couldn't relate to that, and Hall was one."

Two days before the nationally televised Texas–Texas A&M game on Thanksgiving Day in 1957, Mel Allen arrived in College Station to begin his preparation for the NBC broadcast. It was customary for the announcers to spend time with the coaches and their assistants to familiarize themselves with the teams, but of course, Allen needed no introduction to Paul Bryant. Classmates at the University of Alabama in the 1930s, the two remained friends through the years, and Bryant, who was a huge baseball fan, sometimes showed up in the Yankee Stadium press box during the days when the gregarious Melvin Israel was the voice of the most dominant franchise in professional sports history.

After practice, the Bear asked Mel to take a ride with him. He liked to get out on the open road when he had something on his mind, and as the 1957 season wound to a conclusion, he was troubled by something bigger even than the Texas game. Alabama was trying to lure him back as head coach, and he was torn.

The people of Texas had been awfully good to him. His bank

accounts were bulging as a result of his success with the Aggies—in addition to his impressive contract with the university, prominent friends helped him invest in various oil, real-estate, and housing ventures—and as they drove around College Station, the coach pointed out his numerous holdings. He and Mary Harmon were incredibly happy in College Station, but he wanted to know what another 'Bama man thought.

"I don't know what to tell you, Paul," Allen replied in his familiar booming drawl, which dripped with the sound of Alabama. "You've got a lot to keep you here. But there's nothing like being asked to come home."

If Notre Dame had called begging for a rescue from the clutches of mediocrity and Joe Kuharich, he would have told them to find somebody else to wake up the echoes. Southern Cal could have offered a ten picture deal with Warner Brothers. The New York Giants could have thrown in the Statue of Liberty and a skyscraper to be named later. But *Alabama!* Alabama was home. As much sentiment as he retained for his roots in rural Arkansas, he felt a considerable debt to the University of Alabama for helping him escape poverty and grow into a man of strength, confidence, and character. He had always quietly dreamed about someday returning to Tuscaloosa to follow in the footsteps of Frank Thomas and Wallace Wade. He was a part of Alabama, and Alabama was a part of him.

Although he had rebuffed prominent 'Bama alumni during an earlier attempt to lure him back to Tuscaloosa, the Crimson Tide looked like a sinking ship in 1957. Once-mighty Alabama —the program that placed southern football on the map—had won a total of four games in three years under J. B. "Ears" Whitworth, and the phone calls from the Heart of Dixie often contained a note of desperation.

When the contract negotiations turned serious and it appeared he would take the job, Bryant was modest in his salary demand of eighteen thousand dollars—considerably below the twenty-five thousand dollars he was earning at Texas A&M—

but he was adamant about obtaining the title of athletic director. His experiences at Maryland, Kentucky, and Texas A&M taught him the value of having complete control of the athletic program, and he refused to take the Alabama job without reporting directly to the president of the university. But how would that affect Hank Crisp?

No man shaped Paul Bryant's evolution more profoundly than Coach Hank, the crotchety old cuss with the leathery skin who served as the top aide to Wallace Wade, Frank Thomas, and Red Drew for nearly thirty years. It was Crisp's rumble seat that carried the Bear out of Arkansas, Crisp's pleading and threatening that helped turn the Bear into a football player defined more by his heart than his ability, Crisp's roll of one-dollar bills that provided the poor country boy with the only means at his disposal to take a girl out on a date or buy a pair of shoes, Crisp's cracker-barrel psychology that helped keep him from packing it in and quitting college and football during his freshman year. The grown-up mountain of granite Bear Bryant loved Hank Crisp like a son loves a father.

During the Whitworth regime, Crisp served as both athletic director and line coach; he was Ears's boss *and* his aide. Still productive in his early sixties, Coach Hank was an institution at the institution known as the Capstone, and regardless of who replaced Whitworth, it was understood that he would remain as athletic director and assistant football coach until his retirement. But Bryant refused to accept a deal that left a layer of management between him and the president, however benign, and he also could not take his old coach onto his staff.

"Coach Bryant said he couldn't have Coach Hank working for him," recalled Ernest Williams, the chairman of the selection committee, "because giving him an order would be like giving his father an order, and he just couldn't do that."

The selection committee discussed the situation with Crisp, who agreed to take a job as director of intramurals. But Bryant wasn't satisfied. He wanted to hear it from his old coach's lips.

He refused to sign the contract until Coach Hank told him that he wasn't going to be hurt by the move.

"Bear had a lot of old-time values," said Jeff Coleman, Alabama's longtime alumni director, who also served on the selection committee. "He didn't want to do anything to hurt Coach Hank."

The next day, Crisp hopped an airplane to Houston and walked into the Bear's suite at the Shamrock Hotel. The teacher, a rather small man who was slightly stooped and plastered with the residue of a lifetime of hard living, cast a squinty look in the direction of his pupil, who at forty-four remained young, vital, and years away from his greatest triumphs. Before the Bear could say a word, his old coach got right down to business as he stood in the shadow of the doorway.

"Bryant, you old son-of-a-bitch," he said with a somewhat bewildered look, "I don't care about being no athletic director or no assistant coach. Now, come on. Get your ass back to Tuscaloosa so we can start winnin' some football games."

A broad smile rose across the pupil's chiseled face, and he draped his long right arm around his teacher's shoulders. They spent the better part of the afternoon laughing and lying about the old times, and later that evening Bryant signed a ten-year contract to become the University of Alabama's twentieth head football coach.

The Aggies couldn't believe he would leave them, of course, and one of the men who helped lure him away from Kentucky never forgave the Bear, wouldn't even accept his calls. The toughest part was breaking the news to his team—especially the ones he recruited—and although he stayed to coach A&M in the Gator Bowl against Tennessee, the whole affair was one giant anticlimax. The Vols' 3–0 victory was only the second time Bryant's team had been shut out in four years.

On December 8, 1957, the morning after Hank Crisp's visit, Ernest Williams convened a press conference inside one of the ballrooms at the Shamrock Hotel. After he told the assembled newsman that he believed the committee had secured "the finest football coach in the country" to revive the 'Bama program, Paul Bryant took his turn at the podium. As he stood before the lights and cameras in the year of Sputnik and Buddy Holly, Bryant apologized to the A&M fans but said he was returning to 'Bama because he felt like he had "heard Mama calling." If the simple phrase left the shocked and saddened Aggies with a hollow feeling, it resonated perfectly with Alabamians. One of their own was coming home to make everything all right again, Thomas Wolfe be damned.

7

Back to 'Bama

DURING THE ALABAMA COACHING REGIME of J. B. "Ears" Whitworth, Wednesday was dominoes day. Every Wednesday morning, several prominent former Crimson Tide players dropped by Whit's office to play a few leisurely games of dominoes, discuss the progress of the football team, and in many cases, tell him what he was doing wrong—which, considering his 4–24–2 record from 1955 to 1957, was plenty. Sometimes they ordered sandwiches and talked right through lunch. Whit didn't mind; he enjoyed the company and the help.

A few days after Paul Bryant arrived at his new offices in January 1958, the domino bunch stopped by to see him. The half-dozen or so businessmen told the Bear they were ready to help him whip the team into shape; maybe they could play a few games, talk a little strategy. The domino boys didn't know Bear Bryant at all, of course, for the Crimson Tide's new coach was not the kind of man who believed in football—or anything—by committee.

When he told the men he didn't have time to see them, but that he would be happy to set up an appointment for any legitimate business at five-thirty the next morning, they stomped off down the hall, thoroughly enraged.

"Just wait'll that joker starts losing," one of them predicted as they walked away, "and then he'll want our help."

The irresistible plea that Paul Bryant likened to "Mama calling" was more like a Mayday from the *Titanic*. Once-mighty Alabama, with its history of Rose Bowls and national championships as "Dixie's football pride," had sunk deeper and deeper under Whitworth, a well-respected longtime assistant coach who simply wasn't a leader, a general. While Bryant was teaching Texas A&M how to win, 'Bama suffered through four straight losing seasons for the only time in its history, and the poorly equipped Whitworth was dumped after the most painful defeat of all: a 40–0 drubbing at the hands of archrival Auburn, which clinched the hated Tigers' 1957 national championship.

Two weeks after the lame-duck Bryant led his Texas A&M Aggies to a Gator Bowl loss to Tennessee, he arrived in Tuscaloosa and called a meeting of his football team. His reputation as a hard-driver preceded him, and the war stories about the horrors of Junction took on a life of their own in the buzz of players, coaches, and fans, but none of those young men yet understood what it meant to play for the man. The first squad gathering of the new era took place in a dusty meeting room in Friedman Hall near the center of campus in January 1958, and the general with the chiseled face and the voice imported from someplace due south of his kneecaps looked over his troops and laid it on the line:

"How many of y'all have girlfriends?"

About half of the hands in the room shot up.

"Well, all y'all who raised your hands might as well pack your bags now, 'cause you won't have the time to become football players."

Gulp.

Two minutes into his twenty-minute lecture on the importance of commitment and discipline, the door creaked open and four latecomers tiptoed into the room. He stopped in midsentence and looked straight at them. "Get out! Get out!" he screamed, and they meekly retreated out the door. He turned to one of his assistant coaches and said, "Will you have somebody lock the doors? There'll be no interruptions."

Tardiness was, to him, a symbol; a man who showed up late to an appointment was revealing a central character flaw in Paul Bryant's neatly ordered world. It reflected sloppiness and a lack of commitment. Whenever he called a team meeting in his days at Alabama, he made a point of arriving early, walking to the front of the room, and comparing the time on his watch with the various timepieces worn by the players in the front row. What time do you have? And you? And you? At the end of his clock comparison ritual, he would set his timepiece back to match the slowest time of all the players' watches, just to be fair. Then, when the appointed *second* arrived, he started talking. Players knew better than to walk into the room after he began speaking. In their coach's meticulously ordered universe, tardiness, like pregnancy, was never a matter of degree.

"In a situation such as we accepted here," he told reporters during his first spring in Tuscaloosa, "the main thing is getting the material and teaching your kids to forget a losing complex. Teach them to win."

Under the Bear, football at Alabama became a grueling, year-round commitment. His practices were an intricately organized flurry of hitting and instruction. His emphasis on teaching the fundamentals included special classes that the SEC and NCAA rules then permitted, for which the student-athletes received academic credit. He employed a much larger staff than any of his SEC rivals—eighteen assistant coaches at the peak—and he was a master at organization on the field and off. Even before spring practice began in March, he instituted a harrowing off-season conditioning program that, through the years, became the most effective winnower of his huge freshman classes. Such conditioning programs were the exception rather than the rule in those days, and Alabama's emphasis on strength and endurance paid tremendous dividends.

"You walked in that door [to the gymnasium on the top floor of Friedman Hall] and you never stopped for the next hour," recalled Jack Rutledge, who was a freshman when Bryant arrived. Organized into small groups, the players alternated running, wrestling, exercising—and, invariably, puking. The sides of the gym were lined with garbage cans smelling of vomit. No water breaks were allowed. "I don't care how good a shape you were in," Rutledge said, "that was an exhausting endurance contest, like Marine boot camp."

Much as they had at Kentucky and Texas A&M, large numbers of players quit in the first months of the new Bryant regime, unable or unwilling to endure the constant physical and mental strain. He believed he had inherited a lazy, poorly conditioned, largely uncommitted team, and when asked about all the defections that resulted from his methods, he told reporters with a sense of pride, "The riff-raff are fast eliminating themselves."

"My plan was to bleed 'em and gut 'em," Bryant later said, "because I didn't want any well-wishers hanging around."

He made an example of anyone who failed to measure up

to his expectations. During a scrimmage in 1958, Bryant saw something that bothered him, so he stopped the action and ran at full speed toward sophomore guard Russell Stutz, who had been recruited out of suburban Birmingham by the Whitworth regime and was playing on the defensive side of the ball. Stutz was a fighter, and everyone called him Bulldog, but Bryant thought he was loafing.

"Bulldog," the coach asked, "were you giving it 110 percent on that last play?"

"No, sir, Coach, I guess I wasn't," Stutz replied.

"Well, get your sorry ass off the field."

Stutz said the wrong thing at the wrong time, and his 'Bama career was over. Just like that. Stutz lost his scholarship, although he stayed in school and wound up as a Birmingham stockbroker.

"That was an object lesson for the team as much as it was for Russell," said Billy Richardson, who was then a freshman lineman. "You were either going to give it everything you had, or you were liable to be gone."

Richard Williamson, a talented split end from the tiny south central Alabama town of Fort Deposit, got so fed up with the demands of playing for Bryant that he packed his things after a grueling practice, got in his car, and headed for home. About halfway to Fort Deposit, he stopped at a pay phone and called his daddy to tell him he was giving up football and college, that he would be home for supper. His daddy told him, with no room for misinterpretation, that he would not be welcome at home if he quit at Alabama, so Williamson got back in his car and returned to campus. The Bear never knew, and in time, Williamson became a starter and, in later years, a successful coach.

Eight months after arriving on campus, the Bear convened a meeting of his first freshmen class, replete with names such as Pat Trammell, Billy Richardson, Billy Neighbors, and Tommy Brooker, who would be the pillars of a new, incredibly successful era in Alabama football. No one showed up late.

"How many of y'all have called your mamas?" he said after walking to the front of the room. "Let me see a show of hands."

Then he proceeded to advise his young men to telephone their mamas after the meeting, and to write home at least once a week, and he told them the road ahead was not going to be easy. "Look around at the guys sitting next to you," he advised the group, nearly one hundred strong, and heads turned from side to side throughout the room. "Chances are, four years from now, there's probably going to be no more than a double handful of you left. . . . But if you work hard and do the things I ask you to do, you can be national champions by the time you're seniors."

The man from Moro Bottom always kept his word.

For forty-one years, the bitter Alabama–Auburn rivalry existed only in the mind. Although the football teams from the state of Alabama's two largest universities first met at Birmingham's Lakeview Park on February 22, 1893—a seminal victory won by the Tigers, 32–22—a dispute erupted seven years later, leading to the suspension of the series, producing college football's most bizarre cold war. Rather than mollifying both sides, the four-decade disruption of the series deepened the feelings of resentment and polarization among many fans and alumni.

When the schools finally resumed athletic relations at Birmingham's Legion Field on December 4, 1948, Alabama and Auburn met not as equals but as opposite sides of a class war. (The Crimson Tide won the first renewal by the lopsided margin of 55–0). The University of Alabama represented the state's elite; it produced lawyers, doctors, businessmen, and therefore most of the state's political and corporate leadership. Auburn, then known officially as Alabama Polytechnic Institute (API), a land-grant university with strong ties to the state's agricultural system, was more likely to be backed by farmers and other working-class people, and the "cow college" jokes thrown about by 'Bama partisans bespoke a certain cultural elitism.

It was also a clash of the haves and the have-nots of football. During those forty-one years, Alabama emerged as a national power, while Auburn was mired in the SEC's second division throughout most of those years. Long after 'Bama started making regular pilgrimages to the Rose Bowl in Pasadena, the only postseason reward Auburn could boast was a hastily arranged trip to Havana, Cuba, in 1937 to play Villanova in something called the Rhumba Bowl, the first and last. (The game was part of a festival that included one of sport's lower moments: Olympian Jesse Owens racing against a horse.) The Tigers' stadium was so small that most of the school's SEC rivals refused to travel to the loveliest village on the plains, as tiny Auburn referred to itself, so the team was forced to play many of its home games on the road in Birmingham and Montgomery.

"Auburn people felt like second-class citizens," observed former Tiger star Babe McGehee. "We were the butt of the Alabama jokes. They went to Rose Bowls and we couldn't even get Tennessee to come to our place to play."

Ralph "Shug" Jordan understood the plight of the Auburn man. A star center for the Tigers in the early 1930s, Shug spent more than a decade as an Auburn assistant coach, and in 1951, on the heels of a winless season on the plain, the school lured him back from Georgia as head coach. His outstanding teams of the 1950s gave Auburn people their first taste of success, capped by an undefeated, untied season in 1957, which brought the school's first Southeastern Conference and national championships, although the Tigers were serving an NCAA probation for recruiting violations at the time. During the dark days of Alabama football between 1954 and 1957, when the world seemed upside down to the men and women wearing crimson, the Tigers won four straight of the Iron Bowls—so-called because the game was played annually at Legion Field in Birmingham, one of the world's leading steel-producing cities—outscoring the Crimson Tide by an embarrassing 128–7. The road back to the top led straight through Shug Jordan's Auburn Tigers, who had seized 'Bama's birthright of state dominance. What next, 'Bama fans wondered, *locusts?*

Although the talent level was sorely lacking in 1958–exacerbated by the large number of defections in the first year of the new system—the Crimson Tide reversed the trend of the disastrous Whitworth years and finished 5–4–1. Their offense was mostly nonexistent—the quick-kick, unheard of nowadays, became one of 'Bama's most potent weapons in the field-position, three-yards-and-a-cloud-of-dust game of the one-platoon era—but the Tide displayed flashes of the butt-kicking defense that would become its trademark. The quarterback, senior Bobby Jackson, was a battler who had suffered a knee injury, and while he wasn't anywhere near as talented as some of the men who would later fill his shoes, he was the Tide's most valuable player by default. With few offensive weapons at his disposal, Jackson ran the ball on nearly half the snaps, and his toughness made him one of his coach's favorites. Billy Cannon (the 1959 Heisman Trophy winner) and his LSU teammates, headed for the national championship, had to rally in the second half for a 13–3 victory in the premier of the Bryant era. In week eight, 'Bama upset heavily favored Georgia Tech, 17–8. Auburn, unbeaten and once tied, needed a great defensive play to break up a touchdown pass in the waning moments to preserve a 14–8 victory over the Crimson Tide in the season finale.

The program turned the corner in 1959. With several sophomores breaking into the starting lineup—including a feisty quarterback named Pat Trammell, who eventually supplanted the more experienced Bobby Skelton—'Bama finished 7–1–2, earning a number-ten national ranking in the final Associated Press poll and a berth in the first Liberty Bowl against Penn State in frigid Philadelphia. Although the Nittany Lions edged the Tide, 7–0, on a fake field goal at the close of the first half by future Florida head coach Galen Hall, the postseason bid was the first of an NCAA-record twenty-four straight for

Bryant-coached teams. The master's touch was unmistakable. The remnants of the team that had surrendered an SEC-worst 173 points in 1957 held its opponents to a 5.9 average in 1959, third best in the country. Nothing, however, signaled the Tide's reemergence like the 10–0 victory over Auburn.

"Before the game we said it'd take a superhuman effort to win, and I think our boys gave it," Bryant said of the pivotal upset. "If our team played 100 percent against Georgia Tech [a 9–7 win], it played 135 percent to beat Auburn."

Jordan's Tigers entered the 1959 season in firm control of football in the state of Alabama, riding the crest of a twenty-three-game unbeaten string and ranked among the top five teams in the country. But 'Bama's first victory over its archrival in five years represented a turning point in the series. Over the quarter-century of the Bryant era, Alabama would win nineteen and lose only six against the Tigers, and the gentle Shug Jordan, who appeared on the verge of long-term dominance in 1959, was reduced to a marginal figure in the Southeastern Conference. He never won another SEC title, and placed just five more teams in the nation's top ten. During the 1950s, Auburn dominated in-state recruiting, but after Bryant returned, Alabama slowly won over the high-school coaches and set the stage for a quarter-century of recruiting success. Young people with no particular allegiance to either school became more likely to grow up Alabama fans during the dominating reign of the Bear, and the ripple effects of 'Bama's growing constituency were felt in recruiting, where dominance tends to perpetrate itself.

As Bryant's Crimson Tide rocketed to national prominence and stayed there, the rivalry took on a certain have versus have-not tenor that transcended the game. In addition to fielding superior teams throughout most of his time in Tuscaloosa, Bryant fed the psychological gamesmanship of the rivalry, dropping occasional references to the "cow college" and hinting that Auburn just didn't take football as seriously as Alabama, which was, after all, *the* state university. Although Bryant arrived from Texas A&M with a probation in his recent past, he was able to portray Alabama as the team that won the right way by obeying the rules; while Auburn suffered through three NCAA probations for recruiting violations trying to play catch-up to the Bear, 'Bama remained untainted by scandal. When Bryant made a point of saying, "We adhere to the letter and the spirit of the rules," he didn't have to say a word about Auburn. The Tigers' probations were a matter of public record. A generation of Auburn people grew up embittered by Bryant's dominance and attitude.

"There was a time in my life when I hated Alabama and hated Coach Bryant," said Auburn athletic director David Housel, who was raised in the tiny town of Gordo, about twenty miles west of Tuscaloosa, and grew to respect the Bear greatly. "Like many young people, I confused the competitive desire to win with hate and animosity . . . all that was fed by the feeling of Auburn people being looked down on by Alabama people. Coach Bryant was a master of many things. He was able to portray Alabama as better than Auburn in every way, and an awful lot of Auburn people took that to heart, got wrapped up in it."

Through the years, the Iron Bowl emerged as the most important event in the state, the most impossible ticket, the only yardstick for statewide bragging rights. In 1971, when both Alabama and Auburn entered the game undefeated and in the hunt for the national championship, Bryant told a reporter, "The state championship of Alabama means more, means everything. This game is for bragging rights for the next 365 days."

Bigger even than the game, the rivalry grew to influence everything in the state; many people even voted for city councilmen based on their school preference. In fact, in 1978, Bryant publicly backed then–Alabama attorney general Bill Baxley in his run for governor against businessman and former Auburn star running back Fob James, because he believed having an Auburn man in the governor's mansion would adversely affect the funding of the University of Alabama by the legislature. It was one of the few battles he lost against the orange and blue; James swept into office on the Democratic ticket in 1978, and was elected again as a Republican in 1994.

Bryant was never known for Rockne-esque "Win-one-for-the-Gipper" oratory in the locker room before a game. Too often, he believed, such emotional pleas produced only a momentary burst of adrenaline that soon evaporated in the first-quarter head-rattling. He loved to walk out onto the field, lean against the goalpost, and watch an opposing team whoop and holler before kickoff, because he knew his boys, who approached the game with a businesslike attitude, were going to knock them on their ass a few times and then all that extra juice would burn itself off. Keenly attuned to the psychology of the game, he knew how to manipulate his players' minds as well as anyone who ever coached the game, but he reserved most of his mind games for the days leading up to a game.

One of his favorite admonitions to his players on Saturdays was like a Zen riddle: "If you're ahead, play like you're behind . . . and if you're behind, play like you're ahead."

In the first half against Georgia Tech at Atlanta's Grant Field on November 12, 1960, the Crimson Tide appeared headed for its second defeat of the season. The score was 15–0 at the half —no one else had scored more than a touchdown on the Tide in the first thirty minutes—and the 'Bama players expected a tongue-lashing. But Bryant knew his team too well; he realized that if he came down too hard at that particular moment, they might simply tank the game. What they needed, he decided, was a pat on the back, so he became Mr. Wonderful.

"Where are the Cokes?" he started off as he stood before his team in the locker room. "Let's get some Cokes in here. Now, this is great. We got 'em right where we want 'em. They're gonna see what we're made of now."

"We were all kind of shocked," said junior halfback Billy Richardson. "All of us expected to be reamed out pretty good and then he goes the opposite way. He was very cool, very matter-of-fact. All we had to do was make a few adjustments, he said. Brilliant. Just brilliant."

What followed was one of the most improbable rallies in 'Bama history.

After being totally manhandled in the first half, the Tide completely shut down Bobby Dodd's Yellow Jackets in the third quarter, but still trailed 15–0 entering the final period. Midway through the fourth quarter, Pat Trammell was forced out of the game with an ankle injury, which appeared to doom 'Bama. But senior quarterback Bobby Skelton, charging out of his coach's doghouse, led the Tide on two long touchdown drives in the final six minutes to close the gap to 15–13.

With time running out and everyone in the stadium expecting the Tide to attempt an onsides kick, Bryant instructed his placekicker to drill it into the end zone, which put the pressure on his defense. 'Bama held Tech on downs, used all of its remaining time-outs, and after a punt, took over at the Tech forty-five-yard line with less than a minute to go. Skelton hit Butch Wilson with a thirty-three-yard sideline pass that should have been called incomplete, because Wilson had been bumped out of bounds before reentering the playing surface and making the catch and run. No matter; the officials didn't see it. With the final seconds ticking away, the Tide had a chance for a winning field goal.

'Bama's regular placekicker, Tommy Brooker, was nursing an injured leg and standing on the sideline on crutches. (Two weeks later, he recovered and nailed a twenty-two-yarder to beat Auburn, 3–0.) So when Skelton drove the team to the Tech twelve-yard line with no time-outs remaining, the coach turned to his bench and yelled for the last man anyone would have expected to become the game's hero: Richard "Digger" O'Dell. The unheralded, virtually unused junior end from Lincoln, Alabama, had never kicked a field goal before, although he did kick the extra point earlier in the game. But the old man called his name, and he was ready. The snap was clean, and the kick was a quivering knuckleball with a trajectory barely high enough to avoid being blocked, but somehow it wobbled across the goalpost, and 'Bama scored an incredible 16–15 victory. Even the Bear, who played and coached in 509 games over more than a half-century, called the comeback the greatest he had ever seen.

"When Coach Bryant said, 'We got 'em right where we want 'em,' we believed him," said Lee Roy Jordan, then a sophomore linebacker. "So much of it is confidence . . . he made sure we believed we could still win."

Only Tennessee knocked off the Tide in 1960, and the team's 8–1–2 record was the school's best mark since the undefeated "war babies" of 1945. The team was full of ambitious sophomores and juniors, and 'Bama was heading toward the most successful, most dominant decade in Southeastern Conference history.

During the confusion of the incredible comeback against Tech, radio play-by-play man Maury Ferrell mistakenly credited the injured Tommy Brooker with the winning field goal: "Brooker! Brooker! Brooker!" When the team arrived at the Birmingham airport that evening, the deliriously happy crowd —including dozens of screaming, grateful coeds—gathered around Brooker and ignored Digger O'Dell, the real hero, who walked from the terminal to the bus in the shadows of anonymity. It was the only field goal he would ever attempt in a college game, and not a soul in Alabama knew about it. So much for his fifteen minutes of fame.

Bear Bryant's Alabama teams of the 1960s became known as his "quick little boys," and while they were not exactly emaciated compared to the general male population, they were small compared with the players in most major college programs. His linemen, especially, tended to be runts compared with the men they were facing across the neutral zone. Trench soldiers like Jerry Duncan, Jimmy Sharpe, and Charley Pell weighed no more than 185 pounds on average, and some of the behemoths they faced tipped the scales at 230 or more.

Of the resulting battles that the smallish Crimson Tide usually won on the way to one championship after another, *Sports Illustrated* once said, "It was embarrassing, like getting mugged by a kindergarten class."

Although the Bear wasn't averse to large players—All-America tackle Billy Neighbors checked in at five-eleven and 218 pounds in 1961—he disliked fat bellies and he placed a greater premium on quickness and endurance in the sixty-minute war. The smaller players tended to be quicker, and also were better equipped to survive his grueling conditioning program. The Bryant system, which featured more running and fewer trips to the training table, served to make the athletes leaner. He would take a quick, hard-hitting runt over a lumbering refrigerator any day of the week, because one-platoon football coached the way he coached it turned an opposing team's size from a strength into a liability. Throughout the 1960s, the rules forbade the use of the hands at the line of scrimmage, so 'Bama's little boys were taught to hit hard and quick below the knee at the point of the attack, a move that, if executed properly, cut those big trees down to size.

The success of his little boys was stunning. In the 1960s, the Crimson Tide won an NCAA-best 90, lost 16, and tied 4, for an .836 winning percentage. 'Bama captured national championships in 1961, 1964, and 1965, won four Southeastern Conference titles, played in ten straight bowl games, and finished eight times in the nation's top ten. Only the 1969 Tide finished out of the top twenty.

Although his offensive philosophy ranged all over the map through the years, Bryant's defenses always emphasized speed, movement, gang tackling, and a certain defiant attitude. Coaches such as Bobby Dodd, Bud Wilkinson, and Darrell Royal were terrific offensive innovators, but the man from Moro Bottom was a defensive genius. His defenses were a reflection of him—disciplined, hard-nosed, intimidating, and just plain scary—and when the Crimson Tide hunkered down with the game on the line, you could almost hear their steely resolve: *No, you can't do that to me! You can't score on me!*

The schemes changed from time to time, but 'Bama practices always emphasized quickness drills and hitting drills. Film grading was strict, and any player judged to be loafing was graded down heavily; regardless of how much ability he possessed, he was subject to the Russell Stutz treatment.

"Bud Wilkinson told me one time he thought Coach Bryant was the greatest defensive coach of all time," said Penn State's Joe Paterno. "You look at the numbers and the teams, it's hard to disagree."

The numbers from the 1960s make a convincing argument. In the decade of Kennedy, Apollo, and Woodstock, Bryant's Crimson Tide led the major colleges in scoring defense (8.2 points per game), total defense (212.6 yards), and rushing defense (96.7 yards). 'Bama forced more turnovers in the decade than any other SEC team (317), and led the nation in takeaway/giveaway ratio (plus 1.19 per game).

No team in the modern history of the Southeastern Conference played defense like the 1961 Crimson Tide. Living up to their coach's challenge, the senior-dominated unit swept to the national championship with a perfect regular season and then scored a 10–3 victory over Arkansas in the Sugar Bowl. (Of the eighty-nine freshmen who showed up for the first meeting in 1958—when he promised them a national championship—eleven determined souls remained in the autumn of 1961.) In ten regular-season games, Billy Richardson, Tommy Brooker, Billy Neighbors, Pat Trammell, Lee Roy Jordan, Darwin Holt, Charley Pell, Jimmy Sharpe, et al. outscored their opponents 287–22, with six shutouts. Trammell, Jordan, and Neighbors were Alabama's first All-Americas in more than a decade. Opponents scored just three touchdowns against the Tide all year. No team in the country since 1961 has been able to hold the opposition to fewer than three points per game.

"Those guys acted like it was a sin to give up a point," remarked their proud coach.

"After all those years of repetition and sacrifice, it was a matter of pride to us," said the greatest defender of them all, linebacker Lee Roy Jordan, a junior on the 1961 team. "We took every point (against us) as a personal insult."

Recruited out of the tiny South Alabama town of Excel, Jordan was no great physical specimen at five-ten and 190 pounds, but he was a devastating hitter who became the greatest linebacker in Alabama history and an All-Pro with the Dallas Cowboys. In 1989, he was named to the all-time college team selected by ESPN, joining his coach. After his incredible twenty-four-tackle performance in a 17–0 win over Oklahoma in the 1963 Orange Bowl, his coach shook his head and grinned from ear to ear. "If we can keep 'em on the field," Bryant said proudly, "Lee Roy will tackle 'em."

In the Bryant system, the quarterback was entrusted with tremendous responsibilities, including play calling in most instances. Bryant often referred to his quarterback as his "personal representative on the field," and the phrase wasn't thrown about loosely. He held his quarterbacks to a higher standard, but he also allowed them more latitude during the game than might seem consistent with his otherwise controlling nature. "There are several basic rules by which we expect our quarterbacks to operate," he once said, "but I wouldn't give a plug nickel for a quarterback who would not be willing to break every one of these in order to win a game."

Bryant loved Pat Trammell, the six-two, 205-pound doctor's son from Scottsboro who was the leader among leaders on the 1961 national championship team. Sometimes combative, usually profane, always tenacious, he was even tougher on his teammates than his coach. But he was a natural leader, and they loved him like a big brother, followed him like a litter of puppies. During the Auburn game in 1961, he shocked his coach by quick-kicking on second down with the ball at midfield.

"What the hell are you doing?" Bryant demanded when Trammell ran off the field.

"Well, Coach, those damn guys aren't blocking anybody, so I thought we might as well see if they can play defense!"

If anyone else had pulled such a stunt, Bryant would've benched him. But he felt a real kinship with Trammell, who possessed many of his coach's own attributes of leadership and steely determination. He was a fighter who wasn't very talented but didn't know it.

"As a quarterback, Pat had no ability," Bryant said. "He was not a great runner, but he scored touchdowns. He didn't pass with great style, but he completed passes. All he could do was beat you."

Driven and extremely intelligent, Trammell graduated in pre-med, earned his medical degree, and opened a private practice in Birmingham. One day during the 1968 season, he called his coach to tell him the bad news: Trammell had a tumor. A cancer. Determined to beat the disease, he checked himself into an experimental clinic in New York City, and after several months, the cancer went into remission. Then, just as quickly, it reappeared, and within a year he was dead at age twenty-eight. His old coach was devastated, and he cried like a baby the day his boy died.

"Pat Trammell was the favorite person of my life," he said.

The 1961 Alabama football team remains a close-knit bunch, bonded by the four-year endurance test they survived, by the games they won and lost, by the coach who touched them so profoundly. They matured into coaches, business executives, salesmen, and lawyers, but they never stopped feeling a connection to one another and to the football program they rescued from the abyss. On the day of Trammell's funeral, many of them gathered at the Holiday Inn in Scottsboro and created a memorial to their fallen comrade. For more than a quarter-century now, the A-Club Foundation has been providing a lift to former players down on their luck. The nonprofit group, funded entirely by former Crimson Tide players, has paid medical expenses, bought wheelchairs, served as a lifeline to the ever-expanding 'Bama football family.

"The A-Club Foundation is the 1961 football team," Tommy Brooker said. "And the 1961 football team is Coach Bryant."

Stormy Days

DURING HIS TEXAS A&M REVIVAL, Paul Bryant traveled to a small school on the edge of Indian territory near the Oklahoma border to see a star running back named Jack Holt. Every coach in the conference wanted Holt, because he was big and strong and he knew how to run toward the light.

After visiting with the boy for a while, the Bear sat down with the high school's coach to watch film of Gainesville's game the previous week against rival Castleberry. A highlight film it wasn't. The field was a sea of mud, the thermometer was stuck in the single digits, and Gainesville was lucky to escape with a 2–0 victory, so fate was not smiling on the marvelous running talents of Jack Holt that night. But Bryant saw something.

"I want that 'un," he said, pointing to the screen as a smallish center fought over a loose ball in the mud. "That little bitty number 64. He's a battler!"

"But he's just a junior," the high-school coach responded.

"Well, tell him not to get hurt, 'cause he's gonna play for me."

Darwin Holt, who happened to be the star running back's little brother, was a runt by comparison. But he knew how to fight.

Even in Bryant's world, where bigness was measured by the size of one's heart, Darwin Holt was diminutive. He arrived at A&M standing five-nine and weighing 152 pounds, but he was cocky, and as the coach could ascertain by one spool of film, he was the kind of young man who gave everything he had on every single play. As the varsity Aggies climbed to the top of the national rankings in the autumn of 1957, Holt played freshman ball and counted the days until he could show The Man what he could do. But then the Bear heard Mama calling, A&M replaced him with a former Marine named Jim Myers, and the Aggies fell into a 12–24–1 tailspin that rendered the Bryant years no more than a glorious aberration.

Convinced he would never play at A&M, Holt phoned Bryant

in the summer of 1958 about the possibility of transferring to Alabama. "If you can get your release from A&M, then come on," the coach told him. "But we don't want you to come straight to Alabama. Find you a junior college where you can go for a year."

The following summer, in 1959, Holt showed up in Tuscaloosa with his fighting spirit and his belongings, which included an associate's degree from a junior college in his hometown. No one told him not to graduate, but his attention to his studies cost him a year of eligibility.

Down to two years of varsity stage time, Holt battled for a starting berth at fullback and linebacker in preseason practice with the Crimson Tide in 1959. One day, he sustained a hit to his right knee and fell to the ground in excruciating pain. In a later era, he might have been a candidate for arthroscopic surgery, but in those days, the answer was immobilization. For six weeks, doctors kept the injured limb tucked away in a cast, and the closest he came to the action was flying to and from the 'Bama games with Dr. Frank Rose, the university president, in the school's tiny turboprop, which had swivel seats, the better for resting his wounded leg. When the cast came off around midseason, the Texas firebrand would have walked to the away games, he was so hungry. But Bryant refused to use him.

"I had a lot of venom in me . . . because I couldn't figure out why Coach Bryant wasn't playing me," Holt said.

After the season, the coach explained that he had obtained a medical hardship exemption for the frustrated young man, and suddenly, all of the bile building up inside him disappeared. The hardship ruling, one of the first ever granted by the NCAA, restored the year he had lost to the injury by allowing him to play in both 1960 and 1961. Without the strange twist of fate that caused him to become injured and then granted an unusual waiver as a means of compensation, Darwin Holt might have been a footnote in the history of Bear Bryant and Alabama football. Instead, he emerged as a twisted symbol of college football's dark side.

Sometimes lost amid all the pageantry of college football
are some cold hard facts about the game. Although most of
the attention flows to the talented superstars who display their
gifts running, passing, and catching the football, the sport is,
at its heart, defined by a brand of controlled violence. Football
is a game of intimidation and hitting; speed, smarts, and a
sound game plan play an unmistakable role, of course, but the
better team more often than not is the one that wins the battle
at the point of attack, where blood and sweat are commodities
spilled in abundance.

No one taught the physical, hard-hitting style of football
with more success than Bryant. Junction represented the
lengths to which he was willing to go to reinforce his beliefs
about "paying the price," and the on-the-field achievements of
his teams through the years proved his methods could yield
immense dividends. Shorty after Bryant returned to 'Bama,
Harry Mehre, the former Georgia coach who became a sportswriter, joked, "Bryant says that his [brand of football] is 'an
eye for an eye.' Bear must be softening up a bit, because I
heard his Texas A&M squad never offered an eye unless they
could get two in exchange."

"Since Bear Bryant came back to Alabama," Auburn's Shug
Jordan remarked in the early 1960s, "this . . . hell-for-leather,
helmet-bursting, gang-tackling game is the only game which
can win" in the Southeastern Conference.

Vince Dooley, a former aide to Jordan who later won two
hundred games of his own at Georgia, said, "Coach Bryant
changed football in the SEC in two pretty fundamental ways.
One, he elevated the work ethic. He was the hardest-working
guy you've ever seen, and that meant the rest of us had to
work harder coaching, scouting, recruiting, the whole bit. Two,
his teams just played harder, and that meant our teams had to
play harder to try to compete."

The Bear believed games were won with defense and special
teams, and his defenses and special teams were especially

vicious. In the years after two-platoon football took root in the mid-1960s, he always placed his best athletes on defense. He was often described by his peers as a defensive genius, but his schemes weren't any better than anyone else's. His "quick little boys" of the 1960s just played harder; they were intimidating both in their unrelenting pursuit and in the force with which they attacked. Before an Alabama–Auburn game in the early 1960s, a 'Bama fan was overheard boasting, "It'll be easy to pick out the Auburn ballcarrier. He'll be the one who turns white as soon as they hand him the ball."

"I want players who want to go jaw-to-jaw for sixty minutes," Bryant once said in explaining his philosophy. "To go out and be reckless. You have to fight and bleed. You have to be tough, mentally and physically tough."

"What Coach demanded above all else is that you go full speed on every play," said Charley Pell, a guard on the 1961 national championship team. "If you go full speed and the other guy's loafing . . . then you're gonna be more successful."

The delivery of a jarring blow within the rules can be, in the context of the game, a thing of beauty, and the Alabama teams under Bear Bryant were determined to hit their opponents as hard as possible, to "knock their heads off," in the language of the game. Some, no doubt, attacked with the notion of sending an opposing player to an early shower: "You have to out-mean people," Bryant was fond of saying. On his Sunday afternoon television show, whenever he saw a good lick he especially liked, the coach's growl contained a certain lilt and a signature kudo: "Bingo! That's a goodie!"

But there is a big difference between playing hard and playing dirty. Bryant's teams were always extremely sound fundamentally, and he never condoned cheap shots. His teams were consistently among the least-penalized squads in the Southeastern Conference, and a flagrant foul by one of his players was destined to draw a lot more than a flag from the head coach.

"In Coach's mind, one of the worst things you could do was to get a penalty," said Lee Roy Jordan. "He was obsessive about that. If you started making a bunch of stupid mistakes, you weren't going to last long playing for him, because one or two key penalties could lose us a game."

Bobby Dodd was one of the finest coaches of his era. His concepts of offense were superb, and the results spoke for themselves. His Georgia Tech teams won 165, lost 64, and tied 8 between 1945 and 1966, including a share of the 1952 national championship and a record six consecutive bowl victories. Although eight different teams captured or shared Southeastern Conference titles during the parity-riven 1950s, the Yellow Jackets won with the most consistency, and the low-key Dodd was considered the reigning football master of the age in the South. But the 1960s belonged to his old buddy Bear Bryant.

Unlike Bryant, Dodd believed in finesse more than strength. He was a strategist, not a driver. He probably won more games on Saturday than Bryant—he excelled in making adjustments during games—but his philosophy of preparation was less intense, which provided a stark contrast between two outstanding coaches.

When he recruited against Bryant, Dodd often liked to say, "Now, you don't want to go down there and work all the time. Come over here and have fun. Shoot, we play volleyball on Thursdays, and Bryant's still bangin' heads."

Gaylon McCollough, who played center for Alabama from 1962 to 1964 but was recruited out of Enterprise, Alabama, by both men, said of the difference, "Coach Dodd liked to recruit good athletes and play on their intelligence . . . instruction wasn't as important to him. Coach Bryant believed, on the other hand, that repetition, preparation, and conditioning played a tremendous role in molding a team. He wanted to work you so hard that your assignments became second nature to you."

Although Bryant made clear to his players that he respected Dodd's abilities as a play-caller, he firmly believed his own style of football was superior. When his Crimson Tide played

Dodd's Yellow Jackets, the coach and his players always considered it less a game than a referendum on the Bear Bryant way of life.

After rallying to beat the Yellow Jackets on a last-second field goal, 16–15, in 1960, the Crimson Tide scored a pivotal 10–0 triumph at Legion Field on November 18, 1961. Mike Fracchia, who was as graceful a runner as Alabama ever produced before sustaining a career-ending knee injury in 1962, scored on a sixteen-yard run and Tim Davis kicked a thirty-two-yard field goal. The defense held Tech to less than one hundred total yards. 'Bama was undefeated and headed for its first national championship under the Bear, and Dodd's program, which was already on the wane, would never be the same.

If quarterback Pat Trammell was the dominant leader and personality on the Alabama offense, Darwin Holt was Trammell's alter ego on defense. The rules then allowed one substitution during the change from offense to defense and vice versa, and Holt played most of the snaps on the smothering defense that held its opponents to twenty-two points all year.

"Darwin was a tough guy," said his teammate Bill Battle, who later became the head coach at Tennessee. "He knew how to lay a hit on somebody."

In the fourth quarter of the Tech game, with the game firmly in hand, Alabama lined up for a punt return in its own territory. Billy Richardson was to catch the punt, and Holt's job was to block the end man on the line of scrimmage and, in theory, to seal the wall for the ballcarrier to head upfield. But the punter shanked the punt, and Richardson was forced to run at least ten yards upfield to catch it. Richardson called for a fair catch on the run, but Holt didn't know it. At almost the precise moment that Richardson caught the ball, Tech's Chick Graning passed in front of Holt, who laid a block on him that sent the man tumbling to the ground.

What might have been a routine play in a million other instances generated a firestorm of controversy. Graning sustained a concussion and a fractured jaw on the play, lost three

The Bryant clan, circa 1916. Young Paul, standing next to his father on the front left, was influenced more by his mother, seated second from the right. While his father's inability to provide for the family became a burden for his youngest son, his mother's strength and self-reliance marked him for life. Courtesy: Ray Bryant

Known as "the other end" at Alabama, Bryant helped lead the Crimson Tide to the 1934 national championship. The next year, he gained attention throughout the South for playing the game of his life against bitter rival Tennessee—despite a broken leg.
Courtesy: University of Alabama Sports Information Office

At Texas A&M, the Bear turned a perennial loser into a championship program. But not before losing three-quarters of his team at a place called Junction.
Courtesy: Paul W. Bryant Museum

When Alabama sent out a distress signal after the 1957 season, the Bear felt compelled to return to rescue the program that had changed his life. "It was like hearing mama calling," he said.
Courtesy: Paul W. Bryant Museum

In the locker room, Bryant was not known for Rocknesque speeches. But in all situations, he knew how to intimidate and inspire his players.
Courtesy: Paul W. Bryant Museum

Bryant, pictured with several of his assistants after clinching a third national championship, often said one of the keys to his success was his willingness to surround himself "with people smarter than me." Courtesy: Paul W. Bryant Museum

In the early days in Tuscaloosa, the Bear still liked to teach by demonstrating blocking and tackling techniques on his players. Even going against men half his age in full pads, he could throw a punishing lick. Courtesy: Paul W. Bryant Museum

Bryant counted Georgia Tech's Bobby Dodd among his closest friends in the coaching profession—until the Darwin Holt controversy ignited a bitter feud.
Courtesy: Paul W. Bryant Museum

Joe Namath and Johnny Musso, two of the Bear's greatest players, share a joke with the master during an awards dinner in the 1970s.
Courtesy: Paul W. Bryant Museum

Famous friends often stopped by the Alabama practice field to visit with the legendary coach, including President Gerald Ford, pictured with University of Alabama President Dr. David Mathews in the famed tower.
Courtesy: Paul W. Bryant Museum

As Bryant surveyed practice from his tower, players and assistant coaches alike feared the clanking of the chain—which meant that the boss was coming down. Rarely was that good news.
Courtesy: Paul W. Bryant Museum

The master, pictured here with Maryland's Jerry Claiborne, finished with a 43–6 record in games against his former pupils. Courtesy: Paul W. Bryant Museum

Even as he became more of a grandfatherly figure to his players, the aging Bear relished the real-life job of grandpa. Marc Tyson spent many Saturdays walking the sidelines with him in Tuscaloosa. Courtesy: Paul W. Bryant Museum

teeth, and spent four weeks in the hospital. When they discovered the severity of the player's injuries, several members of the Atlanta media seized on the play and portrayed Holt as a thug whose intent was to injure his opponent. He was flooded with hate mail and threatening telephone calls in the weeks after the play.

"Holt forfeited the right to play college football when he intentionally smashed his left forearm into Chick Graning's face," wrote Jesse Outlar in *The Atlanta Constitution*, calling for the Southeastern Conference to suspend the player. "Apologies from Holt won't replace Graning's teeth."

Alan W. Graning, the fallen player's father, raised the emotional pitch of the controversy when he told reporters, "I believe Bryant is encouraging such tactics ... [as] this sneak attack on my son."

Nearly a year after the game, *The Saturday Evening Post* published an article by *Atlanta Journal* sports editor Furman Bisher suggesting that the severity of the hit "was no accident" and that Bryant taught "brutal" football. The coach and his player sued and, as part of the deal to settle for libelous charges in a subsequent *Post* article, were vindicated to the tune of more than three hundred thousand dollars.

Although it is impossible to say for certain what Holt's intentions were at that moment, the facts of the case are more complicated than the sum of Graning's unfortunate injuries. Contrary to some media accounts at the time, the hit did not occur well after the whistle had blown; the film clearly shows that Holt blocked Graning at almost the same exact moment that Richardson caught the ball. The film also shows an official standing within five yards of the play, looking in the direction of the block, and making no effort to throw a flag. In his defense, Holt argued that Graning relaxed before the whistle blew, when he was still in a live football situation and could be hit within the rules; the film confirms this as well. Holt enjoyed a reputation as a hard-hitting player, a "fighter," in the words of his coach, but he had never been accused of cheap shots. When his opponent relaxed and bent his knees, Holt contended, the arm intended for the "hitting zone" on his chest wound up striking his jaw.

"It was a legal play," said Holt, now an insurance salesman who lives in Birmingham. "One of the things that we were always taught by Coach Bryant is that you never stop going full-speed . . . before the whistle blows. He always said that was the easiest way to get hurt. After [Graning] relaxed . . . his jaw came down into the hitting zone . . . and then his face just exploded. There was no intent on my part to hurt him. Hell, yes, I meant to hit him. I meant to hit him hard. But no, I didn't intend to hurt him."

In those days of rather flimsy headgear, Graning's face was protected by a single bar above the chin strap, and the large opening allowed Holt's arm to reach his jaw. "If I'd had a full cage," Graning remarked, "I probably would've had no more than a headache" afterward.

"There is absolutely nothing wrong with good, clean, hard football, but I believe Darwin crossed a line," said Graning, who remains convinced that Holt intended to hurt him. "There's nothing wrong with hitting somebody with the intent of taking a little of the sap out of 'em, but what Darwin did was totally uncalled for."

Although Bryant later conceded that he thought the hit should have resulted in a penalty, he didn't believe it was intentional. "There's no doubt Darwin fouled Chick Graning," he said. "I probably would have disciplined him in my own way if those Atlanta sportswriters hadn't set out to crucify him. A penalty is one thing; a crucifixion is another."

Bryant believed certain members of the media were using the Holt–Graning incident to attack him, and in the minds of many their efforts were successful. But players and coaches who competed against Alabama in those days refute the notion that Bryant taught dirty tactics.

Even Graning, who recovered from his injuries, became a coach, and now sells insurance in Natchez, Mississippi, defended the Bear. "I don't think Coach Bryant taught that," Graning said. "Coach Bryant taught hard, tough, intimidating football . . . but he didn't teach his players to play dirty. There's no doubt in my mind about that."

Even in the best of circumstances, young men get hurt playing football. It's a brutal sport. Even completely legal hits sometimes leave lifelong scars; in rare cases, players are sometimes even paralyzed for life as a result of playing the game. The Holt–Graning affair resulted from a freakish incident; for reporters and others to suggest that Holt's actions fell outside the lines of hard-hitting, jaw-to-jaw football was reckless and irresponsible. After all, no one accused Lawrence Taylor of brutality when he slammed Joe Theisman to the turf, mangling his leg and ending his playing career. Football isn't a tea party; people get hurt.

In addition to casting Holt and Bryant in the role of villains, the incident created a deep rift between Alabama and Georgia Tech. Bryant believed that Dodd, his longtime pal, needlessly played up Graning's injuries in the media, and their friendship soured as a result. In 1962, when Tech edged Alabama 7–6 at Grant Field, a small number of Yellow Jacket fans threw liquor bottles in his direction; two years later, he showed up on the field in Atlanta wearing a football helmet—only partly as a gag. One of his own players was elbowed with his helmet off after the final whistle, but nothing was ever made of it.

After the 1964 game, Tech dropped Alabama from its schedule and withdrew from the Southeastern Conference. Although Dodd and Bryant later reconciled and Tech even played 'Bama again toward the end of the Bryant era, a large segment of the 'Bama faithful continued to carry a grudge about the whole affair. When former Tech player and coach Bill Curry became the second man to attempt to follow the legendary Bear at Alabama in 1987, many Crimson Tide players of that time greeted the hiring with a certain amount of resistance and contempt.

More than three decades after their shared moment in the spotlight, both Darwin Holt and Chick Graning remained scarred by an incident that became part of the lore of southern football.

Doctors advised Graning not to play the sport after sustaining the concussion, but he charged ahead and eventually spent an exhibition season with the St. Louis Cardinals and played briefly in the Canadian Football League. His pro football career was a bust, and he moved into coaching and then insurance.

"It took me two years to remember anything between the day of the game and [the following] Thanksgiving," he said. "I'll never know whether the injury had an effect on whether I didn't make it in pro football."

Rather than stay in the Atlanta area, where the incident made him an unwitting celebrity, Graning moved to Mississippi in the 1960s to escape the constant reminders. He didn't enjoy feeling like a victim; even today, after the passage of so many years, strangers who meet him for the first time often recognize his name and ask him about the play.

"I've gone through a real gamut of feelings," he said. "From anger to frustration to bitterness. I've tried to put it behind me. It doesn't do any good to hold anger in your heart. I don't harbor any ill feelings toward Darwin, but that doesn't mean I would like to spend a great deal of time around him."

The man who inflicted the damage was himself damaged as well. Darwin Holt resented being portrayed as some ignorant, hotheaded redneck, especially when he had already received his undergraduate degree and was working toward his master's during the 1961 season. In addition to the hate mail and death threats that he received in the wake of the play, he believes that the resulting publicity cost him a career in coaching by scaring off potential employers.

"It changed my whole life," Holt said. "I paid a bigger price for it than [Graning] did. I pay every time somebody mentions it, which is just about every day. There's no telling how many opportunities I've lost because somebody recognized my name and just assumed I was some kind of thug."

He also encounters Alabama fans who remember the game and believe he got a bad rap. One time when Holt's eight-year-old daughter Tate was selling Girl Scout cookies around the neighborhood, she knocked on a neighbor's door.

"Are you Darwin Holt's little girl?" the man of the house asked.

"Yessir," she said sheepishly.

"Well, you know, your daddy was the meanest football player who ever played for Alabama."

Tate Holt ran home crying.

"She didn't understand that in football, being mean is a good thing," her daddy said. "That guy wasn't trying to be hateful. He meant it as a compliment, and she just didn't understand."

In the weeks and months after the 1961 Tech–'Bama game, Bryant predictably adopted a defiant stand against those who criticized his boy and his program. He never attempted to visit Graning or showed any sort of public compassion toward him, although he undoubtedly was sorry that the young man had been hurt. He clearly believed that certain factions in the media were out to get him, and by the time he became aware of how seriously Graning had been injured, he was in the middle of a public-relations war. His rhetoric reflected the times.

"Graning wasn't hit that hard," he said. "It was lucky for him it wasn't one of our big guys like Billy Neighbors."

"I always thought it was pretty unfeeling of Coach Bryant to say I wasn't hit hard enough to be hurt that bad," Graning said.

But the rough and tough Bryant mellowed through the years, and the case of Kent Waldrep illustrates how much.

On October 26, 1974, the undefeated, fourth-ranked Crimson Tide was hosting outmanned Texas Christian at Birmingham's Legion Field. The Horned Frogs were destined to be the seventh of eleven victims that autumn, in the middle of the Bear's run of unparalleled Southeastern Conference dominance in the 1970s. With the visiting team on the way to a crushing 41–3 defeat and the vast majority of the seventy thousand fans in attendance loving every minute of it, TCU running back Kent Waldrep took a pitch from his quarterback, charged toward the 'Bama line, and took a clean hit. Then Waldrep remembers everything going numb and the world around him shifting into slow motion.

"It was a feeling of such helplessness," Waldrep said years later. "I wanted to move my legs, but they wouldn't budge."

Although there was never any question about the legality of the tackle, Waldrep's spine snapped on the fall to the turf, a freak accident that left him paralyzed for the rest of his life. In sharp contrast to the earlier incident, Bryant went out of his way to visit the injured player on many occasions, ordered his staff to honor the young man at halftime of a 'Bama game the next season, and organized a hugely successful drive among 'Bama fans to raise money for his hospitalization and rehabilitation expenses.

"I can remember so well waking up in intensive care . . . in the first few days after [the injury] . . . and looking up and seeing Coach Bryant's face," said Waldrep, who now operates a paralysis foundation in Dallas. "It was a real shock. He'd brought Charlie Finley and George Steinbrenner by to see me, and he kept saying, 'We wanta see you get outta here real soon, now, son.' My mama later told me that he was near tears out in the hall waiting to see me. He was a constant presence at the hospital for the next month, and that was the start of a very special friendship."

Waldrep remains embittered by the way TCU treated him after the catastrophic injury—the university refused to pay his medical bills after the first few months—but his feeling of kinship with Bryant is reflected in his spacious Dallas office: While there is no visible reminder that he ever played for TCU, four separate paintings of Paul Bryant hang on the walls.

"I'll always feel a lot closer to Alabama and to Coach Bryant than I ever will to TCU," he said.

On the afternoon of September 22, 1962, before a sellout crowd of some fifty-four thousand at Legion Field in Birmingham, a young talent named Joe Namath was unleashed onto the world. Hard-throwing, confident, with the looks of a movie star, the streetwise transplant from the hills of western Pennsylvania stepped into Pat Trammell's shoes and led the Crimson Tide to a 35–0 season-opening victory over the Georgia Bulldogs. His three touchdown passes seemed effortless, and Alabama was headed to a 10–1 finish behind its sensational sophomore, with only a 7–6 loss to Georgia Tech preventing the Crimson Tide from capturing back-to-back national championships. Georgia, conversely, was on its way to a 3–4–3 thud, the second of three straight losing seasons under Johnny Griffith that served as the precursor to Vince Dooley.

As unremarkable as the game appeared at the time, it was destined to become associated with one of the ugliest phrases in all of sport: the fix.

Five months later, in an edition dated March 23, 1963, *The Saturday Evening Post* charged Bryant and his longtime friend, Georgia athletic director and former head coach Wally Butts, with conspiring to "fix" the 'Bama–Georgia game. The blockbuster article, which bore the stinging title "The Story of a College Football Fix," became front-page news across the nation, threatening even more than the careers of two men. The integrity of the entire sport was being called into question:

> Not since the Chicago White Sox threw the 1919 World Series has there been a sports story as shocking as this one. . . . Before the University of Georgia played the University of Alabama last September 22, Wally Butts, athletic director of Georgia, gave Paul (Bear) Bryant, head coach of Alabama, Georgia's plays, defensive patterns, all the significant secrets Georgia's football team possessed. The corrupt here were not professional ballplayers gone wrong, as in the 1919 Black Sox scandal. The corrupt were not disreputable gamblers, as in the scandals continually afflicting college basketball. The corrupt were two men—Butts and Bryant—employed to educate and to guide young men. How prevalent is the fixing of college football games? How often do teachers sell out their pupils? We don't know—yet. For now we can only be appalled.

As proof, the *Post* offered the bizarre tale of a telephone conversation between Butts and Bryant, supposedly overheard by an Atlanta insurance man named George Burnett. Nine days before the season opener between the two teams, Burnett said, he picked up the telephone at his office and dialed the number of a local public-relations firm. The line was busy, so he kept trying. On the fourth or fifth attempt, Burnett said, he found himself somehow plugged into a conversation between Butts and Bryant, who were discussing football. Burnett, who was curious, pulled out a piece of paper and started making notes. He came away from the conversation believing the two men were sharing information, but he kept quiet. Several months later, feeling the need to unburden his heart of his suspicions, he approached a friend with ties to the University of Georgia and brought the conversation to the attention of the school's administration, and eventually, the *Post* got wind of the story.

The successor to a publication founded by Benjamin Franklin in the 1700s, the *Post* was once the foremost chronicle of conservative, establishment middle American life. It brought to the nation's mailbox fawning profiles of movie stars, political leaders, and sports legends, capped by the ubiquitous cover art by Mr. Americana himself, Norman Rockwell. But the dawn of the television age in the 1950s signaled a new, more competitive era for general-interest magazines—a broad category including *Time*, *Life*, *Look*, *Colliers*, and the *Post*, among others —and the *Post*'s circulation and advertising pages began to decline steadily.

The change to a more aggressive editorial policy came in 1960 when Curtis Publishing Company, parent of the *Post*, hired as the magazine's editor-in-chief a cocky, somewhat kinetic limit-tester named Clay Blair. In his off-hours, Blair loved to scuba dive; he enjoyed diving to incredible depths to see how far he could go without passing out, and his companions often bailed out with throbbing ears while he plunged farther and farther into the deep. As an editor, Blair attacked the *Post*'s blandness with a similar determination, championing a philosophy that he called "sophisticated muckraking" with the

intent of "provoking people . . . making them mad." In his de-
position for the trial that resulted from this particular piece of
raked muck, Blair spoke with pride of several pending lawsuits
against the magazine. "We are hitting them where it hurts," he
said.

One of his early hires was a veteran magazine writer and
editor named Roger Kahn. Kahn, who would later gain fame as
the author of the baseball epic *The Boys of Summer,* accepted
a post as senior editor/sports in 1962, shortly after Furman
Bisher's diatribe against "brutal football" dredged up the details of the Holt–Graning affair. Kahn presided over a change
from warm-and-fuzzy profiles and opinion pieces to features
with greater depth and harder edges, such as "The Anatomy of
a Bookie."

In February 1963, representatives of insurance man George
Burnett secretly started trying to interest several national magazines in the story, including *Sports Illustrated* and *Newsweek,*
which apparently passed on it before it reached the midtown
Manhattan offices of the *Post.* One day around lunchtime, as
Kahn was heading out the door to meet a friend at the journalists' hangout Toots Shor's, Blair pulled him to one side and
filled him in on the alleged fix story, for which Burnett was
eventually paid five thousand dollars.

"I told him I didn't want to touch it," Kahn recalled. "My
original thought was, 'When there's an indictment, then we go
with it,' because, you hear so many 'fix' stories . . . but the only
way to prove something is to let the DA do his job and get an
indictment first. And I should've stuck to that thought. But
then at some point [over the next few days], my journalist's
instincts took over, and I went from a 'We can't do this' mode
to a 'Let's get this story and beat our competition' attitude."

After Kahn assigned the story to Frank Graham, Jr., who had
written several other pieces for the magazine, Blair committed
a horrendous mistake: Fearing a leak that could cost the *Post*
its exclusive, he removed two of his top editors from the loop
on the story, including articles editor William Emerson. Kahn
had the piece thrown in his lap, and his job was to move it

through the pipeline; except for Blair, who was blinded by the
red-meat aspects of the story, there was no check on the feature's accuracy or fairness. His attempt at secrecy undermined
the magazine's ability to get the story right.

"I never saw the piece [prior to publication] and that infuriated me," said Emerson, a native Georgian. "I had no chance
to influence the story . . . no chance to urge that we exercise
all the appropriate due diligence. It was stupidly, clumsily handled by all involved."

The resulting article reflected this rush to judgment. In addition to factual errors and quotations that were later denied in
open court, neither of the men being accused of fixing the
game was given the opportunity to deny the claims, which,
however perfunctory the gesture, would at least have given
the story the appearance of evenhandedness. The participation
of *Atlanta Journal* sports editor Furman Bisher further
clouded the magazine's objectivity; Bisher, who had written
the earlier piece accusing Bryant of teaching "brutal" football,
was paid one thousand dollars for on-site reporting in Athens.
Given the litigation arising from that article, his impartiality
was bound to be questioned. (Bisher refused to be interviewed
for this book.) Perhaps most baffling was that no one at the
Post ever saw the notes that Burnett allegedly scribbled during
his eavesdropping—the closest thing to hard evidence that
any such conspiracy had actually happened.

Within days of the article's publication, Bryant and Butts
filed separate libel suits seeking millions of dollars in damages.

On the Sunday after the magazine appeared on newsstands,
an angry Bryant bought time on statewide television in Alabama to vehemently deny the charges. Although he had managed to emerge from the probation at Texas A&M largely
unscathed, and the earlier brutality charges against him were
widely dismissed as one unfortunate incident being blown out
of proportion, a fix allegation represented a scandal that could
ruin him. He recognized the stakes; if he was found guilty of

such collusion—whether merely to help his team win or, worse, for the purpose of gambling on the outcome—Bryant might never coach another game.

On a live broadcast that interrupted regular programming throughout the state, sitting at a desk dominated by a large nameplate emblazoned with the words "Coach Bryant," he sneered into the camera and defended his good name. "I have been accused in print of collusion or attempted collusion with the athletic director at the University of Georgia to fix or rig the game we won against the University of Georgia by a score of thirty-five to nothing," he said, punching the words *fix* and *rig* as if they contained a foul smell. "I welcome the opportunity to tell the people of Alabama that these charges are false in every sense of the word . . . I want to take this opportunity to deny these charges with every force in my command."

The next day, addressing a large group of students at Foster Auditorium on campus, he said, "Our football team is something sacred to me. I'm proud of them when we win. And I want to win . . . but there's one thing you can bet your life on: that I never would try to use them to win a bet for ten jillion dollars." The place roared with approval.

As the state of Alabama rallied around him, with letters and telegrams of support pouring into his office by the hundreds, Bryant submitted to and passed a lie detector test. Although his own case was bogged down in a tight docket in Birmingham, the coach's testimony in Wally Butts's libel suit against Curtis Publishing Company on August 8, 1963, was widely considered a turning point for the plaintiff. The media attention for the event was predictably huge; Walter Cronkite led the *CBS Evening News* by saying, "Bear Bryant walked into an Atlanta courtroom today and laid it on the line . . . " He was calm, engaging, completely cooperative and, as always, larger than life. At one point during direct examination by Butts's attorney Bill Schroder, he got up from the witness stand, walked over to a chalkboard, and amplified his answers to various football questions with crudely scrawled x's and o's.

Although it eventually exonerated him and Bryant, the trial

ruined Wally Butts's reputation. The *Post*'s lawyers succeeded in making his character an issue in the proceedings. Several university officials reluctantly admitted that Butts had been asked to relinquish the head football coaching duties after the 1960 season because of his rather sordid private life, including the married man's very public, longtime affair, which several prominent alumni believed was damaging the program. They agreed to let him remain as athletic director and replaced him with one of his assistants, Johnny Griffith. Before the fix allegations became public, university officials demanded his resignation as athletic director, and although the plaintiff's attorney tried to portray the dismissal as some sort of vindication, the reality was more complicated; a large segment of the alumni had soured on Butts long before the blockbuster article, and rather than stand behind him until the facts could be ascertained, they used the fix charge as an excuse to dump him.

Neither Bryant nor Butts denied that the telephone conversation took place. Telephone company records confirmed it, and both men dismissed the call as containing no more than routine chalk talk among coaches. Telephone company records also confirmed Bryant's frequent calls to other friends in the coaching profession.

"I used to talk to Coach Woodruff down in Florida," Bryant said on the witness stand, "and I probably shouldn't say this, but Coach Woodruff is longer-winded on the phone than Coach Butts is. You get him on the phone, and you're going to miss dinner."

But were secrets passed, perhaps by a disgruntled Wally Butts, who harbored ill will toward the school that had pushed him upstairs? The *Post*'s lead attorney, former Georgia first baseman Welborn Cody, attempted to portray the somewhat rotund little man who had guided the Bulldogs to their greatest glory—a 140–86–9 record from 1939 to 1960, with four Southeastern Conference championships—as embittered and financially strapped, and therefore, capable of selling out his old school.

Before the trial, the *Post* hired several private investigators to attempt to prove that Butts or Bryant had wagered on football, but they came up dry. (Although the point spread was seventeen, Alabama won by thirty-five; the term "fix" was used to describe an effort to affect the margin of victory as well as the outcome.) The defense's fumbles were legion; incredibly, they decided not to call either the writer or the magazine's editor-in-chief to the stand to defend the piece, and the plaintiff's attorney succeeded in exposing the article's many errors.

Asked under oath if he had conspired to fix the game, Bryant replied angrily, "Absolutely not, and if we did, we ought to go to jail, and anybody that had anything to do with this ought to go to jail, because we didn't. Taking [the *Post*'s] money isn't good enough."

The article alleged, among other things, that Butts had told Bryant of the two formations the Bulldogs were using, and that this was somehow "secret" information. Both of the formations in question—the slot right and the pro set—had been used by Georgia the previous year and, in fact, they had been used to varying degrees by most of the teams in the Southeastern Conference. Not only was such information readily available in the newspapers at the time, the 'Bama staff had scouted the Bulldogs' spring game. Given the Bear's meticulous detail in assembling game plans, he probably knew more about the Bulldogs' tendencies than Johnny Griffith's staff did.

Even Griffith admitted under oath that such information would have been of no help to the Alabama coaching staff. He also pointed out errors of fact in the piece: As proof that the Crimson Tide had advance knowledge of Georgia's plays, the article quoted Bulldog end Mickey Babb as saying the 'Bama players were taunting them at the line of scrimmage, " 'You can't run Eighty-Eight Pop [a key Georgia play] on us.' . . . They knew just what we were going to run, and just what we called it." Griffith revealed that Georgia had no such play, and four Georgia players testified that they did not believe that Alabama knew their plays.

The most damaging testimony came from the eavesdropper

himself. Burnett, heavyset, with slicked-back black hair, was visibly nervous. He conceded that he had initially lied to University of Georgia officials about having a clean record, fearing that his history of passing bad checks might cloud his credibility, which it did. More important, he testified to two factual inaccuracies in the article. The first occurred in the opening line; he said the conversation took place on September 13, not September 14, as the article alleged. Phone company records confirmed the error. Although the date of the conversation might seem meaningless in the larger scheme of the alleged conspiracy, it played to the plaintiff's contention that the *Post* had been fast and loose with the facts, careless in pursuit of a scoop.

Perhaps the biggest bombshell of the trial, however, was Burnett's complete denial of one key passage of the article. The *Post* quoted him as saying Butts told Bryant that Georgia quarterback Larry Rakestraw "tipped off what he was going to do by the way he held his feet. If one foot was behind the other it meant he would drop back to pass. If they were together it meant he was setting himself to spin and hand off." Under oath, Burnett said he had never made such a statement.

(Later in the trial, the jury watched film of the game in question, and various experts testified that Rakestraw did not, in fact, telegraph his actions in such a manner. However, during his first year at Texas A&M in 1954, one of Bryant's assistants was poring over Georgia's game films when he discovered that the Bulldogs' quarterback tipped off his play calling with the position of his feet. A&M won the ballgame over Wally Butts's 'Dogs, 6–0.)

At the outset of the eight-day trial, the plaintiff's counsel placed a large, poster-sized blowup of the article on an easel in front of the jury box. Every time a witness contradicted a statement of fact or a quotation in the article, Schroder marked through the inaccurate passage in red ink. It was a brilliant stroke of showmanship, visible at all times to the all-male jury that would decide Wally Butts's fate.

Charley Pell and Jimmy Sharpe, two of the smallish linemen (weighing 189 and 182, respectively) from Bryant's "quick little boys," took the stand and testified that there had been no special preparation in the week leading up to the Georgia game, no last-minute changes that might have taken place in the presence of new "inside" information on their opponent.

Lee Roy Jordan, the Tide's defensive captain and All-America linebacker, later said of the scandal, "First, that's not something Coach Bryant would have ever done. He didn't want to win that way, didn't have to win that way. And even if [the coaches] had had so-called secret information, they couldn't have put it into the game plan without me knowing it. It just never happened. That whole story was total fiction."

Bob Ford, now a lawyer in Wynne, Arkansas, spent three years on the 'Bama staff before joining Johnny Griffith at Georgia in the spring of 1961. In the weeks leading up to the trial, the *Post*'s lawyers approached him about testifying on their behalf. He was dumbfounded.

"I said, 'When I got here from Alabama, I brought in all my old ['Bama] playbooks and threw 'em on the table [at a staff meeting]. I told [the coaches] everything I knew about the Alabama program, down to the smallest detail. I made myself available to answer all of their questions about the Alabama program. I knew all of the secrets and I told 'em everything I knew. And we still got beat. And you want *me* to testify?' The guy looked at me kinda shocked and said, 'No. No. I don't think we'll be needing you.' "

"Knowing what I know about Paul Bryant and about Wally Butts, I'm absolutely convinced it never happened," Ford said. "The whole thing was ridiculous. Coach Bryant was one of the most honorable men I've ever known."

After deliberating for less than a day, the jury awarded Butts a record $3.06 million judgment, although it was later reduced to $460,000 on appeal. The *Post*'s inability to prove the charges it had made in print represented a slam dunk for the plaintiff. One of the jurors later told a reporter, "Butts was a symbol. He just symbolized any person in the country that a magazine might have charged with 'fixing' or 'rigging' a game and being 'corrupt,' without proving the charges."

Within a year, the U.S. Supreme Court's ruling in the landmark *New York Times* v. *Sullivan* fundamentally altered the parameters of libel law, placing the burden of proof squarely on the plaintiff. Although the *Post* was unsuccessful in winning a new trial according to the *New York Times* doctrine, the case was waged all the way to the Supreme Court, where *Curtis Publishing Co.* v. *Butts* set a precedent on the issue of public figures in the new libel law environment. In June 1967, nearly five years after the game in question, the court held 5–4 that public figures as well as public officials could collect libel damages only by proving that defamatory falsehoods about them were made with a reckless disregard for the truth—and that the *Post* in this case had violated even so lenient a standard. Writing for the majority, Chief Justice Earl Warren said the *Saturday Evening Post*'s conduct was unreasonable and "constituted an extreme departure from the standards of investigation and reporting ordinarily adhered to by responsible publishers."

Six months after the Butts trial, Bryant settled his case for three hundred thousand dollars and a retraction. If the case had reached a courtroom in Birmingham, he most assuredly would have triumphed on the facts, but Curtis's lawyers would have tried to destroy his character, and such a prosecution could only have left him wounded.

Post editors Kahn and Emerson place a large amount of blame for the outcome on the magazine's lawyers, particularly chief counsel Phillip J. Strubing, who approved the piece before publication. "We got into it one day before they settled with Bryant and I was furious," Kahn said, "and I said, 'Look, Strubing, if there's another trial and I'm forced to testify, I'm gonna make sure everybody knows you signed off on this piece.' I think they settled to cover their own asses as much as anything else."

Although the lawyers bore the responsibility of protecting

the *Post*'s liability, Kahn and the rest of the editing staff were charged with getting the story right. And they failed.

In the aftermath of the "fix" story, editor-in-chief Clay Blair experienced a professional meltdown and eventually left the magazine; writer Frank Graham, Jr., lost the faith of some of his editors, although he went on to write several books; and the *Post* slowly descended into the muck. In 1969, the magazine folded.

Could such a betrayal of college football have happened in September 1962? Only two men know for sure, and both are dead. But given the facts and Paul Bryant's history, it seems inconceivable. No one who knew him believed a word of the *Post* story. The game meant too much to him, it was too much a part of him.

"I think that whole affair hurt Coach more than anything he ever faced," said his friend Ellis Taylor. "That some people would actually believe that he would do that . . . that he needed to do that to win. That was a blow he never really got over."

Several days after the lawyers worked out the details of his settlement, Bryant and his chief aide Sam Bailey drove to the Birmingham airport to pick up the man who would ultimately become his new sports information director. On the ride back to Tuscaloosa, Charley Thornton and his boss engaged in the usual idle chit-chat, and somehow the subject of the lawsuit came up.

"By the way, Coach," Thornton asked, "how do they pay you off on one of those deals?"

Without a word, the Bear reached into his shirt pocket and handed Thornton a yellow Western Union moneygram in the amount of three hundred thousand dollars.

"I knew right then it was a good day to come for an interview," Thornton said.

9
Southern Man

ONE NIGHT DURING THE OFF-SEASON of 1960, as he watched John Wayne fill up the screen in the western classic *Rio Bravo*, Tommy Brooker experienced a strange sensation. He couldn't stop thinking about how much the Duke, who was the roughest, toughest, most intimidating, most charismatic man in the movies, reminded him of Paul Bryant, who was the roughest, toughest, most intimidating, most charismatic man on the planet. The chiseled face. The swagger. The voice. The aura. The two giants of American popular culture were cut from the same rough-hewn cloth. Everyone saw it. Even the Bear recognized—and enjoyed—the comparison.

As Brooker walked casually out of the darkened theater alongside several of his Alabama football teammates, he spotted the Bear standing behind the ropes. He nearly swallowed his gum. He wondered, for a moment, if he was hallucinating. Then he nudged his friends and they tried to sneak out of the place without being seen by the man behind the ropes, because even away from practice, he scared the hell out of them. But it was too late. He ambled over to the door and flashed a sly grin in their direction.

"Just wanted to see this guy I'm supposed to act like," he grunted as the players smiled nervously at the surreal collision of life and art.

"Talk about an eerie feeling," said Brooker, one of the leaders on Bryant's first national championship team in 1961. "We walk out of that theater and see the man standing there, it's like John Wayne has jumped off the screen and spoke to us. We got out of there as fast as we could."

The man always seemed ten feet tall. His hands were as big as catcher's mitts. His voice, deepened by a lifetime of unfiltered Chesterfields, was more growl than enunciation. Sometimes he spoke with perfect diction. Sometimes he mumbled incomprehensibly. His face, as wrinkled as a dried-out prune in his later years, looked as if it had been lifted from Mount Rushmore. His walk was all swagger and attitude, like a gunslinger's. Capable of being both intimidating and captivating, he could amble into a room and become the center of attention without saying a word, because he had something, something you could neither define nor distill. Friends, colleagues, former players, and just plain folks invariably use words like "regal," "charismatic," and "magnetic" in describing Paul Bryant's unmistakable presence.

"Even his peers in the coaching business felt in awe of him," said Penn State head coach Joe Paterno. "He had such charisma. Whatever it is that makes great generals, he had it. Tons of it. He was just a giant figure."

On a Sunday afternoon at the end of one regular season in the 1970s, Paterno told his wife that he was going away by himself for two or three days so he could start preparing for the bowl game. He told her how to get in touch with him, but not to give anyone the number except Bryant. She perked up.

"You mean Coach Bryant's going to call? Can I talk to him?"

"Coach Bryant had a kind of magic to him," said Jack Rutledge, who played and coached for him at Alabama. "It was something you couldn't really put your finger on, but you could feel it whenever he walked into the room."

"There were several good football coaches, but there was only one Paul Bryant," said his longtime friend John McKay, the former Southern Cal coach. "With the chiseled face and the walk and the talk, he looked like he was playing a part in a movie every day of his life. But Paul was the genuine article, the last of a breed."

The man who become synonymous with the houndstooth hat he wore like a crown represented a certain American ideal. In an age when a hero was more than just a sandwich, he was the rugged, earthy, tough-as-nails embodiment of everything the American male was supposed to be. His was the face of strength, discipline, sacrifice, decency, and old-time values. The ultimate man's man who could tell a dirty joke but never in the presence of a lady, Bryant was a two-fisted drinker, an avid gambler who liked to shoot craps and bet the horses, a chain-smoker who kept trying to quit, and above all, a dedicated professional who started his day before the sun and routinely worked sixteen hours to become the dominant figure in the coaching profession.

A man with an extraordinary talent to lead tempered by ordinary human frailties, Bryant was a symbol for a part of America itself. Like a mirror held up to the great melting pot, he reflected the characteristics we revere while serving as a constant reminder of our shared origins as pioneers and strivers. Even more than the Madison Avenue distillation of two cars and a split-level in the suburbs, the life of Bear Bryant represented the American dream. If the apocryphal stories about him walking on water sometimes made him seem part Paul Bunyan, his hardscrabble rise from abject poverty to wealth, fame, and the status of American folk hero served as a confirmation of the very idea of America.

"I've always seen Coach as the cowboy figure from our past," observed Charley Pell, who played for him at Alabama and later coached at Clemson and Florida. "If he'd been born a hundred years earlier, he'd have been out west somewhere blazing a trail through the wilderness."

In the South, where football coaches enjoy a status on a par with governors and movie stars, Bryant became the foremost icon of his time. No man ever so dominated the game that lives so close to the southern heart. He considered football a metaphor for life, and southern fathers, who more often than not agreed, wanted their sons to grow up to become men of strength and honor like Bear Bryant. In addition to respecting his unmatched success, southerners of all stripes identified with him because, more than other Americans, they could relate to his struggles against poverty and for respect, and they admired his self-deprecation and humility, which were as much a reflection of their culture as his sandpaper drawl. He won and lost with a certain dignity and class that mirrored the noblesse oblige planter mentality that subtly dominated southern culture well after the age of the gentleman planter, and yet he was always the toughest son-of-a-bitch in the room.

He lived to win, but when he suspended Joe Namath for disciplinary reasons with two big games to play in his junior year, southern fathers understood, because they knew life was sometimes bigger than football, and they respected him for taking a stand on principle. He was the powerful man who played golf with presidents and he was the genuine man who liked to crumple up his cornbread in a glass of buttermilk before bedtime. He was the stubborn man who once went on statewide television and told his critics to go to hell, and he was the gentleman who always took off his hat when he walked indoors. He was an American hero alongside Babe Ruth, Vince Lombardi, and Muhammad Ali, but he belonged to the South. He was the granite-faced embodiment of southern pride.

During the final two decades of his life, Bryant was such a larger-than-life celebrity, it was difficult for him to go anywhere in the Southeast without being mobbed by autograph-seekers and glad-handers. As the perfect southern gentleman, he always obliged them, and as much as he enjoyed his fame, he sometimes felt trapped by it. During the off-season, he often spent a week or two at a time at the Palm Beach home owned by his friend Logan Young; sometimes he didn't leave the place for days, sending his bodyguard Billy Varner out for meals rather than fighting through the inevitable crowds.

"You know, Logan," he once said to the Memphis millionaire, "all I ever wanted to be was the best damn football coach in the country. I never thought people in all these places would give a damn who I was. I never have wanted all this attention."

"I think Coach got to be bigger than he ever wanted to be," Young said. "He wasn't able to get away from his fame, and that had to be a lonely feeling."

In Alabama as throughout much of the South, college football is more than just a game. It is a kind of cultural glue that transcends class, race, sex, income level, and educational attainment, bonding the state's citizens in a way outsiders can never truly appreciate. In the absence of major league sports and other cultural activities, amid the drumbeat of statistics ranking the state among the nation's poorest and worst-educated, college football serves as the foremost extension of the state's pride and self-esteem. Deeply rooted in the southern traditions and a symbol of the state's tendency to favor the physical over the intellectual, the game is, for Alabamians, the great leveler. Football gives them an opportunity to truly compete against the rest of the country and, more often than not, to win.

"The obsession with football gives meaning to everything else," said Wayne Flynt, an Auburn University history professor and the author of several historical books about the state. "If you look at the relative size of Alabama versus other states, the number of outstanding athletes and outstanding teams [produced by Alabama] is disproportionally large. One of the main reasons for that is that football is more important in Alabama. It gives us something to hold on to."

No man ever tapped the intimate relationship between football and life quite like Paul Bryant.

When Bryant's Crimson Tide rocketed to national prominence in the 1960s, the state of Alabama was being bombarded with negative publicity from the often-shameful performance of its leaders on the civil rights issue. The world watched as Bull Connor, the Birmingham public safety commissioner, turned his dogs and fire hoses on black protesters; as George Wallace stood in the schoolhouse door at the University of Alabama in an attempt to prevent court-ordered integration; as state troopers turned the Selma march for voting rights into Bloody Sunday. Virtually every time the name "Alabama" was mentioned on the evening news, it was uttered in the context of racial bigotry or, when the various poverty statistics were released, as one of the nation's poorest states.

But the Bear became the psychological antidote to Alabama's festering inferiority complex. To Alabamians who felt under siege on the race issue, he was a source of tremendous pride when pride was in desperately short supply. Even as the old order was crumbling, the Bear grew in stature, and his unparalleled success was a validation of one portion of the Alabama subculture, proof that the state was not defined simply by hatred and poverty.

Three decades later, the memories of the Alabama fans who grew up during the Bryant era are shaped by the context of those days. They cherish his records and his victories, and they also remember how he made them feel when they desperately needed to feel something other than bitterness.

Even in social situations, Bear Bryant never stopped being defined by his job and his legend. He had great difficulty pushing football out of his mind—he always carried a yellow legal pad to scribble notes about his team—and his dominant presence served as an emotional fence between himself and others. He could be a real charmer, but the same magical aura that drew people to him, that made players want to please him, kept them at arm's length.

Even after their playing days, most of Bryant's pupils felt intimidated by the man. Many loved him, but most could never penetrate the wall between player and coach. "I would see him coming down the hall [at coaching conventions] and I'd go hide in the bathroom," said Danny Ford, who became a successful coach at Clemson and Arkansas. Bryant often talked to his friends in his later years about how he wished more of his former players felt at ease socializing with him, but to most, he was always going to be a larger-than-life figure. They regularly stopped by to see him and sought his advice on matters ranging from marriage to finance, but he never stopped being the coach any more than their father ever truly relinquished the role of parent.

"You always felt like there was a limit to how close you could get to Coach Bryant," said Bob Baumhower, an All-America end for Alabama in the mid-1970s who went on to an All-Pro career with the Miami Dolphins. "As much as he meant to me—and he was very instrumental in my life—I never really stopped feeling in awe of him."

Even his family and their friends felt intimidated by him. The Bryants owned a summer house on Lake Martin in south central Alabama, and the coach and Mary Harmon enjoyed getting away from Tuscaloosa for several days at a time. He was a wily practitioner of the art of poker and gin rummy, and he enjoyed cooking steaks on his large open grill in the backyard; he demanded the biggest cut of meat available, and if a steak wasn't big enough for his tastes, he would send it back to the butcher. When he showed up unexpectedly on Mary Harmon and her friends, there was a definite change in the barometric pressure.

"When he walks in, you go from a very relaxed situation to a feeling among everybody that we should please him," said Martha Gibbs, one of Mary Harmon's closest friends. "That wasn't bad; it was just different. We thought so much of him and enjoyed him, yet we were never completely at ease around him."

He could be moody or positively charming. During their early days at Texas A&M, Mary Harmon became acquainted with Louise Porter through a bridge club, and the Porters invited the coach and his wife to a dinner party one Thursday night in the middle of the football season. She accepted for them. They were new to town and Mary Harmon was anxious to make friends. But when Thursday night rolled around, the coach arrived home in a foul mood after a hard day's work and told his wife to call it off, that he didn't want to spend his evening with a bunch of strangers.

An hour later, after an embarrassed Mary Harmon had phoned the Porters to say they couldn't make it, he came up behind her and put his arms around her. "Now, honey, where was this you wanted us to go tonight?" And Thursday night dinner at the Porters' evolved into a weekly tradition during football season at A&M, as the Porters and the Bryants became the best of friends.

"It was difficult for him to let his guard down," Louise Porter said. "I think he had a hard time relaxing and getting away from all his responsibilities."

Despite his unmistakable aura, Bryant was always very genuine, very human. He never got caught up in the trappings of fame. He felt just as comfortable scarfing down fried okra and meatloaf at the working-class Fyfe's cafeteria in downtown Birmingham—where the factory workers and laborers roll their sleeves up and punctuate a meal with a toothpick—as he did dining on filet mignon at New York's posh 21. Throughout his life, he always made a conscious effort not to let his celebrity change him, and it never did.

"Coach Bryant had this thing about 'plastic people,' " said his friend Butch Baldone, who owns a tailor's shop in Birmingham. "He hated phonies of any kind, and he could spot 'em a mile away. One time we were eating at Fyfe's and he leaned over to me and said, 'There ain't no goddamn plastic people in here.' "

Never one to pull a punch, the coach shocked members of the presidential staff during the 1960s when he was invited to Lyndon Johnson's Texas ranch. Upon greeting Bryant for the first time, LBJ looked him over and said, "Well, now, you're a big 'un, ain't you?"

The Bear gave the president a steely look. "You're a pretty big sonofabitch yourself!"

Bryant's unpretentious nature spilled through his daily life, such as the time in his office when the phone rang during an interview with a sportswriter. He excused himself and picked up the receiver.

"All right, just let me get a pencil," he said to the person on the other end of the line.

"OK. Dozen eggs. Carton of Milk. Loaf of bread . . . "

Even the Bear ran errands for his wife.

Joe Namath never lost the feeling of awe, but he became one of the few former players who regularly socialized with his coach. Bryant often visited his former star quarterback during training camp in his days with the New York Jets, and

in later years, when Namath retired from football and became
a full-time stage actor, the coach sometimes traveled with him
to his plays. After a performance of *Guys and Dolls* one night
in New York, Namath treated the whole cast to dinner at Gallagher's and enjoyed introducing the other actors to the living
legend from Alabama. The group was mesmerized by the Bear,
but one young lady kept leaning over to Namath, unable to
understand a word the coach was saying.

"What'd he say? What'd he say?"

The Bear didn't miss a beat. "Hey, Joe, tell her I teach diction
at Alabama!"

His small circle of close friends consisted mostly of successful businessmen, including Jimmy Hinton, Ellis Taylor,
Preacher Franklin, Johnny Mitchell, Julian Lackey, Logan
Young, and Red Pope. In addition to investing money together
in various ventures, Bryant and one or more members of his
inner circle often traveled to Las Vegas to gamble, to New York
for the annual induction ceremony for the National Football
Foundation Hall of Fame, to California and Florida to play
golf, and to various sites throughout the Southeast to hunt
birds and deer.

"Paul had a real way of making people like him," said John
McKay. Even though "he was bigger than life . . . he had a quality that allowed him to connect with all kinds of people. He
could be a great companion."

A self-taught golfer who learned to play after World War II,
Bryant had a relatively high handicap, but he attacked the
game like everything else he faced. "He was not much of a
player," said his friend Frank Broyles, the former Arkansas
coach who often hit the links with Bryant and former Texas
coach Darrell Royal. "But he was a very competitive golfer. He
would fight you like the dickens over a five-dollar bet."

A frequent golfing partner of such luminaries as Gerald
Ford, Bob Hope, and Jackie Gleason—especially during his
annual outings at the Bob Hope Desert Classic in Palm Springs
—the coach also played with the common folk and attacked
the task with the same enthusiasm. During his annual press

outing at a Florida resort in the mid-1960s, he and sportswriter John Pruett ended a round tied with businessman Red Wells and Gary Sanders of WAPI-TV in Birmingham. Bryant, who was credited with inventing the phrase "a tie is like kissing your sister," turned to Wells and grunted, "Hell, we ain't endin' in no tie! We'll just play these last three holes for fifty dollars a hole!"

"Fifty dollars a hole was chicken feed to Bryant and Wells, but I probably didn't have fifty dollars in my checking account, much less on me," said Pruett, the longtime sports editor of the *Huntsville Times.* "But what could I do? I couldn't say, 'Well, Coach, I don't think I want to do that.' Not to Bear Bryant."

So Pruett pulled Sanders aside and convinced him to disregard their side of the $150 bet, and then Bryant proceeded to birdie two of the three playoff holes to take Wells's money. He hadn't made a single birdie all day, and then he bagged two to win the prize. Pruett wanted to kick himself for not believing in the Bear.

Like most golf addicts, Bryant enjoyed watching and talking golf as much as playing. On the spur of the moment during one of his off-season visits to Florida in the late 1970s, Bryant and Logan Young rented a car and drove up to Jacksonville to watch the Tournament Players Championship. Jerry Pate, who starred collegiately at Alabama, was in his prime and Bryant wanted to see him play a few rounds. When they drove up to the gate, the guard asked for their tickets. The coach thought he could buy tickets at the gate, but when the guard didn't recognize him and told him there were no tickets available, he took out a piece of paper and asked the guard to have it delivered to the television people. Within five minutes, the coach and his friend were escorted into the club with sirens blaring, and the tournament treated them like royalty for the rest of the day.

"Two things impressed me about that day," Young said. "One was how he could scribble a couple of lines on a piece of paper and the whole world would fall at his feet. The other was how he didn't get mad at that boy at the gate. He said the kid was just doing his job. He didn't want anybody to make a fuss over him. He could be real humble about stuff like that. All he wanted was to see Pate play a few holes, and he was willing to buy a ticket like anybody else."

The coach enjoyed horse racing, and his celebrity was never more evident outside the state of Alabama than on one of his annual pilgrimages to the Kentucky Derby with his buddy Ellis Taylor. As much as Bryant loved to gamble, he never bet enough to alter his standard of living, and he rarely wagered more than he carried in cash at any particular moment. But after he and Ello, as he called Taylor, ran out of money before they ran out of races, one of his friends in the breeding business came up to him and urged him to bet on his horse in the next race, which he assured him was a sure thing. The coach told his friend he was out of money.

"People just started coming up to Coach and offering to lend him however much he needed," said Taylor. "He didn't want to borrow money, kept telling them, 'I don't even have a check.' But they just kept offering. They knew he was good for it. All those people wanted to be able to say they loaned Bear Bryant money. So finally he borrows seventy-five hundred dollars from one guy, and the horse wins on a seven-to-one shot . . . and he pays the money back and we walk out of there with money stuffed everywhere on us."

One of the most amazing aspects of Bryant's life was his almost total lack of personal enemies, which, for a man who accumulated so much power and achieved so much, is very unusual. Most of the players who survived four years under his direction would have taken a bullet for him. The men who coached under him universally revered him. Even the competing coaches who kept getting their brains bashed in by his teams couldn't help liking the guy.

In the years after the Darwin Holt/Chick Graning incident, Bryant experienced a falling-out with Georgia Tech head coach Bobby Dodd. They didn't talk for years; Bryant believed Dodd had milked the situation to make him look bad and manipulated it as an excuse to bolt from the Southeastern Conference. After years of silence, they reconciled in the 1970s, and Tech even agreed to play Alabama again. But Bryant never stopped hating Furman Bisher, the *Atlanta Journal* sports editor who fomented the Tech–'Bama split and played a role in *The Saturday Evening Post* article which alleged that Bryant fixed a game with Georgia's Wally Butts. Bisher refused to discuss Bryant for this book.

One afternoon, several years after the "fix" story, Bisher showed up at an Alabama practice and tried to gain admittance. The student manager at the gate sent word to Bryant, and Bryant sent word back that he would be heading for the gate in a few minutes and that the sportswriter from Atlanta had better not be there when he returned.

Ellis Taylor had never seen such a look of contempt in the coach's eyes. "I do believe, if he had been out there when Coach came out, Coach would've hurt him," Taylor said.

Women were drawn to Bryant's fame and his rugged good looks. Rumors of his alleged infidelities nearly cost him the job as Alabama head coach in 1958; several prominent alumni secretly opposed his hiring.

"At first, I was against him because of the things I'd heard about him and other women," said Jeff Coleman, the University of Alabama's longtime alumni director and a member of the search committee. "I did some real soul-searching. But I finally decided that was between him and Mary Harmon."

Women "just threw themselves at him," said Young Boozer, Bryant's college roommate and longtime business partner. "He was such a handsome guy—the most outstanding man in his profession—and the women just threw themselves at him."

On his annual pilgrimage to Las Vegas, the coach sometimes stopped over in Palm Springs to see his friend John McKay and his family. Typically, he would spend two or three days at McKay's condo and then head to Vegas with several thousand dollars in cash on him. Always leery of being robbed, the coach liked to hide his money before he went to bed at night, and the ritual of hiding and recovering became a familiar game to the

McKays' son Richie, who was in elementary school at the time. One morning when the coach was preparing to leave for Vegas, they couldn't remember where they had hidden his stash of five thousand dollars in hundreds.

"We must've searched for two hours before we finally found it," said McKay, who is now general manager of the Tampa Bay Buccaneers. "The coach was really getting steamed. What an image: this giant figure down on his hands and knees searching through potted plants and air vents!"

After narrating the Super Bowl telecast for the crowd gathered around the sports book parlor at The Dunes—a chore he shared for many years with Duffy Daugherty, the longtime Michigan State coach—Bryant headed for the craps tables. He usually went home with money in his pocket, but the money was never as important to him as the release the gambling represented. Like football and every other aspect of his life, however, he pursued his leisure time with a vengeance. His stamina sometimes bewildered his friends. Rather than riding from casino to casino in the limousines provided for dignitaries such as Mr. B, as the dealers and pit bosses called him, the coach demanded that they walk from place to place. He could drink like a fish, shoot craps till dawn, and after sleeping three or four hours while sitting up in his bed, be ready to start all over again.

He always had a lit cigarette in his possession. He liked to smoke his unfiltered Chesterfields down to the butt without dumping the ashes, and the trail of ash sometimes appeared to defy all the laws of physics. For a few months in the late 1970s he tried to cut down to three or four cigarettes a day, but the habit he had picked up as a youth in Arkansas was too powerful for even the Bear to lick. Within a short time, he returned to his three-pack-a-day Chesterfield fix, although for many years he kept an unopened pack of the lower-tar L&M brand in the breast pocket of his jacket as a reminder of his failure.

A short time before dawn every morning, Bryant climbed out of bed, showered, shaved, dressed, drove to his office on the University of Alabama campus, and spent half an hour or so answering his correspondence, and then retreated to a corner booth at a small diner across the Black Warrior River in Northport. The place was usually pretty empty at that hour, and he could have his breakfast and read his newspaper in peace. The tiny reading glasses that hung on the edge of his nose gave him a certain grandfatherly look, and as he waited for his food to arrive, he sipped his coffee and turned to Ann Landers. He and the famed advice columnist corresponded often through the years, and he often shared with his team bits of her column that he found inspirational. After Ann Landers, he flipped to the stock tables; in addition to being a great football coach, the Bear was a very astute businessman.

His salary at Alabama was never very impressive. In fact, he took a substantial pay cut when he arrived in 1958—from twenty-five thousand dollars to eighteen thousand dollars—because he realized it might cause problems for him politically if he earned more than the university deans. Although he always made sure he had several years remaining on a long-term contract to provide him with security, Bryant never pushed for the huge salary increases that he could have easily attained. As late as the early 1970s, when he was already the winningest and most revered coach in the land, his salary of about thirty-five thousand dollars was less than those of many of his Southeastern Conference rivals. His salary paid the bills, but many outside deals made him a millionaire several times over by the time of his death. In the 1970s, he donated some two hundred thousand dollars to the university for faculty raises, an unprecedented gesture for a football coach.

Before most coaches in the South, he recognized the value of television. His original Alabama contract granted him exclusive rights to the Crimson Tide's game films, which he used to build a tremendously lucrative franchise. For a quarter-century, his Sunday afternoon *Bear Bryant Show* was required viewing throughout the state, and the sponsors—Golden Flake Potato Chips and Coca-Cola—paid handsomely for the exposure, coughing up more than two hundred thousand dollars combined per year by the early 1980s.

By the time he returned to Alabama as athletic director and head football coach in 1958, Bryant was already a wealthy man. In addition to his impressive deal with Texas A&M—which included a cut of the gate—the coach benefited from friendly Aggie boosters who helped him (and in some cases staked him) in various real-estate, commodities, and oil and gas ventures. During his days at Alabama, he became a partner in the giant Ziegler's meat-packing company, a large shareholder in the Alfa insurance company, and the owner of a box company, a Volkswagen dealership, and large tracts of commercial and residential real estate throughout the state. He served on the boards of various banks and businesses. He even started a company with his friend Sonny Werblin to manufacture his own line of houndstooth hats. Every man in Alabama had to have a Bear Bryant hat.

"A football coach really lives football, but making a living at the same time is difficult," he said. "I've been lucky that I've had a lot of good friends who've helped me make money. Some of 'em have helped me make money without me taking a chance of losing money, and that's the kind of friend we all want to have."

Except for his television program, the coach eschewed most offers to trade on his name. He endorsed very few products through the years, but his series of television commercials for South Central Bell in the early 1980s touched a powerful chord with the public.

The script of the first commercial, which was a pitch for long distance, called for him to close by staring into the camera and asking, "Have you called your mama today?" After about thirty takes, the man with the almond-shaped face was growing weary. He hit the line and then ad libbed, "Sure wish I could call mine." It was pure magic; unplanned and unrehearsed, the very genuine addition was pure Bryant, and it was tugging at the heartstrings of mothers and sons all across the South on the day he died.

On the eve of the historic clash between Notre Dame and Alabama in the 1973 Sugar Bowl, the Bear Bryant stories were flowing like wine. The table of sportswriters who had arrived in New Orleans to cover the biggest game in the history of the bowl knew Bryant better than most, and as they dined and drank well on their expense accounts at a restaurant in the French Quarter, they took turns regaling each other with tales of a man they genuinely liked and respected. One of the stories involved the coach in a state of inebriation. After a while, the couple sitting at the next table got up to leave. The middle-aged woman, who was obviously an Alabama fan, approached the sportswriters' table and gave them all an angry look.

"I don't appreciate the things you've been saying," she chided. "And I'll have you know that Coach Bryant doesn't even drink!"

The entire table broke out in laughter.

In Alabama, the heart of the Bible Belt, where more than half of the counties forbid the sale of alcoholic beverages and where many consider drinking a sin, a large segment of the population saw the man as a saint. They wanted him to be more than he was; they loved him so much that they wanted him to be perfect, but as great a man as he was, he was a man prone to ordinary human weaknesses. His tendency to drink to excess was well known among his friends and among the news media, yet no one ever reported a word about this glaring flaw.

"In those days, you didn't write about the president's warts and you didn't write about a sports icon's warts," observed Jimmy Smothers, the longtime sports editor of the *Gadsden Times* who covered Bryant's teams for a quarter-century. "It was just sort of understood that we didn't write about Coach Bryant's tendency to drink too much."

Although he never drank at work or let it affect his job in any way, the coach often overindulged in social situations. Through the years, many of his friends attempted to keep him from getting drunk. Jack Hicks, a former 'Bama student manager and Joe Namath's best friend, made a habit of telling bartenders to water down the coach's drinks. Ellis Taylor stopped keeping whiskey around his house and often took drinks away from the coach when he had had too many.

At conference meetings and outings at the lake, when Mary Harmon felt her husband had drunk too much, she would signal for her friend Martha Gibbs and they would gently persuade him that it was time to go to bed. Mary Harmon "loved him so much, and she hated to see him embarrass himself," Gibbs said. "It wasn't that he was ever particularly rowdy or anything, but she just didn't like other people to see him that way, when he wasn't in complete control of himself. He just couldn't drink very much without it affecting him."

"I think he was an alcoholic," said his friend Butch Baldone. Drinking "became too much of a crutch for him."

Sometimes, there is a fine line between social drinking and problem drinking, and at various times in his life, Bryant staggered over the chalk. He could go for months and drink only occasionally and then go through periods when he drank too much more often than not. Whether he was an alcoholic depends upon one's definition. He was not the kind of man to wake up and start drinking before breakfast; on the contrary, he made a clear delineation between work and off-hours, and he never drank at work. He was always all business at work, but he liked to drink to have a good time, and it was difficult for him to stop before he got sloppy drunk.

Many of his friends say they believe he drank as a means of escaping his fame and responsibilities. Although he rarely showed it, the immense pressures of his position and his celebrity weighed heavily on him, especially toward the end of his life, and friends say they sensed a certain loneliness in him. He was always Bear Bryant, always the repository of so much southern pride, and if the drinking was a symptom of something deeper, as it almost always is, it was his one way of turning down the noise in his mind.

In addition to escaping from his various responsibilities, Bryant also lost many of his special qualities when he hit the bottle hard. The drunk Bear Bryant could hurt people who loved him, could hurt them without knowing it. One night in the late 1970s, a longtime Alabama assistant coach spotted his old boss at a hotel in Birmingham and greeted him without realizing he had been into the bottle.

Bryant, bleary-eyed and wobbly, looked him over. "Who the hell are you?"

The man had worked for Bryant for nearly twenty years. He loved the old man like a father, and he had never felt so low in his life.

Mary Harmon Bryant remained an important part of her husband's life until the day he died. He sought her counsel on many of the biggest decisions in his career. Friends say she was instrumental in convincing him to accept the Alabama job when it was offered, and she played a role in his decision to walk away from a deal to coach the Miami Dolphins in 1970. In his later years, she worried about his health—and where he might die—and she tried to convince him to retire for several seasons before he finally made the difficult decision in 1982.

Mary Harmon enjoyed a special relationship with the Alabama football players. On road trips, she joked and played cards with them and got close to them in a way her husband couldn't. Without her husband's knowledge, she invited Joe Namath over for dinner the night after the Bear suspended him from the team in 1963 and gave the star quarterback a combination pep talk and tongue-lashing. She often invited married players and their wives over for dinner when he was away, but they often accepted with a sense of forboding. One Sunday in 1979, Mary Harmon invited Jim Bunch and his wife, Leslie, to watch the taped *Bear Bryant Show*, and as they

munched on Golden Flake chips and swigged on Coca-Cola,
Jim kept looking over his shoulder.

"I was scared to death Coach Bryant was going to walk
in," said the six-two, 233-pound Bunch, who earned three-time
All-SEC acclaim at offensive tackle from 1977 to 1979. "Kind
of late in the show, the front door opened and Paul Junior
walked in, and I was terrified it was Coach Bryant."

Although they endured problems and maintained separate
bedrooms for much of the last twenty years of his life, Paul
and Mary Harmon clearly loved each other and enjoyed a very
playful relationship, even during the darkest of times. In the
weeks after *The Saturday Evening Post* article, the coach and
his wife retreated to their lake house for some much-needed
peace and quiet. After finishing his nightly dose of cornbread
crumpled up in buttermilk, Papa, as Mary Harmon called her
husband, started up the stairs to bed and asked his wife if
there was anything new to read.

"Well, Papa," she said, "there's a *Saturday Evening Post* on
the night table up there. That ought to put you right to sleep."

He rolled his eyes and stomped off to bed.

On another visit to the lake, she walked into a small grocery
store down the road from their house to pick up a few necessi-
ties for dinner, and she struck up a conversation with the clerk.
"Oh, by the way," the checker said. "I think I saw Coach Bryant
in here the other day."

"Oh, yeah? Was he a big man with a real kind face, real
sweet acting?"

"Yes, ma'am."

"Well, that wasn't him."

The public never saw the private man's immense capacity
for compassion and generosity.

"Coach Bryant was the greatest person I ever saw in helping
people who needed it and never letting them know that he
helped them, which is the mark of a great man to me," said

Bill Battle, who played on Alabama's 1961 national champion-ship team and later served as the coach's marketing represen-tative.

The big, mean, scary Bear harbored a soft spot in his heart for handicapped and terminally ill children. He was a regular visitor around the children's wards of the various hospitals around Birmingham and Tuscaloosa, and he was instrumental in helping John Croyle, one of his former players, found the Big Oak Boys and Girls Ranch for troubled children near An-niston. On one occasion in the late 1970s, he showed up at the Children's Hospital in Birmingham and went to see a termi-nally sick little girl who had been asking for him, and he held her in his arms until she died. Although his players and staff rarely saw the tough guy's sentimental side, it became a large part of his legacy.

A chance meeting at a Fordyce pool hall in 1958 fundamen-tally altered Larry Lacewell's life. Lacewell, the son of a child-hood friend of Bryant's who had died when the boy was in high school, was a twenty-year-old knockabout headed no-where fast. Bryant, who found him playing dominoes, paid his way through college, gave him a leg up in the coaching profession, and mentored him for the rest of his life.

"Whatever I am today, I owe to Coach Bryant," said Lace-well, the Dallas Cowboys' director of player personnel. "I got [an education] because of him. I got my first coaching job sight unseen because of his recommendation. [After I got out of the business] he convinced me to get my butt back into coaching. He just changed my life."

Twenty-four years after their fateful first meeting, the rela-tionship came full circle at the American Football Coaches Association convention in Los Angeles. After Rutgers dropped Alabama from its 1982 schedule, Bryant was shopping around for a replacement opponent. One of his colleagues suggested lightly regarded Arkansas State, where his pupil Lacewell had recently been named the head coach. The Bear summoned his boy to his hotel suite to discuss a possible matchup between the Crimson Tide and the Blazers.

"Now, look, Larry, I'm gonna have to play you early—"

"OK, Coach. But why?"

" 'Cause if I play you late I'll be in the hunt for the national championship and I'll have to beat the shit out of you!"

Despite his gruff image, Bryant genuinely cared about his players and tried to help them succeed in life. Many coaches talk a good game on the subject of life after football, but Bryant's record is impossible to ignore. He spent an incredible amount of time helping his former players land jobs, both in coaching and in various other professions. When a former player was down on his luck, Bryant often called his banker and arranged a loan. "He was such a soft touch," said George Shirley, the former president of First National Bank of Tuscaloosa. "If somebody needed something, he wanted to help 'em." On the several occasions when former players failed to repay such notes and he was left holding the bag, he felt like he had failed because he expected his disciples to be men of strong character above all else.

Pat Trammell was the kind of man who never expected to need his help. The very personification of the Bryant football player—"He was," the great linebacker Lee Roy Jordan said of his teammate, "one tough sonofabitch"—Trammell was endowed with a combination of intelligence and drive that marked him for greatness. Bryant loved him like a son, and the Bear cried like a baby on the day Pat Trammell died of cancer.

In the ensuing years, the coach took a special interest in Trammell's son and daughter and tried, as best he could, to fill in the gaps of their lives. He always remembered their birthdays, and was always around when they needed advice or just to talk. Pat Junior regularly walked the sidelines at Alabama games.

"Looking back on those days, it amazes me how kind Coach Bryant was to us," said Pat Trammell, Jr. "Here was a man who was so incredibly busy, but he took time with us and had a way of making us feel like we were the most important people in the world to him. It wasn't like having our dad back, but it was special. He was a special man."

The Trammell children became the first recipients of a truly remarkable and unprecedented scholarship program. Thanks to Bryant's foresight and generosity, the children of any former Crimson Tide player under the Bear may attend the University of Alabama free of charge. Dozens of former players have educated their children on the coach's nickel over the last sixteen years. In the mid-1980s, when Jimmy Fuller's youngest was preparing to attend the University of Alabama, the former Tide lineman at first decided not to take advantage of the Bryant scholarship; as a 'Bama assistant coach, he was earning a good living and he could afford to send his little girl to college on his own.

But Ray Perkins changed his mind. "That's not the point," explained the man who followed Bryant as the 'Bama head coach. "The point is, Coach Bryant wanted to do something for all of us. He wanted to give something back."

His generosity seemed driven at times by a sense of personal debt to those who had helped make him successful, but he was also capable of moments of simple kindness that can only be attributed to the old-time values that marked him so deeply. Tommy Brooker often flashes back to the day when, more than a decade after his Alabama playing career had ended, the coach showed up for his daddy's funeral. He can still see the old man standing in the middle of the street like a stoplight, with his houndstooth hat in his hand, as the hearse pulled away from the funeral home. He can still remember how the sight made him feel. He can still feel the lump in his throat.

"He didn't have to come to my daddy's funeral . . . but he did. That's just the kind of guy he was."

10
Arms and the Man

JOE NAMATH WAS A GIFT. During the recruiting season of 1960–61, the immensely talented quarterback from Beaver Falls, Pennsylvania, signed with the University of Maryland, but his college boards fell a few points shy of the school's minimum requirements, so late in the summer he suddenly was up for grabs, like a lottery ticket tossed to the winds. Recruiting buzz was more subdued in those pre-ESPN, pre–sports talk radio days, but Tide assistant Charley Bradshaw got a call from a friend on the Maryland staff. The Terps were crushed to lose such a promising prospect, of course, and were frightened of playing against him at Penn State, which was hot on his trail. Alabama, which didn't appear on the Maryland schedule, was a more palatable alternative; that Joe's older brother had been recruited by Bryant at Kentucky certainly didn't hurt 'Bama's chances. So the coach dispatched former Wildcat Howard Schnellenberger to the hills of western Pennsylvania, and after more than a week of fending off the various other suitors—including Notre Dame—for the greatest passer since Johnny Unitas, they hopped a plane headed south for an official visit.

After all those days on the road with only two changes of clothes, the tall, mustachioed Schnellenberger looked like a sailor staggering home after a week's shore leave. His clothes were wrinkled, he smelled of sweat and cigarettes, and he was flat broke. The thirtysomething Schnellenberger, with a wife and two children to support on the modest salary of an Alabama assistant coach, had expected to be on the road no more than two or three days, so when two or three days ran into a week and then ten days, he ran out of money; rather than risk losing the prospect by waiting for a wire from home, he wrote a bum check for Namath's plane ticket. Like the Marines, Bryant men were taught to improvise, adapt, overcome!

The Birmingham airport was fogged in, so the coach and his prize were forced to fly into Atlanta and spend the night, which necessitated another rubber check for a hotel room. The next morning, when they got up and returned to the airport to fly on to Birmingham, Schnellenberger dug deep into his pants pocket and retrieved fifteen cents.

"Luckily, Joe didn't want breakfast," said Schnellenberger, who later led Miami to the 1983 national championship. "If he had, I'm not sure what I would've said. But he wanted a cup of coffee, so I bought him a cup of coffee and I did without."

Two-a-days were in full swing by the time they arrived on campus, and Schnellenberger wasted no time in getting his prospect in front of the boss, although he was worried what the coach would think about the young man's appearance. The product of a broken home and a modest environment in steel-mill country, Namath looked like a street hustler, sucking on a toothpick and wearing a checkered sport coat with a pocket watch dangling from the breast pocket. When he climbed up on the Bear's tower and stood there, toothpick in tow, talking to the legend, every head on the field turned in amazement. No player had ever been invited upstairs with the boss. They didn't know who he was, but they knew he was somebody special.

The Bear worked his magic, and Namath signed with the Tide.

Anyone who watched Namath take a ball in his hands could see he was going to be a superstar. He possessed the combination of arm strength, quickness, size, toughness, and football smarts that comes along once in a generation. Also, there was an air of supreme, unshakable confidence about him, even as an uninitiated rookie. Bryant later called him the most talented athlete he had ever seen. Although he was unaccustomed to the South, Namath blended easily. He even started answering to the name Joe Willie, like a good ol' boy from Albertville. The coeds flocked to him like a Beatle.

In his first college game, Namath looked like a veteran, tossing three touchdown passes to lead the Crimson Tide to the 35–0 victory over Georgia in the 1962 season opener that cost *The Saturday Evening Post* so dearly. The sensational sophomore led the Tide to a 10–1 season, including a 17–0 victory over Oklahoma in the Orange Bowl. Although the numbers pale in comparison to modern-day passing offenses like Miami's and Florida's, the Namath-era Crimson Tide moved the ball downfield at a torrid pace for the times. Coaches like Bear Bryant didn't toss it on first down or in short-yardage situations, of course, but Joe Willie set a new school record for completions (76) and passing yardage (1,192) while tying Harry Gilmer's mark for touchdown passes in a season (13).

One play prevented the Tide from repeating as the national champion in 1962. Ranked number one, with a twenty-three-game unbeaten string riding in the balance, and trailing Georgia Tech 7–0, 'Bama scored a late touchdown and opted for a two-point run attempt by backup quarterback Jack Hurlbut.

"There was no question . . . we had to go for two points," Bryant said in defending the decision. "When you're number one in the country you don't play for the tie."

In the spring of 1963, Bryant brought in passing game specialist Ken Meyer—future head coach of the San Francisco 49ers—as the quarterback coach to open up the offense a bit more. Namath was impressive as he gained experience, but 'Bama lost two games it should have won: 10–6 to Florida (one of only two losses for Bryant-coached teams at Bryant-Denny Stadium) and 10–8 to Auburn.

Most memorable, however, are the two games Joe Willie didn't play.

The Sunday after John Kennedy was assassinated in Dallas, Paul Bryant received word that his star quarterback had been seen drinking and causing a disturbance at an off-campus hamburger joint the night before. Drinking during the season was a violation of training regulations, and while many similar incidents came to the attention of assistant coaches and were handled without bothering the boss, whenever something caused enough of a stir to reach him, he felt compelled to handle things, and he wasn't likely to let it pass with a few early morning gassers. There was little to tell except that Namath, head manager Jack "Hoot Owl" Hicks (Namath's best friend), and two other players had drunk a few beers and were hanging out at a diner called Captain Cooke's. In those days, girls had to be back in their dorms and sorority houses by midnight, so after the coeds were locked up for the evening, it was common for Captain Cooke's to fill up with guys who had left the bars or had dropped off their dates. There was no fight or major disturbance; some of the guys got loud, and Namath got nailed only because the owner of the place recognized him and called Bryant.

The coach walked into the dining room at Bryant Hall and collared Namath. They walked into the coach's private room at the dorm, and he told Namath what he had heard and asked him if it was true.

"Yessir," Namath said. "I had a beer."

Bryant nearly fainted, because he knew what he had to do, and he figured it was going to cost him two big ballgames against Miami and Ole Miss in the Sugar Bowl.

"I can either suspend you or I can let you play in these last two games and then I'll have to resign," the coach told his star quarterback. " 'Cause if I let you play I'll be violating all my principles of coaching."

"No, Coach, I don't want that to happen," Namath said, his eyes welling up with tears. "I'll take my punishment."

Before making his decision, the coach called a meeting of his assistant coaches and apprised them of the situation. Every man in the room favored keeping Namath on the team except twenty-seven-year-old Gene Stallings, the slow-talking boy wonder who had played under the Bear at Texas A&M. "If it'd been me," Stallings said forcefully, "you'd have kicked me off."

"I wasn't thinking about what was best for the team or for Joe Namath," admitted line coach Dude Hennessey, who favored keeping Namath on the team. "I was wondering how in the world we were gonna beat Miami and Ole Miss without our quarterback . . . thinking about my bowl bonus."

After every coach had his say, Bryant adjourned the meeting and told his staff he would make his decision and let them know. The next day, he called them together to tell them he was suspending Namath.

"Y'all aren't thinking of Joe," he scolded his coaches. "This is the best thing for Joe."

No one outside the coaching staff knew about Namath's activities, so it would have been easy for Bryant to ignore the incident or give his star quarterback some meaningless punishment. But Bryant firmly believed that Namath needed to be taught a lesson about rules and responsibility, and he knew if he let the situation pass without taking action, team discipline might suffer. The decision also reflected the coach's remarkable sense of fairness; he was determined to let the football team know that rules were rules, and that if the star quarterback was caught violating the rules, he was going to be punished with as much force as a scout-team blocking dummy.

When word started spreading around Bryant Hall that the starting quarterback and the head manager had been suspended for the rest of the season and moved out of the athletic dorm, sophomore fullback Steve Bowman, who had been out on the town with Namath and Hicks, returned to his room and started packing.

"I just sat there waiting for the knock on the door," said Bowman, who was destined to become an All-SEC fullback on 'Bama's national championship teams in 1964 and 1965. "I knew if they were kicking Joe and Jack off, I didn't have a prayer. That's the only time in my life I've ever been scared of losing something, and I was scared of losing everything."

Bowman's teammates never ratted on him, and the knock never came.

The coach arranged for Namath to move into a regular student dorm on campus and told the quarterback he could return to the team in the spring if he kept his nose clean. He warned his staff against helping Namath in any way. The day his suspension hit the newspapers in bold type, Joe Willie stopped by Bryant's office with one last request: "Would you call my mother?" he asked. "Just to explain it to her. Tell her it's gonna be all right."

Meanwhile, Alabama struggled to a 17–12 win over Miami

on national television under backup quarterback Jack Hurlbut. Sophomore Steve Sloan, the top high-school quarterback in the state of Tennessee in 1961, took the reins against SEC champ Ole Miss in the Sugar Bowl. The Tide was an underdog without Namath, but the day after a freak snowstorm in New Orleans, Tim Davis kicked four field goals for a 12–7 'Bama win.

"Coach Bryant taught me about paying the price," Namath said later. "He was right and I was wrong."

Friends of Namath's say the punishment was a wake-up call that played a large role in his maturation from brash kid to dedicated professional.

"Joe loved Coach Bryant like a father," said Jack Hicks, who remains one of Namath's closest friends. "That time when he was suspended was probably the toughest time of his life, but he respected what Coach Bryant was doing. Joe knew Coach Bryant was right, and it made him a better man."

Several colleges tried to lure Namath out of Bryant's dog-house, but he decided to stay and prove to his coach that he was worthy of a second chance. After rejoining to the team in the spring, Joe Willie helped lead 'Bama to an undefeated season and the national championship in 1964. The bomber from Beaver Falls returned in impressive fashion, but in the fourth game of the season against North Carolina State, he suffered the first of a series of knee injuries that would dog him for the rest of his career, and as he nursed the sore leg, he shared playing time with Steve Sloan for the rest of the season.

Of all his great performances in a crimson uniform, Namath's most unforgettable was in a loss. Already crowned the national champion, Alabama trailed Texas 14–0 in the second quarter of the 1965 Orange Bowl when Namath replaced Sloan off the bench.

Like the crippled Kirk Gibson limping out of the dugout to stroke the game-winning home run in the first game of the 1988 World Series, Namath hobbled onto the field with his right knee heavily bandaged. Two days earlier, he had retorn the cartilage, and the pain was intense. He was no threat to run, since he could barely walk. But he stood in the pocket and put on a passing clinic, firing perfect strikes in the face of an unrelenting rush, time and again. The numbers read eighteen completions out of thirty-seven attempts for 255 yards and two touchdowns, but the performance transcended the statistics. The second half belonged to him like an empty stage.

Down 21–7 at the half, Namath rallied the Tide to within 21–17 early in the fourth quarter and then, in the closing moments, Jimmy Fuller picked off a Texas pass to give 'Bama new life at the Longhorns' thirty-four. Namath completed passes to Ray Ogden and Steve Bowman, and then three stabs by Bowman took 'Bama to the one with fourth and goal. Ignoring the pain, Namath called his own number and disappeared in a sea of orange-and-white jerseys. It was close, too close for most television viewers to say for certain. When he got up, he dusted chalk off his jersey, but the officials said he hadn't scored.

After the game, Bryant marveled at his quarterback's gutty performance but refused to second-guess the officials on the touchdown call. "When you're that close, you should score where there's no doubt about it," he said.

The next morning, Joe Namath signed the richest contract in the history of professional sports—$427,000—with the New York Jets. The brash wiseguy with the effortless charm was on his way to the history books as the cocky quarterback who guaranteed a victory over the Colts in Super Bowl III, the ultimate marquee player of his time who gave the American Football League the stature to merge with the National Football League in 1970.

No one was prouder than the man who had punished him for drinking a few beers.

Bryant studied the rule book like a Bible. Coaches of his era say that he probably was responsible for the implementation of more new regulations than any coach who ever lived, because he was determined to use every loophole to his advantage. In his early days at Alabama, he signed football players as wrestlers, baseball players, track athletes, and so forth, to avoid the limits on football scholarships—and then the SEC outlawed the practice. He placed his athletes in for-credit classes during the winter months in which they put on shoulder pads and helmets and learned about fundamentals; the NCAA stepped in and passed a new rule forbidding such classes. He bought fancy crimson travel jackets to give his players a touch of class, until the national governing body ruled that such items exceeded the necessary attire of a college football player. He also knew how to use obscure rules to help his team win on Saturdays, as evidenced by the third game of the 1965 season against Ole Miss.

The defending national champions limped into Legion Field with a 1–1 record. In the opener, Georgia used a controversial flea-flicker to stage an 18–17 upset. The film showed that Pat Hodgson had both knees on the ground when he lateraled to Bob Taylor, who scored the winning touchdown, but the officials ruled that he batted the ball, which was legal. It was the earliest loss for a Bryant-coached 'Bama team since Billy Cannon and company knocked off the Tide in their 1958 opener.

With under five minutes to play against Ole Miss, 'Bama trailed 16–10. But Steve Sloan led the Crimson Tide on a heart-pounding, fourteen-play, eighty-eight-yard march capped by his nine-yard touchdown run to win, 17–16. Three times, 'Bama converted fourth and short to keep the drive alive. During the march to victory, Bryant called a tackle eligible play with one-time fullback Jerry Duncan, who rambled for twenty-two yards and a first down. The ultimate gadget play, the tackle eligible allowed an offensive lineman to become a legal ball-carrier by lining up just behind the line of scrimmage; run correctly, it caught defenses napping.

Ole Miss coach Johnny Vaught was hopping mad. The long-time Rebels coach represented the SEC on the NCAA's football rules committee at the time, and during an off-season committee meeting, he demanded that the tackle eligible be outlawed. "I went on a personal campaign to get rid of that rule," he said.

"Johnny wasn't going to let us adjourn the meeting until we got rid of that play," said former Arkansas coach Frank Broyles, who chaired the committee. "And so we changed the rule."

Two weeks after coming from behind to beat Ole Miss, 'Bama was tied with Tennessee and driving for a go-ahead touchdown in the waning moments. Then a hotshot sophomore quarterback named Kenny Stabler threw the ball out of bounds on fourth down at the Vols' two-yard line. Stabler thought it was third down, and he was trying to kill the clock. After the horn sounded on the frustrating 7–7 tie, the managers couldn't find the key to the dressing room, and the fifty-two-year-old Bryant was so mad that he pushed the players out of the way and rammed into the door with his shoulder. One crack and it splintered, just like on *Mannix*.

Bryant took full responsibility for the tie, which might as well have been a loss to him. But he told his players they could still accomplish their annual goal of winning the national title, which seemed ridiculous, except for those who believed in miracles. "You can still be national champions if you want to be," he said. "If you don't, then I've misjudged you."

Five weeks later, Alabama crushed Auburn, 30–3, to capture the SEC championship and finish the regular season 8–1–1 and ranked fourth. Several days later, the coach called his nine seniors into his office to discuss their bowl plans. The seniors wanted to go to the Cotton Bowl to play Arkansas. As sophomores and juniors, they had traveled to the Sugar Bowl in New Orleans and the Orange Bowl in Miami, so, being young men who hailed mostly from small towns in Alabama, they were eager to see as much of the world on somebody else's nickel as possible. Playing in the Cotton Bowl in Dallas sounded like a great idea to them.

"*Cotton* Bowl?" Bryant interrupted, shaking his head. "We don't wanna go to the Cotton Bowl. Go to the Cotton Bowl and you can't play for the national championship. But if we go to the Orange Bowl . . ."

Then he walked over to the chalkboard and diagramed the

wackiest day in bowl history. Pure fantasy. UCLA, he said, would upset number-one-ranked Michigan State in the Rose Bowl. LSU would go to the Cotton Bowl and shock number-two Arkansas. Then, because the Associated Press's poll of sportswriters and broadcasters was holding its final balloting after the bowl games for the first time, number-four Alabama could back into the big prize by knocking off number-three Nebraska in the Orange Bowl. Not in a million years would such a combination of upsets propel such a longshot to the national title, but the Alabama seniors bought his incredible daydream and started preparing for Nebraska. Then it all happened just as he predicted.

In the afternoon, Michigan State and Arkansas fell. Then, in the prime-time Orange Bowl, Alabama won an offensive slugfest with Bob Devaney's unbeaten Nebraska Cornhuskers, 39–28. Alabama, which finished a roller-coaster season 9–1–1, became the first team to win the national championship with a loss and a tie.

The victory was a showcase for the passing talents of All-America senior quarterback Steve Sloan. Although not as flashy a passer as the cover boy Namath, the reserved, deeply religious Sloan broke Namath's school record for yards (1,453) and completions (ninety-seven) in 1965. He entered the Orange Bowl brimming with confidence, especially after a pregame talk with his coach.

The relationship between Bryant and his quarterbacks was much more intimate than those between the coach and his other players, and before every game, usually after the team meal, he took a walk with all his personal field representatives. "Just a few reminders," he would say, and then he would go on to discuss the game plan, that particular team's strengths and weaknesses, and the importance of various fundamental virtues in the Bryant school of football and life, such as always knowing your down and distance. Invariably, in the years after 1965, he told his men the infamous Kenny Stabler story at least once a year, as an example of how even the best can make stupid mistakes that cost games. Mostly, the walking and talking was the coach's way of pumping up his quarterbacks' self-esteem before the big bout.

As Bryant and his quarterbacks walked around a pier near their hotel in Miami, he pulled Sloan aside and deviated from the usual reminders. "Look, Steve," he said, "I don't think we're gonna be able to stop Nebraska. They've got too much talent. We're gonna have to outscore 'em. So I want you to throw any time you want to, on any down."

Sloan was shocked. "That was a total depature for Coach Bryant," he said. "We were only averaging about sixteen passes a game, and there were pretty strict rules about when you could pass and when you couldn't. You never passed on first down. If you had second and six or less, you always ran the ball. So here he was giving me the authority to pass from my own one-yard line if I wanted to. It was such a foreign concept."

In the previous year's Orange Bowl, Namath had passed much more often than Bryant usually allowed, but only because the Tide was behind and desperate. The Bear was telling Sloan to play as if he were behind from the first series. Unleashed from the normal restrictions of 'Bama football, Sloan took his coach at his word. He threw short from deep in his own territory. He threw deep on first down. The huge Nebraska linemen kept chasing him and knocking him down, but he always kept getting up, even after tearing cartilage in his shoulder. When they lunged for him, he sometimes stood on his toes and cocked the ball a little higher, just out of their grasp, and Ray Perkins and the other 'Bama receivers kept catching and running for daylight. For the night, Sloan completed twenty of thirty-seven passes for 296 yards and two touchdowns, leading the Tide to a 24–7 halftime lead from which Nebraska never recovered. Alabama outgained the 'Huskers, 512–378, but it wasn't nearly so close.

Toward the end of the first half, with the game firmly in hand, the coach sent in a substitute guard with a message: "You don't have to pass on every down, Steve."

Nebraska's Devaney called the performance "the greatest offensive show I've ever seen."

The Orange Bowl demonstrated one of Bryant's fundamental strengths: Knowing his quick little boys faced a tremendous challenge against the bigger, more talented Nebraska team, he changed his entire offensive strategy, even though such a shift represented a complete departure from everything he believed about offensive football. Rather than being chained to a set of beliefs, Bryant was a pragmatist who was strengthened by the ability to adapt in order to give his team the best chance of winning.

Ken Stabler's old man drank to escape the pain. The booze turned down the noise in his mind, helped him escape the lingering horrors of the war against Hitler, helped him forget the lifetime of disappointments, the wasted time, the guilt. But the drinking also unleashed other demons. One night when Kenny was a strapping sixteen-year-old quarterback for the Foley High School Tigers, he arrived home and found his father pointing a shotgun at his mother. The old machine-gunner had her backed into a corner with the other kids and said he was going to blow them all away. He didn't say why. Kenny and his father struggled over the gun, and the son finally managed to take the weapon away from his old man, who was bigger and meaner, and he took it and hid it. He tucked away the gun, but held on to the memories.

"When you've stared down the barrel of a shotgun in your own home at sixteen," Stabler remarked, "third and twenty's not so bad."

The four All-America quarterbacks who guided Alabama to championships in the 1960s brought to Tuscaloosa four very distinct backgrounds and personalities. Pat Trammell grew up the son of a doctor in Scottsboro, Alabama, and was defined by his mental toughness as much as his intelligence. Joe Namath was the product of a broken home in the hills of Pennsylvania, the son of a steelworker, and was streetwise and cocky. Steve Sloan sprang from a typical southern middle-class family in Cleveland, Tennessee, and was devout and unassuming.

Kenny Stabler was a country boy from Foley, Alabama, who fled an alcoholic father, his makeup an odd mix of maturity and immaturity.

"Coach Bryant had a special knack for being able to relate to all kinds of young people, regardless of their background," Stabler said. "He had tremendous instincts about people. He knew how to make us all want to reach and please him."

Inheriting the mantle of Trammell, Namath, and Sloan, Stabler won the starting job as a junior in 1966 and took his place in 'Bama history. Often described as a left-handed Namath, the man called Snake was a natural-born passer: terrific release, great arm strength, good touch. He could stand in the pocket and throw into an oncoming rush, or roll out and chunk it while throwing off his back leg. An elusive scrambler, he led the Crimson Tide in rushing as well as passing his junior season. A talented pitcher, he turned down a fifty-thousand-dollar signing bonus from the Yankees to play for the Bear. As a young quarterback, he could be reckless, impatient, and undisciplined, and those qualities got him into trouble on and off the field.

Without any glaring flaw, the veteran Tide was loaded and experienced on both sides of the ball in 1966. By year's end, Bryant would anoint the bunch as his finest team of all. 'Bama featured outstanding passing and receiving (a pair of All-Americas in Ray Perkins and Dennis Homan), a solid running game (Les Kelly), excellent protection, and as usual, a killer defense, led by junior All-America defensive back Bobby Johns. The Crimson Tide won all ten regular-season games, outscoring its opponents 267–37. For the second time in six years, Alabama led the nation in scoring defense (3.7 per game), with six shutouts and just five touchdowns allowed the entire year.

Only the Tennessee game was close, and it was a classic. Down 10–0 at the start of the fourth quarter, Stabler rallied the Tide for a touchdown and then drove his team to the Volunteers' one-yard line with 3:23 left. Steve Davis kicked a field goal to make it 11–10 in 'Bama's favor. With less than a minute to play, Tennessee drove the length of the field on two long pass plays and set up for a winning field goal . . . which missed wide right.

The rematch with Nebraska in the Sugar Bowl was ugly. MVP Stabler completed twelve of seventeen for 218 yards and two touchdowns. The defense held the 9–1 Big Eight champions to 128 total yards. The final score was 34–7, but it could have been worse.

"They are better than the score indicates," a frustrated Bob Devaney lamented afterward. "Alabama is the best football team I have ever seen."

Bidding for an unprecedented third consecutive national championship, Alabama's coronation should have been a no-brainer. But for the only time in the history of college football, the two-time defending national champion finished unbeaten, untied, and uncrowned. The snub was the football equivalent of Muhammad Ali knocking out Joe Frazier in the first round and subsequently being stripped of his belt by a roomful of accountants.

On November 19 in East Lansing, Michigan, number-one-ranked Notre Dame tied number-two Michigan State, 10–10, in a classic ballgame hailed by many as the greatest game of the century. With possession of the ball and time running out, Irish coach Ara Parseghian refused to try to win the game, which was anathema to the man from Moro Bottom. But both the Associated Press poll of sportswriters and the United Press International board of coaches awarded the national championship to 9–0–1 Notre Dame, with 9–0–1 Michigan State ranked second and 11–0 Alabama rated third.

During spring practice in 1967, Stabler tore cartilage in his knee during a running drill. The wound would take a few weeks to heal, so Bryant told him to sit out spring practice and concentrate on getting well. But Snake was frustrated by the layoff, and he stopped going to class, quit attending study hall, and eventually ran off to Foley and started partying and chasing girls all day and all night. Cutting class was a serious offense in Bryant's world; the assistant coaches would bang on your door at the crack of dawn and physically pull you out of bed if necessary. Flunking out was death, and Snake was in danger of flunking out and losing his scholarship, although he didn't know that his coach knew that he wasn't going to class. Out of the blue, he received a telegram:

YOU HAVE BEEN INDEFINITELY SUSPENDED
COACH PAUL W. BRYANT

"I was very capable of throwing it all away," Stabler said more than three decades later, his memories shaded by his own experiences as a father of two little girls. "I could've tossed my whole life in the trash can and not thought another thing of it. I just didn't care. Coach Bryant understood what I was doing but I didn't."

His father, who was not without redeeming characteristics when he was sober, tricked Kenny into going back to school. An uneducated but wily auto mechanic, the elder Stabler conspired with a local lawyer to write a bogus letter from the U.S. Army declaring that the Snake would be drafted unless he returned to college. The war in Vietnam had been raging for more than two years, and the daily death tolls cast a pall over the evening news. The peace demonstrations were starting to catch fire in 1967, the summer of love. "Make love not war!" Stabler wanted no part of Vietnam, so the phony dispatch worked perfectly. He returned to Tuscaloosa and, with the help of 'Bama assistants Jimmy Sharpe and Pat Dye, begged the university for mercy and re-enrolled in school, which was the easy part. Then he summoned his courage and went to see The Man.

From Stabler's seat on the office couch, Paul Bryant looked like a giant. The couch swallowed a player deep, like quicksand, while the boss's desk was slightly elevated, which served only to distort his already intimidating presence, like a funhouse mirror. The Bear listened to his quarterback's story in silence, the rat-a-tat cadance of Stabler's twangy, nervous voice filing up the room. Stabler's whole body was shaking like a wet dog and he wondered if The Man could tell. Bryant held an unfiltered Chesterfield cigarette between his fingers, periodically taking a drag and then spitting the loose tobacco off the side of his mouth. The billowing smoke was like a fog between the two men, and The Man's gaze was a squint, a piercing squint.

"Stabler," the deep voice finally broke through the fog, "you don't deserve to be on this team."

The nervous quarterback continued to plead his case, but The Man seemed oblivious. The audience was over. "Coach," the twangy voice said on the way out, "I'm coming back out anyway."

"We'll see about that," Bryant responded, and he instructed the boy to shut the door.

A week or so later, Jimmy Sharpe went looking for his renegade. He wore a wide grin. "Coach Bryant says you can come back," he said. "The reason is because you wouldn't take no for an answer."

Although Stabler was too young and immature to realize it at the time, the meeting in The Man's office was a test. The boss wanted to see not only if his boy wanted to come back, but how much. Was he willing to fight? So after passing the crucial first test—many who showed up begging for a second chance wound up pumping gas—Stabler arrived for the first day of preseason practice and walked up to the equipment room to retrieve his basket. In it, he found his practice jersey and other essentials. All his comrades on the first-team offense wore red jerseys. The second team wore white. There were baskets with jerseys of blue, orange, green, and so forth. Stabler's basket contained a brown practice jersey. Brown. More psychological warfare from The Man, who made sure the prodigal son, the MVP of the previous year's Sugar Bowl, received a jersey dyed to the lowest color on the scale, a color to match the boss's pet phrase for someone or something he despised: a turd. Not even the scout team wore brown jerseys.

"So for the next few weeks, I worked my way up through all

those teams and got the shit beat out of me every day," Stabler said. "He was going to make it so tough on me to see if I would quit. But I wasn't about to quit. I was going to take whatever he dished out."

In the season opener against Florida State, Joe Kelley started at quarterback. Stabler took the reins on the second series, and second-ranked 'Bama needed every ounce of his talent to survive a wild 37–37 tie with the unranked Seminoles. The Tide's defense surrendered as many points to FSU that night as it had allowed the entire 1966 season. The All-America Snake proved his dedication and led the Tide to an 8–2–1 season that included a 20–16 loss to Texas A&M, coached by former Bryant player and assistant Gene Stallings, in the Cotton Bowl. In the most memorable play of his career, Snake trudged forty-seven yards in the mud for the winning touchdown in 'Bama's 7–3 victory over Auburn.

Although Stabler never lost his reputation as a wild man, his life turned on the suspension and redemption orchestrated by his coach. In the early 1970s, the Snake became the leader of professional football's own renegades, the Oakland Raiders, and piloted John Madden's team to a Super Bowl championship as the centerpiece of a fifteen-year pro career in which he earned millions. Although the coach later wondered if he had been too easy on Stabler, the Snake looks back on Bryant as the single greatest influence in his life, as the man who introduced him to concepts like discipline, hard work, and sacrifice, as the man who taught him how to be a man.

"He saved my ass," Stabler said. "I was going to throw it all away, but he saw something in me worth saving. He disciplined me and challenged me at exactly the moment when I needed it. Without him, I'd probably be tending bar or pumping gas or hustlin'."

The seeds of Alabama's late-1960s nosedive were sown during the championship days of Joe Namath and the quick little boys. Recruiting, the lifeblood of any successful college foot-

ball program, suffered for a number of reasons. Rivals succeeded in convincing many of the best prospects that they
would never play with all those great athletes on the 'Bama
roster. Bryant, flush with ambition, erred by going after more
boys from outside Alabama and the South, and many quit when
the going got tough because the Crimson Tide didn't mean as
much to them. The coaching staff proved to be slow in ad-
justing to the evolution of the specialist in the early years of
the two-platoon game. The boss, flush with fame, spent an
increasing amount of time off-campus.

The 'Bama defense descended from dominant to mediocre
to atrocious. During an 8–3 run in 1968, the Tide surrendered
more points (139) than the 1960, 1961, and 1962 teams combined. Then it got worse. During a 6–5 season in 1969—which
included an embarrassing 47–33 loss to Colorado in the Liberty Bowl—'Bama's defense allowed more points (268) than
in the winless season of 1955 (256). In a nationally televised
classic that the Tide won over Ole Miss, 33–32, Archie Manning
alone accounted for more points than Alabama gave up in the
entire 1961 season. Even Vanderbilt beat the Tide in the year
of the first moon landing, and it was hard to say which event
was more incredible.

"We were just outmanned in a lot of our games," said running back Johnny Musso, who was a sophomore on the 1969
team. "There were a lot of teams who had been taking it on
the chin from Alabama for a long time, and they ran it up on
us when they got the chance."

As his once-vaunted defense crumbled, the boss became
enamored of the pro-style drop-back passing game. He knew
the only way he could win was to outscore his opponents.
Although the days of Namath, Sloan, and Stabler featured one
of college football's most potent passing attacks, the pass was
always a tactical weapon in the larger scheme of establishing
the run and controlling the game at the line of scrimmage. The
Scott Hunter era featured the pass more as the main strategy,
and in 1969, the junior from Mobile attempted more passes
(266) than Namath threw in his final *two* years as the starter,

and he rewrote the school record book. The offensive line was ill equipped for pass protection, and although 'Bama scored more, it also suffered a corresponding jump in turnovers and sacks.

In 1970, as Hunter continued to pile up yardage, touchdowns, and interceptions, and the defense wilted en route to a 6–5–1 finish, a special NCAA survey proclaimed Alabama the team of the decade for the 1960s. Not much suspense there, but the honor served only to remind Alabama people how far their once-dominant program had fallen—and to underscore how thoroughly they were taking for granted the man who had restored it to prominence. The slide proved the mighty Bear was not infallible, and the whispers about his future grew louder with each devastating defeat.

On his Sunday television program during the 1970 season, the coach defiantly advised the "fair-weather fans" to "go to hell" because Paul Bryant the athletic director would decide when it was time for Paul Bryant the coach to step aside. Many wondered if he had been drinking. No, he was just mad. He came close to leaving Alabama to accept a lucrative offer to coach the Miami Dolphins the same year. Several months later, with the stench of three poor seasons hanging over the program, Bryant and his friend John McKay of Southern Cal and their wives spent a few days at a condo on the beach in Point Clear, near Mobile. He needed to get away, but he never could, not really. A prominent alumnus stopped by for dinner, and when the coach took a walk on the beach alone, the booster pulled McKay aside.

"I think he's losing it," the man said. "I think the game's passed him by."

McKay laughed out loud. He told the guy he was nuts. Bryant's genius for adaptation was about to carry him to even greater glory.

11
Motivator

ONE OF THE TWO MEN in pinstriped suits started scrawling words on the blackboard in the meeting room on the second floor of Memorial Coliseum. His partner hurriedly arranged stacks of written material on the conference table. Several minutes later, with dawn breaking on another day in the late 1960s, Paul Bryant ambled in and took a seat. He had told the two motivational experts they had fifteen minutes to dazzle him with their approaches to getting the most out of the people you lead.

Fifteen minutes turned into five hours, and after each motivational technique was explained by the duo, the coach took a drag on his Chesterfield and pronounced his mastery of the device. "Hell, I've been doin' that for years," he'd say. "I didn't know what I was doin', but I've been doin' that for years."

Although he never received any formal training in dealing with young people, Bryant was a born leader with tremendous instincts about human psychology. He was a master at concepts such as goal setting, repetition, reverse psychology, incentive motivation, and immediate reinforcement long before they became buzzwords in a blur of seminars and self-help tapes.

Dr. John Geier, a University of Minnesota psychologist who produced a motivational video with Bryant in 1982, lauded the Bear for "blending inspiration and perspiration to a degree perhaps unmatched in our society."

"He was what I call 'country smart,' " opined former 'Bama quarterback Steve Sloan. "He might not have known the Pythagorean theorem, but he knew people. Boy, did he ever know people. He knew how to look inside somebody and figure out how to make him play."

Bryant's uncanny ability to motivate his players and coaches, equal parts mysterious and calculating, was central to his success. Other coaches innovated; Bryant's career was defined by the intangibles of leadership.

"He was probably the best there's ever been at putting players in position to perform," said Mississippi State head coach Jackie Sherrill, who played on 'Bama teams of the mid-1960s.

"He could coach an average player to become a good player or a good player up to an outstanding player."

The Bryant philosophy was built on organization. Every man had a job, and every man knew in intricate detail what his job entailed. In his first meeting with each year's freshman class, Bryant instructed his players to write down their goals for the team and their personal goals as students and athletes. "I want you to have a plan for everything," he often told them. "A plan if you're ahead at the half, a plan if you're behind." He always looked beyond short-term goals; everything at Alabama was geared toward competing for the national championship. His kind of player desperately wanted a national championship ring like his predecessors'—what the consultants would call a form of incentive motivation.

Although he recruited all kinds of athletes, Bryant loved overachievers. "I don't want ordinary people," he said. "I want people who are willing to sacrifice and do without a lot of those things ordinary students get to do . . . that's what it takes to win." He treated his Alabama players like thoroughbreds, with plush accommodations in a modern dormitory often referred to snidely as the "Bear Bryant Hilton," which was a palace compared to most athletic dorms in the 1960s.

Many of the men who helped Alabama win championships under Bryant were the first members of their families to attend college, and they were hungry to achieve, to overcome their modest backgrounds, just as their coach had. Professional football was not the lure in those days that it would become later in the era of million-dollar contracts; most of the young men who played for him saw football primarily as a way to earn an education. He instilled a tremendous sense of pride in his players, pride not just in representing him and the University of Alabama, but in succeeding on behalf of all their mamas, papas, and hometowns, to which he often alluded.

He was always able to subordinate all those egos to the team concept. There were no stars on the Alabama football team. "Coach Bryant was our franchise player," remarked former 'Bama quarterback Steadman Shealy, now a lawyer in

Dothan. "If you were the kind of player who was more interested in personal glory than winning, you went somewhere
else." No Crimson Tide player ever seriously contended for the
Heisman Trophy; campaigning for such an individual award
was anathema to the coach, and in most cases no 'Bama player
could hope to compile the kind of stats needed to capture such
an honor, because Bryant believed in playing his whole squad
if possible.

"To Coach Bryant, that guy who played three plays was just
as important as Joe Namath," Jackie Sherrill said.

In order to reinforce the team concept, Bryant sometimes
picked the biggest stud in his pasture and humiliated him,
just to make a point. Mike Hall looked like a Coke machine
compared to most of the skinny runts on the 'Bama team in
the late 1960s, but in one of the first practices of his freshman
year, Bryant saw something he didn't like about Hall's play, ran
up to him, grabbed him by the face mask, spun him around,
and kicked him right in the ass. Made him feel about two
feet tall, just to prove a point. Two years later, Hall made
All-America.

During a scrimmage at Denny Stadium in 1965, sophomore
quarterback Kenny Stabler called his own number on third and
short but was tackled shy of the first down. A smartass to
begin with, Stabler got up and clenched his fist as if he were
going to hit his tackler. Bryant was in his face before he could
turn around.

"Stabler," he said, "you're like a bush league baseball player!
You'll always be bush league!"

"He had a way of humbling you in front of your teammates,"
Stabler said. "It didn't matter who you were."

Everything revolved around fear, which flowed from the
coach's intimidating, charismatic presence. In the early days,
he pushed his teams so relentlessly that players feared losing
their scholarships if they didn't perform to his liking. While
this feeling of insecurity never abated, even more powerful
during his Alabama days was their fear of disappointing him.
The kind of player who survived his grueling mental and physi-

cal tests could not imagine letting the man down; the game invariably meant more to the athlete who had made such a commitment.

"You had to have some motivation inside that was bigger than yourself to play for him," said Charley Pell, who played guard on Alabama's 1961 national championship team.

Pell, who grew up on Sand Mountain in northern Alabama, fell victim to one of his coach's legendary psychological ploys during the spring before his senior season in 1962. For no apparent reason, Bryant demoted Pell to the second team. He was crushed; he had invested so much of his self-worth in his achievements as a football player that he believed the demotion devalued him as a man. Pell became a terror on the practice field that day, eventually facing off against the player who had taken his place and grinding him into the dirt, time and again. By the end of the day, he had recaptured his first-team jersey.

"He was taking my identity," Pell said. "I had to get my identity back."

Bryant raised the bar, and Pell struggled against his own will to surmount it.

"Coach Bryant taught us that you can always give more than you think you can," said Arkansas head coach Danny Ford, who played offensive guard for the Tide in the late 1960s. "Everybody has limits, but he trained our minds to push on further than we thought we could go."

"There's a difference in being a great performer and a great player," Bryant once said. "A great performer can give a great performance and lose. A great player will do the things it takes to win."

Bryant's tower magnified the mystique and the fear. Thirty-three steps above Thomas Field, armed with a bullhorn and a keen eye, he watched the meticulously organized drills like a general surveying the front. He usually wore a crimson-and-white baseball cap, a coaching shirt, and khaki pants. Every man on the field, assistant coach and player alike, feared the sound of the chain clanking against the gate at the top of the tower, because it meant the coach was on his way down. The sound was ominous and familiar. On many occasions, hearing the sound echoing in the breeze, the various assistant coaches started chewing out the nearest player, lest the boss be headed in their direction.

On the first day of spring practice in 1964, Bryant snaked down the ladder and ran up to freshman lineman Jimmy Fuller, who was in the midst of an outstanding practice. "How you think you're doing, Jimmy?" he asked.

"I think I'm having a great day, Coach."

"Well, let me tell you something. If you think that's anywhere close for you to become a winning football player at Alabama, you're badly mistaken."

"I was blown away," recalled Fuller, who now coaches offensive linemen for Gene Stallings. "But I realized later, he knew I was having a good day but he didn't want me to become satisfied. He was challenging me to reach."

Bryant instinctively knew how far he could push each player. He knew, as coaches like to say, where the line was. Alabama players invariably praise his remarkable ability to know when an athlete needed praising and when he needed scolding.

"He could push you till you hated him and then he could say one or two words and . . . you loved him again," remarked former Tennessee coach Bill Battle, who played on his teams in the early 1960s.

Sometimes, the mind games were more overt. After a lackluster victory over Vanderbilt in 1962, the coach scheduled a practice before dawn on Monday morning. Visibly angry, he guided his team through a practice dominated by the fundamentals of blocking and tackling, and at one point, he demonstrated a blocking technique by knocking one of the assistant coaches halfway to the fieldhouse. "Tonight," he said with a sneer, "we're going to start all over again, like it was spring, and find out who really wants to play."

That day, five players packed their gear and left, fearing what was to come. "It was a very taxing day for us to endure

mentally," recalled center Gaylon McCollough, now a Birmingham plastic surgeon. "We all had an uneasy feeling, because we knew [that night] was going to be one of those 'gut
check' practices. Then it turns out that we didn't even go out
in pads. Just sweat clothes. He had made his point. Everybody
who showed up made the statement that they were willing to
take whatever he dished out."

One of Bryant's favorite drills was aimed at training their
minds as well as their bodies. He always waited for one of the
hottest days of the year, when the temperature hovered around
one hundred degrees; until the late 1960s, he allowed no water
breaks, which pushed many of his players close to dehydration
as well as exhaustion. The first-team offense would be given
the ball on the twenty-yard line, with four plays to make a first
down against the third-team defense. No passes were allowed.
If it didn't make the first down, the offense was penalized by
having to run wild sprints around the practice field, and then
it had to go back to the twenty and try again.

"As a member of that first-team offense, you're thinking this
is going to be a piece of cake," McCollough recalled. "But then
you don't make the first down every time, and you start running and coming back to try again, and running again. . . .
Pretty soon, you're exhausted. You want to quit. I remember
one of those times when I thought I couldn't walk another
step, but I kept going. He used that to find out who would
break—physically, emotionally, and mentally."

Bryant was more than a slave driver. He could just as easily
display a gentle side in dealing with his players' problems. He
had their respect and, eventually, their love, because he was
always honest and fair; a player knew he could always count
on his coach, regardless of the problem or circumstance.
"Coach Bryant was the most tender-hearted man I've ever been
around," said Jim Goostree, his trainer for all twenty-five years
at Alabama, "but he didn't want anybody to know it."

The real measure of Bryant's leadership skill was his ability
to motivate average athletes to become winning players on
championship teams. This was especially evident during the

1960s, when his quick little boys were outweighed by most of their opponents. "I'm not much of a coach with great players," he once said, "but I'm a champion with that player that isn't very talented but doesn't know it."

Ohio State coaching legend Woody Hayes once said his colleague was "a master at taking average athletes and making them believe they are invincible. I don't know of any coach who instills such an iron resolution in his players."

"Alabama didn't have better players than the rest of us [in the Southeastern Conference]," said Florida head coach Steve Spurrier, who won a Heisman Trophy for the Gators in 1966. "But [the Alabama players] thought they were better than everybody else, and everybody else in the SEC got to believing Alabama was better."

The men who pulled on those crimson uniforms believed in Paul Bryant without reservation. Most would have followed him to hell and back, had he asked. His ability to instill such a powerful sense of loyalty, belief, and confidence defies explanation. If it could be reduced to a formula, the world would be filled with Bear Bryants; like all great leaders, he possessed something mysterious that made people around him want to reach to please him.

"He had a quality that would make you want to run through a wall for him," Kenny Stabler said. "Anything to get a slap on the back from him. That was everything, for him to recognize you in a positive way."

At noon on Sundays during the season, players crowded around the television set in the Bryant Hall lounge, hoping the boss would mention their names on the *Bear Bryant Show*. In 1974, sophomore defensive tackle Bob Baumhower was surrounded by his teammates when the Bear complimented a jarring tackle—by Bob Bellhouse! "I was shattered," Baumhower said. "Just crushed. I was determined from then on to play so well, he would learn my name."

Some players he never reached. Many packed their bags and bought a bus ticket home, no doubt believing that Bear Bryant was the meanest, most unreasonable jerk on the face of the earth. Although the vast majority of the players who stayed at Alabama for four years idolize him and love him, former lineman Steven Wright provides a stark contrast.

An all-everything tackle who grew up in Louisville, Kentucky, and was recruited by every major school in the country, the six-six, 280-pound Wright arrived at Alabama in 1960 and was immediately told to lose sixty pounds. In the era of the quick little boys, he was too big to play football for Bear Bryant. So Wright lost the weight, and along the way lost much of his strength. He grew to resent his coach.

"I was damned if I do, damned if I don't," Wright said. "I was bitter as hell at Coach Bryant. I didn't really fit their program with all those small players, but why did they recruit me? It took me a long time to get over that bitterness."

Wright, who played sparingly for Bryant in 1962–63 and later started for the Green Bay Packers, also believes he was a poor fit for the 'Bama system because he didn't respond to motivation by fear, and because he came from an educated background. "A certain kind of athlete, Bryant could motivate better than anybody," he said. "I was different. I never feared him, and I needed a different kind of motivation."

In comparing Bryant with Packers legend Vince Lombardi, Wright said, "Bear Bryant would tell you to run your head through that wall. If you were brave enough—and most weren't—you'd ask him why. And he'd say because if you don't I'll kick you off the team and make sure you never play football anymore and embarrass you and your mama and daddy because you're the only person in your family who's ever been to college. Vince Lombardi, on the other hand, would say run your head through that wall and you'd ask him why, and he'd say, because it will make you a better football player. For me, Lombardi was better."

Lee Roy Jordan, the All-America linebacker for Alabama who later became an All-Pro for the Dallas Cowboys, gives the edge to Bryant over longtime Cowboys coach Tom Landry. "Coach Landry was a great tactician—probably the best I've ever seen," he said. "But he lacked something on the emotional side. Coach Bryant was a master at making you feel like you could take on the world and whip their butts. We just felt like, with him on our side, we couldn't be beaten."

Although he sometimes stirred his team to emotion during the week, Bryant rarely attempted gimmicks on game day. He believed such pep talks were more likely to backfire. But he was known to play mind games with his teams when the situation called for it—as in the 1960 game when the Tide entered the locker room trailing Georgia Tech 15–0 at the half, after his "got 'em right where we want 'em" speech, which left his team dumbfounded, the Crimson Tide rallied for an improbable 16–15 victory.

"Coach tried to take the emotion out of Saturdays," said McCollough. "Everything was very methodical and business-like. He wanted us to be thinking about our assignments. Of course, in the back of our minds was all the mental training he'd put us through . . . all the hard work and sacrifice . . . all the people we were representing."

"You knew doggone well you'd better lay it on the line," said Bill Oliver, a member of the 1961 national champions who is now defensive coordinator at Auburn. "You've already been put through the mill. You felt like you could beat anybody with him on your side. You knew darn well that whatever happened on Saturday was gonna be easier than what you went through in practice."

When a Bryant-coached team won, he always heaped praise on his players and assistant coaches, while minimizing his own contributions. Regardless of the circumstances, he always took all the blame for a loss. If his team wasn't ready to play, then it was his fault. In addition to reducing finger-pointing in the organization, this humble attitude struck a chord among the players, giving them yet another reason not to let their coach down.

Bryant often found a way to relieve the tension before games. He sometimes cracked a joke or related an event from his own life. One unusual example came before a nationally televised 1982 game against Penn State in Birmingham. Neckties were usually mandatory for the pregame meal, but this day Bryant didn't tell his players to wear ties. Most of the players assumed the policy was being relaxed because of the unusually early team meal before the noon kickoff, so when they convened the morning of the game, only about a dozen of the seventy-three-member travel squad showed up wearing ties. The boss hit the roof and demanded that every man meet the dress code immediately. The players—and several tieless assistant coaches—scavenged through the hotel borrowing strands of silk from fans and employees. Defensive back Rocky Colburn conned a waiter out of a clip-on bow tie.

When they reconvened for the meal, the old coach smiled broadly into the sea of polka dots and stripes. His assistant coaches believe Bryant intentionally let the players think the dress code had been relaxed in order to use the great tie hunt to break the tension of a big game. A very loose 'Bama then crushed the eventual national champion Nittany Lions 42–21 in the last great victory of the Bryant era.

Just past eleven o'clock on a school night during his senior year of high school in 1968, Jeff Rouzie was awakened by the sound of his mother calling his name. "It's Coach Paul Bryant on the phone," she said nervously. At first, the outstanding linebacker prospect from Jacksonville, Florida, thought one of his friends was playing a joke, but as soon as he picked up the receiver, he knew it was him. The voice was unmistakable. The Crimson Tide had been recruiting Rouzie for several months, and he was considering 'Bama along with several other schools, but the Bear said he was making his plans for the next four years and he wanted to know, right then.

"Can I count on you?" the gruff voice asked.

Without thinking, Rouzie blurted out, "Yessir!"

After he hung up the phone, Rouzie's father, who was listening at the door, asked his son if he realized he had made a commitment.

"Yessir," he said, still a bit dazed. "I just couldn't tell Coach Bryant no."

Bryant's charisma and his legendary status made him difficult for many high-school athletes to spurn. Like a good salesman, he knew all the buttons to push—and he knew how to close the sale. He understood players who wanted to make something of themselves, and of equal importance, he was a magnet for mamas and papas. Parents saw him as a surrogate father, because of his reputation as a disciplinarian. They believed he would make his boys go to class and keep them out of trouble, and he did.

"People probably thought all that stuff about the mamas and daddys was just PR, but Coach really wanted to know about the player's background," said his longtime recruiting coordinator, Clem Gryska. "He knew that it mattered whether the kid had a good background, whether he had a work ethic, whether he had values."

As the Bear's mystique grew, his assistants assumed greater responsibility for evaluating and procuring talent, but his unrivaled status gave the Crimson Tide a cachet few programs could match. Players signed with Georgia to play for Georgia, but they signed with Alabama to play for Bear Bryant.

"All of us as coaches would like to think a player comes to our school to play for us," said John McKay. "But I honestly don't believe too many kids came to Southern Cal to play for me. With Paul, there was no doubt. They might've majored in business or education or whatever, but their mamas and papas sent them to Tuscaloosa to play for him."

The Bear's reputation for toughness, year-round work, and high standards probably turned off as many athletes as it attracted. "I had a friend in high school who was a good athlete who heard about the man's reputation and didn't want any part of that," said Bill Battle. "So he went to Auburn." The ones who signed with Alabama were motivated to prove they could measure up, which made them more susceptible to Bryant's psychological warfare once on campus.

Through the years, Bryant learned from his mistakes and became a wiser coach—especially in the way he handled problem players.

During casual time with friends toward the end of his life, he often lamented the way he lost halfback Kenneth Hall. Hall, perhaps the most talented athlete recruited to Texas A&M during Bryant's four-year tenure, failed to show up for practice twice and begged for a third chance with his coach, who refused. He symbolized how Bryant sometimes played the part of the gruff, unyielding coach a little too well.

Although he never stopped demanding the highest standards of his players, and never became any more tolerant of rule breaking or lack of effort, the Bear learned to use his own earthy form of psychology to save some troubled athletes.

Bob Baumhower had all the tools. A six-four, 250-pound defensive tackle with tremendous quickness and strength, Baumhower grew up in Florida but moved to Tuscaloosa during high school. Although he didn't play as a freshman, he quickly moved up the depth chart during the following spring, and was listed as a first-teamer heading into the 1974 season. But he reported in poor shape in August, failed to make his appointed time in the mile run required of all 'Bama players, and found himself wearing the yellow jersey of the fourth team when two-a-days commenced. Frustrated and embarrassed, he quit.

"I had the typical attitude of a nineteen-year-old kid who thought he knew it all," Baumhower said. "I thought they were just messing with me, and I didn't need that. I could go somewhere else."

The next day, Baumhower received word from one of the assistant coaches that Bryant wanted to see him and his father. *The old man knows he made a mistake,* Baumhower surmised, *and now he's going to beg me to come back.*

When the father and son showed up at Bryant's office, the

coach greeted the father warmly and gave the kid a sneer. "What the hell are you doing here? I wanted to talk to your daddy!"

"Well, I heard you wanted to talk to me—"

"I don't need to talk to a quitter!"

But, Bryant said, since he was there, he might as well sit down. The Baumhowers sank deep into the couch and peered up at Bryant, who sat behind his slightly elevated desk puffing his cigarette. The coach asked Baumhower why he had quit, and the young man told him.

Then Bryant told him why he was demoted. "You've got more ability than every one of those players ahead of you," he said, but the game obviously meant more to the others, because they had worked hard and showed up in good shape, and in Bryant's world, hard work was rewarded. Bryant told Baumhower he couldn't use him unless he was willing to make a commitment to working hard and becoming a winner. He never asked the boy to come back, but by the end of the meeting, Baumhower was begging for a second chance.

"That meeting changed my life," Baumhower said. "Coach Bryant taught me to look at the big picture. Up to that point, I had just been happy to be on the team. Didn't have a focus. And I thought I was so good that I could just do whatever I wanted to do and get by. But that meeting fired me up, motivated me to make a commitment to being the best player I could be. That meeting was the turning point of how I thought as a man."

A starter by midseason in 1974, Baumhower eventually became one of the leaders of the 'Bama defense, earning All-America honors in 1976 and graduating to an eleven-year career with the Miami Dolphins. Now the owner of a chain of restaurants in Alabama, he attributes a large measure of his success on and off the field to Bryant.

In early 1960, former Kentucky lineman Dude Hennessey was coaching high-school football in Louisville, Kentucky, and waited for his big break. One night while he was watching television at home, the telephone rang. It was his old coach.

"Dude, I got a job—"

"At Alabama?"

"Yeah, at Alabama."

"I'll take it!"

"How the hell do you know you'll take it? You've never even been to Tuscaloosa."

Hennessey accepted the job without discussing his salary. Two weeks later, he got his first check and realized he had left a high-school head coaching job paying eighty-five hundred dollars for a college assistant's job paying six thousand dollars. He didn't care. All that mattered was working for the best coach in the business.

"Most of us would've paid him," said Hennessey, who served sixteen years on the 'Bama coaching staff. "We'd have worked for nothing. Really. That's how much we thought of him."

Notorious for paying his assistants less than many of his Southeastern Conference rivals, Bryant once offered Danny Ford a job making ten thousand dollars at the same time the recent 'Bama grad was weighing a chance to go to Eastern Kentucky for twelve thousand dollars. Ford and his wife, who were expecting their first child, wanted to chase the bigger salary at the smaller school.

"I just couldn't go in and face him," Ford said. "I couldn't tell him I was turning him down. I was scared to death to tell him. So about four or five days passed, and I worked up the courage to go see him and tell him that I wanted to stay. And he said that he'd already called Coach Kidd [at Eastern Kentucky] and told him that I wouldn't be coming."

When Mississippi State assistant Ken Donahue arrived to interview for an opening on the staff in 1964, Bryant told trainer Jim Goostree to spend the morning with him and tell him everything bad about working at 'Bama. "I told him that we didn't make much money, and how it was hard to get your expense reports approved, and how awful that old paper mill smelled in the mornings—anything I could think of," Goostree said. "I could tell he was having second thoughts about wanting to come."

After meeting with the job seeker for a half hour or so, Bryant walked Donahue into his outer office and offered him the position. "I appreciate the offer, but I believe I'll have to think it over," Donahue said nervously.

"Well, don't think about it too long."

"OK. I'll take it."

Bryant walked out the door to an appointment while Donahue just stood there shaking his head as Goostree laughed heartily.

"Coach Bryant was a hard man to say no to," Donahue said years later.

Throughout his Alabama coaching career, Bryant filled his staff with many of his former players, along with a smattering of outsiders—a conscious decision that shaped the leadership dynamic of the entire program. Even as assistant coaches, they remained pupils and always felt in awe of the boss. The player-coach relationship never ceased; having been tested as players by his various mental and physical tests, their loyalty was unquestioned, and there was never any dissension on the 'Bama staff. Everyone believed in the boss, felt a debt to him, loved and feared him.

"Having all those former players on the staff made him an even more dominant person," observed Howard Schnellenberger, another former Kentucky player who joined the 'Bama staff in the early 1960s.

They also knew, better than any uninitiated outsiders would, how Bryant liked his coaches to coach, providing a tremendous degree of continuity in the level of instruction at Alabama. He encouraged—and aided—his assistants in moving up the ladder to better jobs, sometimes as head coaches, and he never fired a single assistant in his thirty-eight years on the sidelines.

"You're talking about a guy who was loyal to you," Hennessey said. "The attitude on that staff was great. Everybody had a smile on their face. As long as you told him the truth, you knew he was going to be loyal to you and treat you right."

Although their salaries often were mediocre compared to the competition, Bryant's assistants were rewarded for their long hours and dedication with bowl bonuses and the free use of dealer cars.

"You just wanted to bust your butt for him," said Bob Ford, who coached for Bryant from 1958 to 1962.

Although the coach and his aides shared a mutual respect, the staff knew the limitations of their relationship. One afternoon during the 1958 season, Bryant left practice early so he could make it to a speaking engagement on time, and when the staff returned to the locker room, he was tying his necktie at his locker. Bob Ford, a recent addition to the staff, walked past his boss and said, matter-of-factly, "What's your hurry?"

Bryant slammed his locker shut and glared at Ford.

"What did you say?"

"I just said, 'What's your hurry?'"

The Bear's look was deadly. "What did you say?"

"All the while," Ford said later, "Carney [Laslie] and Gene Stallings are back there hiding in the showers. They knew the rookie had said the wrong thing. I was just making small talk, but that's not the way Coach Bryant operated. When he was at work, there was nothing casual about it."

Although he demanded loyalty, Bryant despised yes-men. He demanded that his coaches speak their minds. The constant influx of new blood and new ideas also played a vital role in his success. "A lot of coaches are guilty of surrounding themselves with the same old same old," he said. "But I never hire a coach unless he knows something about the game that I don't know."

In meetings with his team, Bryant often talked about various aspects of life outside football as his players sat rapt, sometimes literally on the edge of their seats in order to hear him. ("There was an incredible silence when he spoke," said Bill Oliver, who played on the 1961 national championship team. "A deafness," remarked Jimmy Fuller, "as if nothing else existed in the world.") Sometimes, he read a poem that had touched him. On other occasions, he spoke from the heart about situations his players were likely to face in their lives. Every summer, when the new crop of freshmen arrived with faces all aglow, he pulled out a favorite letter, clipped from an Ann Landers column, that told a cautionary tale of teenage excess from the perspective of a young man watching his own funeral.

One of Bryant's great strengths as a motivator was his ability to make football seem like more than a game to the young men who played for him. To him, it had always been bigger than a game; it had been his life. He believed the sport taught valuable lessons that could not be learned in school or at home, such as commitment, perseverance, sacrifice, responsibility, and discipline. Although many coaches give lip service to "turning boys into men," Bryant truly cared for his players and wanted them to grow into successful men of strong character. He spent a great deal of time helping his former players land jobs, and they often telephoned him for advice on career and family problems. Even after college, they could not stand to feel that they had let him down.

"Coach was about striving for excellence in everything you do," said Steadman Shealy, one of his Alabama quarterbacks. "He taught us the little things that make your successful in life: setting high goals, working hard, living right."

Near the end of his life, Bryant told a reporter, "I'm proudest of all the people we have doing well in society, regardless of what they're doing. That's more important than all the victories to me."

Although the hundreds of Bryant disciples who finished college and attained success in various fields were not placed on some road to preordained fame, fortune, and happiness, their lives were shaped by the lessons he taught in the framework of football. He motivated them not just to perform on the football field but, as he often liked to say, "to win in life." The vast majority of the players who survived four years under his guidance revere him. Many proudly hail him as the most important influence in their lives.

"He taught us a way of life," said Dr. Gaylon McCollough.

More amazing than all his records and accomplishments is the place he continues to own in the lives of so many of his former players, who still view him with a combination of affection and awe.

"There's not a day that goes by that I don't think about him," said Jimmy Fuller. "I've never had anybody have that kind of effect on me. There are days when I don't think about my father, and I loved him dearly. But there's not a day that goes by that I don't think about Coach Bryant and something he taught me."

12
Integration

ONE SATURDAY DURING THE COLLEGE game of the week telecast in the 1960s, ten-year-old Terry Jones rushed into the kitchen of his family's modest home in Sandersville, Georgia, where his mama was cooking supper, and proclaimed his life's ambition.

"Hey, Mama!" he said with a sense of urgency, "when I grow up, I'm gonna play college football on TV!"

His mother looked down at him tenderly and placed her hand on his shoulder. "Now, Terry," she said, "don't be filling your head with no dreams like that. They don't let little black boys from Georgia play on TV."

He looked up at her in disbelief. "But why not, Mama? Why not?"

Institutional racism was prevalent throughout all areas of the country in 1955, but nowhere was it so central to the social and political order as in the South. The region was rigidly divided along racial lines into two separate and very unequal societies; segregation was the law of the land in everything from public drinking fountains to schools, and whites held all political power, including the authority to prevent blacks from acquiring the right to vote. Blacks were considered second-class citizens in the eyes of the law, and until the Supreme Court's landmark 1954 ruling in *Brown* v. *Board of Education* that overturned the tenet of "separate but equal" in public education—and the Montgomery bus boycott fifteen months later that was set off by Rosa Parks's refusal to give up her seat—focused the nation's attention on the inequities of segregation, blacks in the South mostly accepted their lack of power as inevitable.

In the decade after the bus boycott, the region exploded along racial lines. As Dr. Martin Luther King, Jr., and others challenged various segregation laws and slowly whittled away at the foundations of the system on the way to the landmark Civil Rights Act of 1964, many southern politicians assumed a bunker mentality, and none was more tragically successful than Alabama governor George C. Wallace. Elected on a platform of "Segregation Forever" in 1962, Wallace became the foremost symbol of southern defiance, and while he succeeded to a tremendous degree politically, he failed his state when it desperately needed political leadership instead of demagoguery.

The nation's image of Alabama in the 1960s was formed by one horror after another: the bombing of the Sixteenth Street Baptist Church in Birmingham, which killed four little black girls; Birmingham police commissioner Bull Connor's decision to attack black demonstrators with dogs and fire hoses; the clash between Alabama state troopers and voting rights demonstrators on the Selma march that became known as Bloody Sunday; Governor Wallace's symbolic stand in the schoolhouse door at the University of Alabama in 1963 in a futile attempt to prevent the court-ordered enrollment of two black students, Vivian Malone and James Hood.

To the majority of Alabamians who believed that their heritage was riding in the balance, George Wallace was a hero. But many others favored various degrees of accommodation, and some even marched on Bloody Sunday. The battles in the streets of Alabama were not so much between blacks and whites as between the past and the future. But it was a time of shrill voices, and progressive opinions were more often whispered in private.

"The real tragedy was all those good people who remained silent," said former Alabama attorney general Richmond Flowers.

The issue touched all facets of southern society, and athletics was not immune. The schools of the Southeastern Conference had a gentleman's agreement forbidding the recruitment of black athletes well into the late 1960s, and even as segregated lunch counters and schools began to disappear, the all-white teams of the SEC represented yet another fist shaken defiantly toward Washington. In fact, well after the various major universities had been integrated under pressure from the federal government, state laws throughout the former Confederacy forbade blacks and whites from playing on the same field together; they also prevented teams such as Ole Miss and Alabama from competing against integrated squads from the North. In Mississippi, the state legislature threatened to suspend funding of the University of Mississippi and Mississippi State if they participated against integrated teams. During the 1950s and 1960s, Johnny Vaught's Ole Miss football powerhouse refused to participate in bowl games against integrated northern programs, and Babe McCarthy's Mississippi State basketball team spurned invitations to the NCAA tournament for the same reason.

Paul Bryant moved into a difficult situation when he returned to the University of Alabama in 1958. On the one hand, the tremendous success of his program during the 1960s gave Alabamians a much-needed respite from the beating their state was taking on the race issue. He gave them a reason to feel proud rather than bitter, a kind of inner satisfaction that transcended sports. But, contrary to his wishes, he and his program also became a symbol of segregation. The three national championships his all-white teams captured in the 1960s were held up as proof by many segregationists that the southern way of life was superior, a fallacy that disturbed him. No racist, Bryant had attempted to integrate his Kentucky team in the late 1940s, and he would have recruited black athletes at Alabama from day one if the climate had been different.

"Bryant was a progressive on the race issue," said Richmond Flowers, who openly challenged the extremely popular Wallace by urging compliance with federal laws. "We talked about it several times, and it was clear to me that he was all for integration . . . he knew it was just a matter of time [before segregation was abolished]. If he could've waved a magic wand and made [the issue] go away, he would've, but he knew it was something the South had to work through."

In his autobiography, Bryant said, "When folks are ignorant you don't condemn them, you teach 'em. . . . You don't change people's thinking overnight."

Flowers, who was later driven from office for opposing segregation, became an easy target for the minority of activists who wanted to retain the southern way of life by any means necessary. He was vilified as a Judas in the press and among segregationist groups; his life was threatened on many occasions, and his family was ostracized by the Montgomery community. More than once, the Flowers family awoke to find a cross burning on their front lawn. At the same time, Richmond Junior emerged as an outstanding athlete; one of the most highly recruited receivers in the South in 1965, he also set a world high-school record in the high hurdles. When he chose to play football and run track for Tennessee rather than his home-state Crimson Tide, he, too, was branded a traitor by some.

Several months after he signed a letter of intent to play for the Volunteers, Richmond Junior was sitting in the stands at a track meet in Pritchard, near Mobile, waiting to receive a special award recognizing his world record. When the announcer introduced his father, the attorney general, the stadium erupted in boos. Richmond Junior, who had been forced to simply take and take while his father and the entire family were treated as outcasts, stood up and faced the crowd.

"That's why I'm leaving this state," he shouted angrily. "That's why I'm not gonna play football for Alabama!"

Although he had attempted to recruit Flowers, Bryant understood the boy's decision. In addition to wanting to flee the state for personal reasons, the younger Flowers chose Tennessee because it offered a stronger track program; he went on to earn All-America acclaim in both football and track for the Vols. Several years later, Richmond Junior returned to his home state and applied to the University of Alabama Law School. His tests scores were on the margin, and he was rejected for admission. Rather than holding a grudge against the young man who had helped to beat him twice in the late 1960s, Paul Bryant paid a visit to the dean of the law school and asked him to make an exception and admit Richmond Junior as a personal favor. Richmond Junior finished in the top 10 percent of his law-school class and is now a respected attorney living in Birmingham.

Like the coaches at Ole Miss, Tennessee, Georgia, and other major state universities, Bryant faced tremendous pressure from segregationist factions to avoid any kind of "race mixing." But, even as he realized it would be politically impossible for him to recruit blacks as long as the climate was so rife with fear and hatred, he refused to pander to the segregationists. State laws prevented him from inviting integrated teams to visit Tuscaloosa or Birmingham, but, unlike many of his peers, he resisted pressure to avoid playing them in bowl games. He was determined to separate, to the extent that he could, the Alabama football program from the policies of the state government.

In 1959, after leading his Crimson Tide to a 7–1–2 mark that represented the second milepost on the march to the 1961 national championship, Bryant accepted a bid for 'Bama to play Penn State in the Liberty Bowl in Philadelphia. Penn State had five black players on its roster at the time, including running back Charley Jenrett. At least one member of the University of Alabama board of trustees boycotted the game when he realized he could not stop it. Several of the prosegregation citizens councils across the state openly opposed the matchup. James Laester, the chairman of the Tuscaloosa citizens council, spoke for many in a telegram he sent to university president Dr. Frank Rose: "We strongly oppose our boys playing an integrated team. . . . The Tide belongs to all Alabama and Alabamians favor continued segregation." Rose also received many veiled threats of violence, including one that harked back to the aborted attempt to integrate the campus in 1956:

> Dont [*sic*] you realize the consequences of a most certain repitition [*sic*] of trouble and a very probable unhappy return of such trouble to your doorstep. . . . May God have mercy on you at this Christmas season and the days to folllow.

Despite the opposition, Bryant refused to back out of the game, and the first Liberty Bowl was contested without incident. The worst thing to happen, at least for Alabama fans, was the fake field goal in the closing moments of the first half that allowed Rip Engle's Nittany Lions to snag a 7–0 victory. Over the next several years, Bryant's all-white Crimson Tide played integrated teams from Oklahoma, Nebraska, Missouri, and Colorado in bowl games, and as Alabama kept winning and segregation died a slow and painful death, opposition to such contests gradually waned.

But even as he engendered the wrath of avowed segregationists, Bryant was criticized for continuing to field an all-white team. In the eyes of many across the nation, Alabama was Alabama; there was no separating the blood of Selma from the segregated Crimson Tide. The most dominant football program of the 1960s could not avoid being splattered by Bull Connor's water hoses.

In 1961, Bryant produced one of the greatest teams ever assembled in the era of one-platoon football, a unanimous choice for the national championship. The Rose Bowl, which had been tied to the champions of the Big Ten and Pac-Eight conferences for fifteen years, let word leak out that it was considering inviting Alabama to face UCLA. Several prominent Los Angeles writers pounced on the story and made it sound as if the folks in Pasadena were going to invite the Ku Klux Klan to face the integrated Bruins, and the invitation was never extended.

In 1966, the Crimson Tide opened preseason camp as the two-time defending national champion and then proceeded to win eleven straight games. By all rights, 'Bama should have captured an unprecedented third straight national championship; no other team had ever accomplished such a remarkable run. But the Associated Press and United Press International trophies were awarded to Notre Dame, which had fought to a famous 10–10 tie with also unbeaten Michigan State. Alabama finished third. It was the only time in the history of college football that a two-time defending national champion had gone undefeated, untied, and uncrowned.

Writing in the *Boston Globe*, columnist Bud Collins conceded that Alabama was the victim of some degree of poll bias because of the race issue. His comments said more about the tenor of the times than the world of sports: "Alabama. . . . It's a great place to march, but you wouldn't want to stay. . . . Obviously, the U.S. would be better off by trading the state to Europe for Spain or Switzerland, but until the deal can be made we may as well recognize that our best team is located in Tuscaloosa."

(Despite the sanctimony of the northern press, neither racism nor racial violence were limited to Alabama or to the South. Riots broke out in more than a dozen cities nationwide well after Birmingham, and on the night in 1965 when Watts burned, the *Los Angeles Times* didn't have a single black face on its reporting staff. In 1975, when rioting erupted in South Boston over forced busing, every school in the state of Alabama had been integrated—peacefully—for years.)

The previous season, in 1965, Alabama had used a 39–28 Orange Bowl upset of Nebraska to catapult to its second straight title. On the opening kickoff, a frightened black Cornhusker standing near the ballcarrier fell to his knees.

"Don't kick me!" he shouted toward the oncoming crimson jerseys. "Don't kick me!" To him, Alabama was Selma and Bull Connor, hatred and violence.

"That guy just didn't understand that that's not what we were about," said Jackie Sherrill, who was running downfield on the 'Bama kickoff team that night. "I remember before that game, because some of us were playing against blacks for the first time, Coach sat us down as a team and made a point of telling us that he wanted us to treat 'em just like any other players: 'Knock 'em on their ass, and then help 'em up.' Coach wasn't going to tolerate any cheap stuff. Nobody who did stuff like that could play for him anyway."

Bryant was enough of a visionary to attempt to break the SEC color barrier immediately after World War II, but he was also enough of a realist not to push the issue too soon at Alabama. Despite his dominant presence at the university and throughout the state in 1963, he avoided any involvement in the integration of the campus. The governor and several members of the board of trustees strongly opposed integrating the athletic program, and Bryant, who was never known as an innovator on the field, decided to bide his time.

The passing of the years and 'Bama's frequent bowl match-ups against integrated teams slowly melted the resistance to black football players. Five blacks walked on to the 'Bama squad in the spring of 1967—two even played in the spring game—but like most walk-ons, they didn't survive. During the 1960s, the coach often picked up his friend Butch Baldone and drove over to Legion Field to watch Birmingham's all-black Parker High School powerhouse. Sitting in the press box, he would see some fine young player, no doubt headed to a black college or to the Big Ten, and shake his head. Someday, he thought to himself. Someday.

"We're not recruiting Negro athletes; that's a policy decision for others to make," he told *Look* magazine in 1965. "But Negro players in Southeastern Conference games are coming."

In 1968, after consultation with several prominent university alumni—including Wallace, who was then out of the governor's mansion but was running for president—Bryant gave his staff the go-ahead to start recruiting black athletes. It is not clear if anyone in power actively opposed his decision, but given that the SEC color line had already been broken by

Florida, Kentucky, and Vanderbilt, the future was clear for all to see: Alabama could be a leader in the new era or it could fall behind. In 1969, cross-state rival Auburn signed its first black football player, James Owens, shortly before basketball star Wendell Hudson became 'Bama's first black scholarship athlete in any sport. But neither event carried the historical weight of the signing of Wilbur Jackson.

On December 13, 1969—fourteen years after Rosa Parks was jailed because she demanded simple human dignity—talented receiver Wilbur Jackson sat in his parents' living room in Ozark, Alabama, and signed a grant-in-aid to become the University of Alabama's first black scholarship football player. Parks and Jackson stand as generational bookends in the history of the state of Alabama; one wanted only to keep her seat on a bus, and she was punished for asking so much; the other was recruited by whites to fill the most important role in the state's subculture: the Crimson Tide football hero. Without Rosa Parks, there could have been no Wilbur Jackson, but without Wilbur Jackson and the progress he represented, the hope Rosa Parks inspired would have remained unfulfilled. Jackson's signing was the last nail in the coffin of segregation in the state, an undeniable signal that Alabama would never be the same.

"I'm not sure I fully understood how big a thing it was," said Jackson, who now owns a commercial cleaning business in his hometown. "I just wanted to go to college, get an education, and play football. I didn't want to be Jackie Robinson."

In 1969 and 1970, the man in the houndstooth hat suffered through the only slump of his illustrious career. To many programs, of course, seasons of 6–5 and 6–5–1 constitute some form of success, especially when they include bowl invitations. But the Crimson Tide—which had finished among the nation's top ten for nine straight years, including five times in the top five—was not accustomed to rebuilding. In Alabama, the twin fives were met with alarm, hand-wringing, predictions of the apocalypse, and stray thoughts that the Bear had lost his touch.

The most humiliating of all the losses during those two years came at the hands of Southern Cal at Legion Field on September 12, 1970. The 42–21 licking was one of the worst ever laid on a Bryant-coached team, and it could have been worse. The Crimson Tide's defense was horrendous, and no small number of 'Bama people walked into the shadows that night believing their once-mighty program had fallen to a new low. And the most noteworthy aspect of the game was the skin color of the men who delivered many of the biggest blows.

Sam (Bam) Cunningham, who later starred for the New England Patriots, broke a barrier of his own by running up and down the artificial surface not three miles from the site where Bull Connor had pushed Alabama deeper into the darkness. As one of the first blacks to take the field against a Crimson Tide team at home that night, Cunningham rushed for 212 yards and scored three touchdowns.

"Cunningham," Bryant later quipped, "did more for integration in Alabama in sixty minutes than Martin Luther King did in twenty years."

Another star for the Trojans that night was Birmingham native Clarence Davis, a halfback who scored two touchdowns of his own. The gates to home-state stardom had been barred to him when he left, but they were swinging wide by the time he returned. Watching that game that night, even the most diehard of segregationists could not deny the obvious: Alabama could no longer play the "whites-only" game. An era was over.

Jim Murray, the Pulitzer Prize–winning sports columnist for the *Los Angeles Times*, observed, "The point of the game is not the score, the Bear, the Trojans; the point of the game will be reason, democracy, hope. The real winner will be Alabama."

Murray was right, of course, but lost in all the hype was Wilbur Jackson's presence in the stands that night. Recruited the previous fall, Jackson was a freshman receiver for the

Crimson Tide at the time, but because freshmen were ineligible to play in those days, he would not be able to take the field in a varsity game until 1971. Sam Cunningham played an unmistakable role in smoothing acceptance of the integration of the Alabama football program, but it was already underway when he broke through the 'Bama line.

For a pioneer, Jackson was a real introvert. He didn't go to Alabama to be the first, it just worked out that way. When he wasn't practicing or studying, he often could be found sunk deep into the couch in the players' lounge at Bryant Hall watching soap operas. Yet he says he never felt isolated; he blended easily into the otherwise white-only establishment.

"I remember when I was first being recruited, Coach Bryant told me if I ever had a [racial] problem to come to him with it," Jackson said. "And I never had the first problem. Not one."

Although Jackson was recruited as a receiver, he was moved to halfback his sophomore season and became an elusive runner in the Crimson Tide's wishbone-based resurgence of the early 1970s, earning first-team All-SEC honors on 'Bama's 1973 national championship team.

During the off-season in 1971, John McKay and his good friend Paul Bryant had just finished playing golf in the Bob Hope Desert Classic. They were sitting around the clubhouse having a drink or two when the subject of the coming integration of southern football came up. For some reason McKay mentioned a big, fast linebacker he was on the verge of snagging from Eastern Arizona Junior College. John Mitchell, McKay told Bryant, had been born and raised in Mobile, right under his buddy's nose, and come September it was likely that the junior-college recruit would wind up in the starting lineup in the opener against 'Bama.

After a few minutes, the Bear excused himself and placed a call to his recruiting coordinator, Clem Gryska; unbeknownst to McKay, he told his assistant to see if this Mitchell was still unsigned, and if he was, to go after him.

"Next thing I know," McKay said, "we didn't get John Mitchell. And not only that, he ends up playing against us."

Although Jackson had signed with the Crimson Tide nearly two years earlier, Mitchell arrived at Alabama as a junior in the summer of 1971 and became the first black to play and start for the Tide. Like Clarence Davis, he grew up with a seemingly unrealizable desire to play for the Crimson Tide, and then, after that fluke conversation, he became the school's first black All-America, and later its first black assistant coach.

"Wilbur and John changed everything," said Calvin Parker, a running back on the Tide teams of the mid-70s. "They opened the doors for the rest of us."

When the doors to Alabama and other SEC teams swung open, Terry Jones, who once had been so puzzled by his mother's response to his childhood dream, fulfilled his ambition and signed with the Crimson Tide. Now a strength coach on the 'Bama staff, he grew up big and strong and was a stellar defensive end on the 1977 SEC championship team. He got to play on TV nearly a dozen times, and even hugged a cheerleader or two.

When the change happened, it was immediate and complete. Unlike many programs in the South and elsewhere, Alabama never practiced tokenism. Two years after Mitchell and Jackson joined the team, when the Crimson Tide battled Notre Dame in the Sugar Bowl in one of the classic college football games of all time, one-third of the 'Bama starters were black, skill players and grunts alike.

"Coach Bryant didn't have black players or white players," noted Sylvester Croom, an All-America center in 1974. "He just had football players. The only thing he cared about was how much effort [you gave]; he didn't care about the color of your skin."

This is not to say that Bryant wasn't painfully aware of the prevailing bigotry, which was not simply wiped clean by his decision.

Condredge Holloway grew up in Huntsville the son of educated parents; his father was a schoolteacher and his mother was a civilian employee at the city's Marshall Space Flight Center, which played a fundamental role in America's race to beat the Russians to the moon. He didn't know he was black, he says, until he entered public school in the ninth grader—or at least he didn't fully understand what it meant to be black as the walls were coming down.

"I went to school with [whites] for eight years [in Catholic school], and then I start going to public school, and all of a sudden, because I'm black I'm supposed to be bad?" recalled Holloway, who is now an executive with a minor league hockey franchise in his hometown. "It cut both ways. Whites hated blacks and blacks hated whites. One day [during the first year of integration] the black students staged a boycott, and for what? To continue the hatred? I said to heck with that. I wasn't going to be dragged down by their stupidity. I showed up for school and it was just me and one black girl. We were the only blacks in school that day. I wasn't going to let them pull me under."

Instead, Holloway dedicated himself to his studies and to football, starring for the Lee Generals from 1969 to 1970. A talented passer with a gift for tucking the ball under his arm and running for the tough yards, he remains perhaps the finest quarterback ever produced by a northern Alabama high school. The year Sam Cunningham ran wild at Legion Field, the Alabama coaches started calling.

On his official visit to the campus in Tuscaloosa, Holloway was shocked by Bryant's candor. "He said, 'I'd love to have you at Alabama, but Alabama's not ready for a black quarterback.' A lot of the other coaches, when I asked them about playing quarterback, they'd hem and haw. They'd dodge the question. But Coach Bryant was honest. He knew it would be awfully tough for a black to play quarterback for Alabama at that time. I really respected that. He didn't have to be honest with me. He could've signed me and then made me change positions, which is probably what a lot of schools would have done." Instead, Holloway signed with the University of Tennessee and led the Volunteers to twenty-five victories and three bowl bids in three years as the starting quarterback.

Nine years after Holloway chose to become a quarterback

at Tennessee instead of a running back at Alabama, the Crimson Tide signed highly recruited quarterback Walter Lewis of Brewton, who emerged as the first black to start at the position for Alabama. Fleet of foot in the mold of several of Alabama's wishbone quarterbacks of the 1970s, Lewis unveiled his impressive scrambling ability when he came off the bench against Notre Dame in his freshman year of 1980. The Crimson Tide lost the game, 7–0, as the Fighting Irish's hex over Bryant continued, but Lewis was impressive enough to win more playing time and eventually the starting job. Quiet and deeply religious, he was calling the signals the night the Bear surpassed Amos Alonzo Stagg to become the winningest major college coach of all time, and he was at the controls a year later when the music stopped.

His career also provides a reminder that, despite all the talk about inclusiveness and opportunity, race can be never be completely eradicated as a topic of division. In 1982, the Crimson Tide was expected to contend for yet another national championship, which is to say, it was supposed to be a routine year under Bear Bryant. But 'Bama faltered; it lost to rival Tennessee for the first time in twelve years, and then, in the most devastating month in the history of the program, sustained losses to LSU, to Southern Mississippi in Tuscaloosa—which ended an NCAA-record fifty-seven-game home winning streak—and then to archrival Auburn as Bo Jackson scaled the goal line in the waning moments. The Bryant era was over; all that remained was an anticlimatic victory over Illinois in the Liberty Bowl.

The Tide struggled on both sides of the ball, but nothing pronounced the end of an era quite as dramatically as the first half of the LSU game in Birmingham, when 'Bama was unable to muster even a single first down. The offensive line that once so dominated its SEC rivals was manhandled in the losses to LSU and Auburn, and Lewis found himself scrambling for his life. A rumor began circulating that the 'Bama offensive line had stopped blocking for Lewis because he had taken up with a white girlfriend. Although the story never appeared in print, it spread across the state like wildfire and even got back to the team. It wasn't true in any way. Lewis did not have a white girlfriend, and the offensive line certainly didn't care one way or another; they wanted to win every bit as much as their quarterback. But rather than face the fact that the Tide simply wasn't a very good team that season, a small minority of fans needed a scapegoat. So they believed what they wanted to believe, falling into a habit of seeing the world in racial terms.

Bryant's hardscrabble rise from poverty allowed him to relate to black athletes very easily. Most of the blacks he brought into his program in the 1970s sprang from modest roots, as he had, and he succeeded in motivating and disciplining them with as much ease as with the coal miners' kids in Kentucky and the ranch hands' sons at Texas A&M.

"Coach handled integration like it was nothing," said Dude Hennessey, who played and coached for the man. "There was no difference. We just kept on winning, 'cause Coach Bryant had a gift for relating to kids—and a gift for being able to change with the times."

Almost all of his contemporaries in southern football retired before or shortly after integration. Georgia's Wally Butts, Tennessee's Robert Neyland, LSU's Paul Dietzel, and Clemson's Frank Howard all cashed in their chips before the rules of the game changed. Darrell Royal, whose 1970 Texas Longhorns were the last all-white team to capture a national championship, successfully integrated his team and retired five years later, on the same day as his friend and rival, Arkansas's Frank Broyles.

In the 1960s, Ole Miss emerged as 'Bama's biggest challenger for supremacy in the Southeastern Conference, capturing league championships in 1960, 1962, and 1963, but coach Johnny Vaught quit after the 1971 season rather than integrate, and the program never recovered. Ole Miss never lived down its past in the minds of many of the state's blacks, and in the late 1960s and early 1970s, white flight created dozens of private schools and drained the public schools of money and pupils, which decimated high-school football in the state.

By contrast, high-school football in Alabama grew stronger, and Bryant's Crimson Tide kicked into overdrive. After integration, 'Bama captured nine SEC titles and three national championships over the next eleven years. No team has ever dominated or will ever dominate the country's toughest football conference so completely. Between 1971 and 1981, 'Bama lost a total of four conference games, total. Thousands of Alabama schoolchildren grew up without knowing what it felt like not to have a top-ten team, because the Tide finished in the money every year between the death of segregation and the birth of MTV.

Of course, the 1970s (103–16–1), when college teams were allowed to play eleven regular-season games instead of ten, were only slightly more successful at 'Bama than the 1960s (90–16–4). Bryant's Tide posted the nation's best record in both decades. No other man won national championships with both segregated and integrated teams.

In the thirteen seasons when he was forced to watch so many of the state's best players head to historically black colleges or to major teams in the North, the Bear won 108, lost 27, and tied 8, for a winning percentage of 78.3, with three national championships, four Southeastern Conference titles, thirteen bowl appearances, and nine finishes in the Associated Press top ten. (Six of those losses came in the first two years, as he rebuilt the program from the bottom of the SEC.) In the twelve seasons when he could choose from all players, he won 124, lost 19, and tied 1, for a winning percentage of 86.5, with three national championships, nine SEC titles, twelve bowl appearances, and eleven finishes in the nation's top ten.

'Bama's success in the 1970s was not a result simply of integration, of course. Other changes included Bryant's gutsy decision to "sink or swim" with the wishbone offense; the shift from one-platoon to two-platoon football (which occured in the mid-1960s but had a gradual effect on the game into the early 1970s); the corresponding liberalization of substitution rules, which allowed him to develop a system in which he played three and sometimes four complete units, which accentuated his strengths; and the abandonment of his "quick little boys" strategy in favor of using behemoths to take advantage of new blocking rules. Even as he marched toward social security, the Bear kept pushing and prodding and working sixteen-hour days. Bryant won more games, it is worth noting, after his fifty-fourth birthday (152) than Knute Rockne (105), Frank Leahy (107), Bud Wilkinson (145), Bob Devaney (136), and Frank Broyles (149) won, period.

Segregated. Integrated. Didn't matter. He would have won at Vassar.

To the world outside Alabama, George Wallace and Paul Bryant seemed like twin icons of a culture based less on intellect than strength and emotion. They were, without a doubt, the two most powerful, influential, and beloved figures in the state during the 1960s and 1970s, and if they had ever become political rivals, it would have been extremely difficult for the average Alabamian to choose between them. The two men always maintained a very warm, cordial relationship. But in the context of history, Wallace and Bryant represent two opposite views on the issue that defined a generation. In many ways, Bryant was the Anti-Wallace.

Alabama has been paying for Wallace's demagoguery on the subject of race for more than three decades. When the state needed a leader to step forward and enforce the law and guide the citizenry into an inevitable new era of integration, Wallace exploited the traumatic experience of desegregation for political gain, first in the governor's office and then as a presidential candidate. Although he later repented his earlier racist stands and actually won a majority of the black vote in the gubernatorial elections of 1974 and 1982, Wallace's record during the 1960s and early 1970s left an indelible stain on Alabama's reputation, self-image, and view of the world. In the early 1970s, when the combative governor was railing against court-ordered busing and churning the divisive issue into political capital on the presidential campaign trail, Bryant was quietly integrating his football team. The contrast was stark.

"No one has done more to promote racial harmony in Alabama than Bryant," observed Auburn University history professor Wayne Flint, coauthor of *Alabama: The History of a Deep South State.* "When he started to recruit and play black athletes, Alabamians were so deeply wedded to college football that they were willing to celebrate the achievement of blacks as athletes when they weren't willing to celebrate the achievements of blacks in other areas. That had a ripple effect throughout many things in this state."

Of course, the coach did not integrate his team to promote social harmony. He integrated his team because he thought it would help him win, and it did. He also believed that it was the right thing to do, and the social ramifications were profound.

By the time Wilbur Jackson and John Mitchell pulled on crimson jerseys for the first time, schools throughout Alabama were well on the way to complete and irrevocable integration. All traces of the insidious "whites-only" signs were long gone from public water fountains and restrooms. The Voting Rights Act of 1965, passed in the wake of the Selma march, guaranteed the full rights of citizenship to hundreds of thousands of Alabama blacks. But Bryant's decision to integrate the Alabama football team when he did represented a different kind of progress. Having blacks and whites compete together on the state's most important cultural asset closed the door on a turbulent era with more force than a thousand marches. It compelled the races to share something more personal: their heros.

Even as they cheered the exploits of some talented Crimson Tide player with a darker pigmentation than their own, of course, some Alabamians would not have wanted the player to drop by for dinner. But many other hearts were stirred, and their minds followed. If it was all right for Coach Bryant, many reasoned, it must be all right for the rest of us. Bigotry of the heart remains alive in Birmingham and Montgomery as surely as it continues to flower in New York and Jerusalem, and it will never be completely stamped out, but Alabama today is closer to a color-blind society than Martin Luther King could have imagined in his wildest dreams. In the 1970s, Bryant's example was rife with symbolism.

Alabamians tend to be deeply religious people, and many of the same people who once believed so fervently in segregation as part of God's great plan experienced a change of heart. Even Wallace admitted he was wrong, and black people forgave him. Bryant, who never stood in the schoolhouse door, was a symbol not only of integration for integration's sake, but also of the power of redemption in which so many Alabamians believe so forcefully. They cheered his integrated teams and they slowly changed their hearts and then their minds on some facets of the race question, and they slowly redeemed themselves.

Nowadays, when someone in another part of the country thinks of Alabama and his first image is of Bear Bryant—and not Bull Connor—Alabama wins.

Once during his career as an All-Pro tight end with the Cleveland Browns, former Tide star Ozzie Newsome was asked where he thought his former coach belonged in a continuum with Martin Luther King. "King preached opportunity," he observed, "but without people like Coach Bryant who gave us the opportunity and really treated us as equals, where would we be?"

13
Wishbone

IN THE WINTER OF 1969-70, Joe Robbie approached Paul Bryant about becoming the head coach of the Miami Dolphins. Other professional teams had dangled job offers in front of him in the past, and he always turned them down with little hesitation, but the Dolphins caught him at the right time. His Alabama program had fallen from the nation's best to the middle of the SEC, and even he was beginning to wonder if he had lost his touch—or at least his drive. Retirement crossed his mind, but he knew deep down that he couldn't live without football. Part of him felt as though he needed a new challenge, and building an NFL team virtually from scratch sounded like a great adventure for a fifty-six-year-old legend who had transformed three college programs from chumps to champs.

But it was the money that turned his head. After several weeks of haggling, Robbie and the Bear agreed to terms and Winston McCall, Bryant's lawyer, drew up a contract. The staggering deal amounted to more than $1.7 million over five years, which dwarfed his Alabama salary and perks, which totaled less than one hundred thousand dollars per year. Bryant gave Robbie his word, which was like gold. Only a select few associates knew about the negotiations, and the news shocked John David Crow. The former Texas A&M Heisman Trophy winner, then the running backs coach on Bryant's staff, received a rather cryptic call from his boss one evening in January, instructing him to come over to the Bryants' house. When he arrived, the coach shared the secret and told him to be prepared to fly to Miami the next day.

"He said he wanted me to fire everybody but the girl answering the phone," Crow recalled. "He was already thinking about the people he was going to hire for his staff, and he wanted me to go down and wipe the slate clean and run the office for a few days."

The next morning, after losing a night's sleep and consulting various friends and members of the board of trustees, Bryant stuck his head into Crow's office on the second floor of Memorial Coliseum. The deal was off. He had gone back on his word to Joe Robbie.

"But how could you turn that down, Coach?" Crow asked.

"Well, John," he said, "that would have been the first job I ever took for the money. We've got enough money. I couldn't leave Alabama just for money."

Several days later, the boss called a staff meeting. He walked in the door, took a long drag on his cigarette, and started talking about how poor recruiting had been and how all the fair-weather fans were beginning to call for his scalp. "Now, I'm not worried about myself," he said. "I can get a job. I'm not sure about the rest of y'all. If I was you, I'd get out there and get us some players."

"We about knocked each other down getting to the door," said line coach Dude Hennessey.

The drop-back passing game was never Bryant's brand of football. It was too passive for his tastes. He preferred knocking the other guy into the next county and moving the ball up his gut, and the drop-back game was too dependent on reading defenses and all that standing around at the point of attack. "Three things can happen when you pass the ball," he was fond of saying, "and two of 'em are bad." An NFL-inspired passing craze swept through the college game in the late 1960s, and the Bear joined the crowd. Two bad things happened: 1969 and 1970. Scott Hunter, a future starter for the Atlanta Falcons, passed for 3,428 yards over two years and 'Bama still finished 6–5 and 6–5–1, thanks in part to a porous defense. With Hunter graduating and a mediocre passer named Terry Davis the heir apparent in 1971, the Bear knew he couldn't win with a pro-style attack.

Forever a student of the game, Bryant "was always wanting to know what you were doing new," said Charley McClendon, the longtime LSU coach. "He and Woody Hayes were a lot alike on that. Both of 'em called me more than all the young coaches put together. They never assumed they knew it all just 'cause they'd won so many games."

In the summer of 1971, Bryant flew out to Austin to huddle

with his buddy Darrell Royal. He wanted to know more about the wishbone, the triple-option running formation that the Texas coach and his top assistant, Emory Bellard, had developed in the late 1960s. Oklahoma's wishbone ran up and down the field on 'Bama en route to a 24–24 tie in the 1970 Bluebonnet Bowl, and Bryant was intrigued by the possibilities. The Royals were remodeling their home when the Bear came to town, and the place was filled with carpenters and painters, so the two coaches rented a motel room on the outskirts of town and plugged in the projector.

"I showed him a running game reel and a passing game reel, and that made up his mind pretty quick," said Royal, who won consecutive national championships with the offense in 1969 and 1970. "He decided he was going to the wishbone."

For Bryant, the wishbone was less a depature than a return to his coaching roots. The formation is, at its most fundamental level, an instrument of power, blast-off-the-line, hard-nosed football—but with two unique twists. One was the triple option: The quarterback can either give the ball to the fullback for a run up the middle, keep the ball on a run around end, or run as if on a keeper but pitch the ball wide to a trailing tailback. After establishing the fullback up the middle, a good wishbone quarterback can keep a defense off-balance by forcing it to protect against both the keep and the pitch. Second, the wishbone is an extremely effective offense for passing the ball, because the triple option almost always guaranteed the receivers one-on-one coverage since so many defenders had to stay up front to protect against the run.

Although his team had practiced running the pro set all spring, Bryant returned to Tuscaloosa less than a month before the start of preseason practice and shocked his coaches by announcing the switch to the wishbone. Some of them probably thought the old man had lost his mind, making a change so late. They didn't even have a playbook. But when he said, "We're going to sink or swim with the wishbone," they didn't need a translation.

"What he was doing was putting the pressure on us to make

it work," said quarterbacks coach Mal Moore, who later became offensive coordinator. *"Sink or swim* meant we damn well better make it work."

Determined to keep the switch secret and spring it on Southern Cal in the season opener, Bryant arranged for Royal and Bellard to come to Tuscaloosa, ostensibly to attend the 'Bama coaches clinic. For four days, the architects of the wishbone guzzled coffee and munched on take-out pizza late into the night while dissecting film with 'Bama offensive coaches Mal Moore, Jimmy Sharpe, John David Crow, and Jack Rutledge at the Holiday Inn.

"It was like cramming for a final exam," Crow said.

When the players returned to campus for the start of two-a-days the second week in August, the offensive coaches started with the fundamentals: the new blocking schemes, a half-dozen basic plays, the pitch versus the keep. Success or failure of the new offense would hinge disproportionately on Terry Davis, the junior from Bogalusa, Louisiana, who would be forced to master in three weeks what most quarterbacks learn in two or three years.

When the Southeastern Conference Skywriters Tour stopped in Tuscaloosa, the Crimson Tide switched back to the pro set for the day. Same old Alabama, the writers surmised. Most expected the Tide to be mauled by fifth-ranked USC—which had embarrassed 'Bama in the Sam Cunningham game the previous season—and to finish no better than the middle of the pack in the SEC, which was exactly what the Bear wanted them to think. The bookies were giving Alabama bettors two touchdowns.

The night before the season opener in the Coliseum, Darrell Royal called the Bear in his Los Angeles hotel room.

"Do you think they know?"

"I don't think they have any idea."

On September 10, 1971, when Alabama lined up in the wishbone against Southern Cal, John McKay was stunned. So were his players, who spent most of the first half trying to figure out where to line up. Prepared to defend against the Crimson Tide's pro set, the Trojans looked completely lost on defense, and by halftime 'Bama led 17–0 en route to a monumental 17–10 upset victory.

"I was completely shocked," McKay said. "They had the element of surprise . . . that was probably the difference. Paul set a trap and we walked right into it."

Terry Davis ran the option like a veteran. Johnny Musso, the hard-charging senior halfback from Birmingham nicknamed the "Italian Stallion," scored on runs of eight and thirteen yards. Bill Davis booted a thirty-seven-yard field goal and two extra points. The often maligned defense returned to 'Bama form behind Robin Parkhouse, Tom Surlas, Jeff Rouzie, and Steve Higginbotham.

"The program was on the line," said Musso, who later played for the Chicago Bears and became a successful commodities trader on the Chicago Board of Trade. "Even if we'd played well and not won, I don't know what kind of year we would have had. That game gave us a lot of confidence, gave us back that Alabama attitude. We brought Alabama back."

A brilliant stroke of leadership, the clandestine switch to the wishbone represented a turning point in the coaching career of Paul "Bear" Bryant, who was just catching his second wind. Three days shy of his fifty-eighth birthday, the old man in the houndstooth hat, whose age was beginning to show in his increasingly wrinkled face, won his two hundredth game and ignited the winningest decade in college football history.

"I've been around better teams," Bryant beamed, "but I've never been prouder of one."

In addition to the switch to the new offense and the resurrection of the butt-kicking defense of old, the 1971 season saw the integration of the Alabama program and the emergence of much larger linemen.

The evolution of the two-platoon game that began in the mid-1960s doomed Alabama's quick-little-boys strategy. The age of the specialist gradually eroded the value of versatility, conditioning, and endurance, and the rules changes that allowed linemen to use their hands at the point of attack forever tilted the game in the trenches toward size and strength. Two young men from Albertville on northern Alabama's Sand Mountain, separated by a decade, provide a sharp contrast: In the early 1960s, Charley Pell played winning football on the 'Bama line as a five-ten, 182-pound splinter, going both ways. In the early 1970s, six-three, 274-pound bruiser John Hannah became the prototypical offensive lineman for the new age, first as an Alabama All-America and then as an All-Pro for the New England Patriots.

The Southern Cal game ignited a 10–0 tear, setting up the biggest game in the history of the state. For the first time, both Alabama and Auburn entered the Iron Bowl undefeated and contending for the national championship. Shug Jordan's finest team since the 1957 national champions featured the nation's most prolific passing battery: Heisman Trophy–winning quarterback Pat Sullivan and All-America receiver Terry Beasley. But Alabama had Johnny Musso.

As a grammar-school boy in the early 1960s, he climbed a fence at Legion Field to see his first Alabama–Auburn game, and the experience ensnared him. He grew up dreaming of playing for the Bear, of joining the parade of names and handprints smashed by the Tide's annual captains into the concrete alongside Denny Chimes. And then it came true: He became the Italian Stallion, the Joe Namath of his era, and the Alabama fans who showed up in their best Sunday-go-to-meeting clothes to work up a Saturday afternoon sweat sometimes held tiny cardboard cutouts of him aloft, just to feel a little closer to number 22: "Mu-sso! Mu-sso!" With a rather big nose and sideburns that framed his square face like bookends, he looked like Joe Average, your good-natured frat brother with all the latest jokes, but when he took the field, he was an animal. He was relentless. A two-time All-America and the first thousand-yard rusher in Alabama history—he accomplished the milestone in both 1970 and 1971—Musso is remembered by grateful 'Bama fans not for racing down the sideline, untouched, toward an inevitable touchdown, but for pumping his legs and avoiding certain tackle, for lowering his shoulder and twisting and contorting and breaking free from the defenders who lunged for his legs, the ball tucked under his left arm and his right arm held aloft, like a rodeo rider counting to eight.

After suffering through consecutive losses to the hated Auburn Tigers in 1969 and 1970—for the only time of the Bryant era—Musso injured his foot the week before the nationally televised 1971 Iron Bowl. He desperately wanted the ball. "Coach Bryant didn't want me to start," he recalled. "His thinking was that if I started and got hurt worse, it would be a letdown to the team. Coach Crow, our backfield coach, convinced him I should start."

With Musso rushing for 167 yards and two touchdowns, Alabama turned a 14–7 game in the fourth quarter into a 31–7 rout, clinching an undefeated season and the Southeastern Conference championship.

The victory set up a showdown for the national championship between number-one Nebraska and number-two Alabama in the Orange Bowl, a game that was hyped beyond belief, like a Super Bowl. And it disappointed like a Super Bowl; the Tide was crushed, 38–6. Quarterback Jerry Tagge and flanker Johnny Rodgers, the future Heisman Trophy winner, plundered the Tide defense virtually at will. The 'Huskers exposed the flaws of 'Bama's still-rudimentary wishbone. Bob Devaney, once outcoached and outplayed by 'Bama in the mid-1960s, exacted a measure of revenge by trumping the Bear completely and laying an undisputed claim to a second straight year of national superiority.

"We were beaten soundly by a far superior team," Bryant said. "They toyed with us most of the game. They might have been the greatest I've ever seen."

The season ended with a flat tire, but Alabama was back.

In 1972, the Crimson Tide streaked to another SEC championship and a 10–2 finish. Terry Davis returned for his senior season and the coaching staff started adding dimensions to the wishbone, which zoomed into high gear as the Tide set a school record for points (33.8 per game). Undefeated once again heading into the Iron Bowl, Alabama led 16–3 with six minutes left, but Auburn blocked two punts, scored two touchdowns and two extra points to win an amazing 17–16 victory. One of the biggest and most improbable wins of Shug Jordan's career, the 1972 Iron Bowl was forever immortalized by the bumper stickers it spawned: "Punt, 'Bama, Punt." Auburn fans bragged about the magical victory for a decade—until they managed to beat Alabama again.

American society changed profoundly between the early 1960s and early 1970s. The young people of the early 1960s tended to respect or at least accept the rules and mores of the establishment, but the Vietnam War and the social upheaval of the 1960s created a more cynical generation determined to challenge society's boundaries at all levels. Dozens of colleges and universities—including the University of Alabama—experienced student protest marches and other challenges to the old order, acts that would have been unthinkable a decade earlier. College football was not immune to the changes; many student-athletes resisted the kind of rigidity the previous generation would have accepted without discussion as part of "paying the price" to become one of Saturday's heroes.

Bryant, who was a virtual poster boy for the establishment, believed most fervently in the military way of life. Paul Bryant Hall was run more like a Marine barracks than a dormitory. He told his players when to get up, when to eat, when to sleep, when to go to class, when to go to study hall, how much to weigh, how fast to run the annual mile, what to do during the summer, how to wear their hair, how to dress, how long they could stay out at night. Well into the 1970s, 'Bama players needed permission from The Man to get married. Those who were not prepared to conform to his standards of discipline and commitment were asked to leave. Period.

Although none of the 'Bama players of the late 1960s and early 1970s openly challenged Bryant on the rigidity of the system, many privately resented some of the rules that they considered outdated. Hair length was a symbol, and a legitimate concern for the athletes. During the spring of 1970, a committee of players stopped by to see their coach and asked him to consider a more flexible policy on hair. For years, Bryant's mandates basically matched the military's: high and tight. If players showed up with hair not to his liking, he sent them to the barbershop or back home, their choice. But only old men wore crewcuts and flattops in 1970, and the girls liked the guys with long hair, and the football players liked the girls.

As he pondered the situation one day, Bryant spotted Lyndon Johnson on television. He couldn't believe his eyes: The former president looked like a rock 'n' roller, with a long gray mane falling across his collar. So he talked to some of his friends in the business and decided to lighten up a bit: The hair could rest on the top of the ear but it couldn't touch the collar; sideburns were acceptable to a certain length; facial hair remained forbidden. All hair had to be neatly trimmed. "I don't want you to look like girls," he commanded.

"That might sound like a little bit thing, but it was awful big to us," said Jeff Rouzie, who played linebacker from 1970 to 1972. "Everybody had long hair, but we had to look like the Marines. When he showed some flexibility on that, and relaxed some of the little things around the dorm to make it a little less like a military camp, that had a great impact on morale."

One of the amazing aspects of Bryant's career is how he managed to win with three distinct generations of young people who viewed the world and football in different ways. He related to and motivated all kinds, and when necessary he adapted without compromising his standards of discipline. In contrast to his early and middle years as a coach, when his motivational techniques centered on fear, Bryant in the 1970s was more of a grandfatherly, commanding general figure. His tolerance for mistakes and lack of effort remained low, and he continued to run off the slackers, but he became less of a driver as he moved into his sixties.

"We were taught not to question, to do whatever the authority figure asked us to do," noted fullback-linebacker Jackie Sherrill, who played on the 'Bama teams of 1963–65 and subsequently coached on Bryant's staff. "Those guys who came later grew up during all that unrest, and the world was telling them to question the authority figures, and yet the great disciplinarian was able to prosper during that time."

Although he was willing to show flexibility on the hair issue, Bryant refused to tolerate the most pervasive and destructive by-product of the new era: illegal drug use. Early in 1970, after hearing rumblings about widespread drug experimentation among his football players—which mirrored the society as a whole—he and his staff secretly cooperated with state and federal investigators to engage in surveillance of some of the suspected users.

"We had people watching the [dope] houses to see who came in and out," said Jack Rutledge, then the director of Bryant Hall, who was responsible for many of the disciplinary aspects of the football program. "They'd have a brochure and be able to compare [the players to their pictures]. We were trying to help [the authorities] gather information to break up the suppliers and solve our problem."

On a memorable spring afternoon, the coach called a meeting in the projection room in Memorial Coliseum and laid it on the line. "Gentlemen," he said, "we've got some illegal activity going on around here, and it's gonna stop." In one hour, he said, the dorm would be searched from top to bottom. Any illegal substances had better be gone "or you'll be gone."

At once sobering and oddly comedic, the resulting sweep featured middle-aged, high-and-tight football men such as Clem Gryska, Ken Donahue, and Jack Rutledge searching closets, desk drawers, and cooling vents for marijuana plants, acid tablets, amphetamines, needles, and other paraphernalia. Trainer Jim Goostree supervised the detail, since he knew more about drugs than the coaches. The search was revealing, and the next day, seven members of the Crimson Tide were given a choice: Withdraw from school or take it up with the cops. No one stuck around to get busted.

"We collected boxes and bags full of stuff," said Gryska, who coached under Bryant for more than two decades. "It was all pretty foreign to us, and certainly to Coach, but he knew we couldn't tolerate that kind of activity."

"I don't think he could've handled it any better," said Rouzie, who was then a freshman and now coaches linebackers for Gene Stallings. "A lot of guys were experimenting with marijuana, especially, and there were some guys who had some serious problems, and they were forced to leave. It could've destroyed the program."

Not everyone was caught, of course.

Robin Parkhouse played football like a wild animal, which made him one of his coach's favorites. A big, fast, red-haired defensive end from Orlando, Parkhouse attacked with a recklessness and a sense of abandon that made him an All-America. A natural leader, he cocaptained the comeback team as a senior in 1971. But he was also emotionally immature, lacking in direction, something of a troublemaker who drove a motorcycle and liked to start bar fights. Early in his college career, he started experimenting with marijuana, then with such psychedelics as angel dust and LSD.

After Southern Cal crushed the Crimson Tide in the 1970 season opener in Birmingham, Parkhouse, distraught, decided to quit. After he failed to show up for practice on Monday afternoon, several of the assistant coaches started calling and trying to convince him he was making a big mistake. His parents phoned from Florida, worried. So he thought it over and decided he was wrong to throw it all away, and he got up before dawn the next morning to plead for mercy with the boss.

Bryant listened to what he had to say and told him he needed time to think it over. Come back after lunch, he said, and I'll give you my decision. After all those hours of watching the clock, Parkhouse returned to his coach's office at the appointed time and caught a break: Bryant decided to suspend him for four weeks, which meant he would have to move out of the dorm, but if he kept his nose clean during those four weeks he could rejoin the team. Although relieved by the second chance, he was disturbed by one thing his coach said:

"I think it's the biggest mistake I've ever made, Robin, but I've decided to let you back on the team."

"For years after that, when I'd be getting high late into the night, I would torture myself over that line, replaying it in my mind," Parkhouse said. "What did he mean by that: *the biggest mistake he'd ever made?* I was stoned out of my mind half the time, and I couldn't figure it out. It really tormented me."

Soon after playing his final season for the Crimson Tide in 1971, Robin Parkhouse, All-America, became a drug dealer. In early 1973, more than a year after leaving the university, he traveled to Mexico to buy a large supply of marijuana for resale, which placed him more in the realm of an entrepreneur, looking for the big score. He got caught, busted with 150 pounds of grass in the trunk of his car soon after crossing the border, he wound up in the El Paso, Texas, county jail, staring at fifteen years of hard time, minimum. He knew he couldn't do fifteen *days* in the joint with all those badasses; he was too much of a hotheaded badass himself, and he'd mouth off and start a fight and they'd thrust a knife in his gut. He just knew he was a goner. He just knew.

The arrest of Robin Parkhouse, All-America, made all the papers back in Alabama, becoming an embarrassment to the university and his old coach. But the Bear remembered how Parkhouse had played, how he had thrown his guts onto the turf on every down. He always told his boys that if they worked hard for him he would always be there for them, and so he was for Robin Parkhouse.

"He saved my life," Parkhouse said.

Rather than avoiding the subject of a former player gone astray, Bryant quietly pulled some strings with some politically connected friends in Texas, and his personal attorney, Francis Hare, arranged to have the case remanded to the federal circuit court in Birmingham, where the bench was likely to look more kindly on a former Crimson Tide star. Instead of doing fifteen years in a joint brimming with the stench of death, his own death, Parkhouse served four months and eighteen days at Eglin Air Force Base in Florida, a white-collar minimum-security facility where he played tennis and lifted weights like a Watergate burglar.

"I couldn't play another down for him," Parkhouse remarked. "All I could be to him was an embarrassment. But he helped me because I was one of his boys. He absolutely saved my life."

Although Bryant's intervention after this arrest speaks volumes about his loyalty to his former players, it sent the message that Parkhouse was not accountable for his own actions. Although he "saved" Parkhouse, Bryant prevented him from learning a difficult lesson about consequences and responsibility. Just as he had feared, he made a mistake by being too easy on Parkhouse.

Instead of being scared straight, Parkhouse soon descended back into the drug culture. A decade later, he returned to prison on a cocaine-trafficking charge. For years and years, his coach's self-admonishment from 1970 tormented him to no end. *The biggest mistake I've ever made!* After he walked out of prison in 1989 and at last straightened his life out, starting his own business in his hometown of Orlando and becoming a born-again Christian, he finally figured out the old man's riddle.

"He thought it was a mistake because he knew I had the potential to lead people in the wrong direction off the field, be a bad influence, and he was right," Parkhouse said.

On a beautiful, windswept October afternoon in 1973, Birmingham's Legion Field was packed in a sea of crimson. The sky glowed orange in the distance, a constant reminder of the Magic City's steel-making prowess. The air hung heavy with a mass of sweet-smelling perfumes wafting from all the fine-looking southern ladies, young and old, dressed to the nines, their arms around well-groomed men in coats and ties. They wore wide smiles and shared knowing glances, because it was the middle of the dominating reign of the Bear, and like Florence during the Renaissance, like Vegas during the age of the rat pack, like Yankee Stadium during the epochs of Ruth, DiMaggio, and Mantle, Alabama was the center of the college football universe, and life was sweet.

Undefeated and ranked second in the nation after five games, the 1973 Crimson Tide was already being compared to some of the best teams in school history, but to the man in the houndstooth hat, such talk was premature. The Tennessee game always represented a special test to him, second only to the Iron Bowl against Auburn. The third Saturday in October was a barometer on the road to greatness. During his playing days in the 1930s, when 'Bama and Auburn refused to schedule each other, the Volunteers and the Crimson Tide attacked each other like the Hatfields and the McCoys, and the Bear hated the men in orange so much he had played the 1935 game with a broken leg, played the finest game of his life.

General Robert Neyland, the Volunteers' coach from the 1920s to the 1950s, was both an idol and a curse. Bryant respected him and copied him, but he could never beat him during his days as a young coach at Kentucky. The Bear turned the tables on Neyland's successors during his quarter-century at Alabama, however, posting a 16–7–2 record against Tennessee, including eleven straight victories from 1971 to 1981. In the glow of each of those wins, the Bear and his coaches lit a ritual cigar and filled the locker room with smoke and backpatting.

In the fourth quarter of the 1973 game, no one on the 'Bama sideline was searching for a match. Tennessee quarterback Condredge Holloway had turned Legion Field into his own personal stage, completing passes from the pocket and on the run, scrambling for first downs on busted plays and scoring three touchdowns to lead the Vols to a 21–21 tie with six minutes left in the battle of unbeatens. Then, without warning, the complexion of the game turned decidedly crimson.

Robin Cary gathered in a Tennessee punt deep in his own territory, followed a wall of blockers, and rambled sixty-four yards for a touchdown. Then, after the Tide forced the Vols to punt once again, halfback Wilbur Jackson turned a routine sweep into an eighty-yard touchdown. Seconds later, Tennessee fumbled, 'Bama recovered, and three plays later it owned a head-shaking 42–21 victory.

The Bear was so happy that he mounted a bench in the locker room after the game, his victory stogie dangling from his lips, and told his boys, "You're the greatest bunch I've ever been around. Either that, or the greatest bunch of con men."

Against Tennessee as with most other teams on its schedule, Alabama dominated not only because of its talent but also because of its enormous depth. Unlike the one-platoon teams of the 1960s, which relied on the sixty-minute man's quickness, endurance, and heart—the '61 national champions consisted of about eighteen rugged souls who played most of the snaps—the 'Bama teams of the 1970s rotated three complete units in and out of the game. In a typical game of the period, 'Bama used seventy to eighty players, and while most teams couldn't reach so deep without a tremendous dropoff, the Crimson Tide's units sometimes seemed indistinguishable in performance. They just kept coming.

"In the 1973 game, we had been playing against the second and third teams for two quarters," recalled Holloway, "and then we came back and tied it up and they put the first team back in, and the first team's rested and fresh and they just crushed us."

"They had so many players who could play," observed former Tennessee coach Bill Battle, who was chased from Knoxville after losing six of seven to 'Bama. "They could put in their second and third teams and not get beat, whereas most of the others [in the conference] were going to get their butts whipped if they put their second and third teams in. They spent more hours on preparation and did a better job of preparation than the rest of us."

Winning so consistently allowed Bryant to use so many players, and using so many players helped him win. The more experience those second- and third-teamers gained, the better they performed, and unlike the players in many lesser programs, those players brought loads of experience with them when they moved up to the first team. The strategy proved a morale boost for nonstarters, but it sometimes frustrated the first-teamers. "You look out there and see [the second team] giving up a touchdown or a bunch of yards and you think, 'Hey, you're ruining our stats,' " said Bob Baumhower, an All-SEC defensive tackle in 1975–76.

After rallying to knock off Tennessee, the 1973 Tide finished 11–0 without another serious challenge, won its third straight SEC title, and captured the UPI national championship, awarded before the bowls. An offensive juggernaut that averaged a school-record 41.2 points per game behind quarterbacks Richard Todd and Gary Rutledge, Alabama earned a historic date with number-three Notre Dame in the Sugar Bowl on New Year's Eve to decide the AP national championship.

After all those years of chasing each other from afar, college football's two most successful programs were meeting for the first time in a game that truly seemed to warrant all the hype. This matchup *was* the Game of the Century: Notre Dame's tradition of Rockne, Leahy, and Parseghian versus Alabama's tradition of Wade, Thomas, and Bryant. "People have been looking forward to this game for years," Bryant said before they kicked off. Alabama was favored by three points.

In one of the all-time classics at old Tulane Stadium, Notre Dame and Alabama slugged it out like a pair of heavyweight prizefighters. It was ugly, bloody, bone-rattling football at its best. The most electrifying moment of the night occurred toward the end of the second quarter when Notre Dame's Al Hunter returned an Alabama kickoff ninety-three yards for a touchdown. But there was also the flea-flicker play Alabama pulled in the fourth quarter, with halfback Mike Stock passing to quarterback Richard Todd, who showed his speed by streaking twenty-five yards down the sideline for the go-ahead touchdown at 23–21. Notre Dame responded by driving from its own nineteen-yard line into field-goal range, and Bob Thomas booted a nineteen-yarder for a 24–23 Irish lead with four minutes left.

After downing a punt on the Notre Dame one-yard line with less than two minutes remaining, 'Bama's defense held the Irish to two yards in two stabs. Third down would likely decide the ballgame. 'Bama needed the ball back, and Notre Dame didn't want to punt out of its end zone. The football game suddenly became a chess match, and Ara Parseghian and quarterback Tom Clements won the war of nerves. On the biggest third-and-eight call of his life, Clements faked a belly play to the fullback, pulled back into the end zone, and lofted a perfect spiral to tight end Robin Weber near the thirty-five-yard line. That was the ballgame, and the championship.

"Losing that ballgame was a sick feeling," said Sylvester Croom, the Tide's All-America center. "We were so close and it just slipped away."

After another undefeated run and an unprecedented fourth straight SEC championship in 1974, Bryant got a rematch for his Tide in the Orange Bowl. Although Notre Dame finished 9–2 and out of the hunt for the national championship, Alabama entered the game ranked second and within grasp of another trophy. But Notre Dame, playing the last game in the Era of Ara, deprived the Tide of another championship, 13–11.

As the 1970s rolled on—and the Bear aged into his sixties —the boss delegated more and more responsibility to his staff, becoming less an in-your-face drill sergeant and more a commanding officer. In a typical staff meeting during the 1960s, he was likely to ask his assistants to demonstrate in intricate detail every technique they would be teaching on that particular day—and correct them, for instance, on how they showed the guards to "pull" at the line of scrimmage; as the 1970s progressed, the key members of the staff had been in place for so long that he no longer needed to drill them so often on fundamentals and tactics. "You always felt on edge during those staff meetings," said offensive coordinator Mal Moore. "You were always concerned that he was going to ask you a question you didn't know the answer to." He let his coaches coach on the field and, as he often liked to say during the period, his main job was "coaching the coaches." He continued to work grueling eighteen-hour days during the season, formulating game plans, handling personnel problems. During practice, he spent more time in the tower, but everyone on the field —coaches and players alike—feared the moment he snaked down the steps, because it meant someone was in for a tongue-lashing.

"I think Coach Bryant became wiser as he got older," said Jeff Rouzie, who played linebacker for him in the early 1970s and coached on his staff from 1977 to 1982. "He had more patience and tried to understand and get closer to his players."

He continued to make all personnel decisions, sometimes to the dismay of his assistants—because he was usually right. Before a nationally televised game against Southern Cal in 1977, Bryant walked into a staff meeting and told Ken Donahue, his defensive coordinator, to start sophomore Curtis McGriff at defensive end that week. Donahue couldn't believe it. McGriff, a six-five, 265-pound monster from Cottonwood, Alabama, had played only sparingly on the varsity, and Donahue believed he needed more time to develop. But the boss didn't. The Bear had been watching the young man and believed he was ready to become a winner. Donahue fussed and fumed—but McGriff started and made several big plays in Alabama's 21–20 victory over the Trojans in Los Angeles.

The following Monday morning, the Bear walked into the staff meeting, took a long pull from his cigarette, and flashed a sly smile at Donahue. "Now, Kenno," he said, "you think you can get McGriff a little more playing time?"

"Coach Bryant didn't like yes-men," Donahue said. "Wouldn't tolerate 'em. He wanted us coaches to speak our minds in the staff meeting, but I always knew how far I could take it. You always knew who the boss was. We were all scared to death of him—and respected him so much."

Like any successful leader, Bryant surrounded himself with good assistants—probably the best staff in college football at its peak. Forty-five of his former players and assistants eventually became head coaches at the college or professional level, which would be a record if anyone kept such a stat. "You're only as good as your assistant coaches," he said, "and I've always tried to hire assistant coaches who are smarter than I am." He constantly gave all the credit to his assistants and his players when he won—and, like Lee at Gettysburg, he accepted all the blame when he lost. Although he felt close to many members of his staff through the years, he avoided socializing with them, because he had seen other head coaches experience the inevitable problems caused by conflicting roles. Late in his career, he said of the policy, "I simply don't want to take any chance of creating problems that might develop between women, children, and kinfolks."

Among the dozens of dedicated assistants who toiled in his shadow through the years, two in particular never received enough credit: Ken Donahue and Mal Moore, the architects of Alabama's dominating defenses and offenses, respectively, in the 1970s.

Donahue looked like a drill sergeant. Tall and lanky, with a buzz cut and perpetual scowl, he was the toughest, meanest, most demanding man any of his players had ever met. He played for the general at Tennessee, and his leadership on Bryant's staff was a link to the Neyland brand of football that the Bear so admired. "I used to try to think of ways to get rid of [Donahue]," admitted defensive star Bob Baumhower, "until I realized why he was so tough on me: He was trying to make me a better football player, and he did." If he thought a player wasn't giving it everything he had, Donahue was known to appear at said athlete's door at the crack of dawn and lead him to the practice field for a series of wake-up gassers.

Moore, who played on the 1961 national championship team, seemed low-key until he got in your face. Although Alabama's wishbone was rather one-dimensional in the breakthrough year of 1971, the cerebral former quarterback from Dozier,

Alabama, was largely responsible for adding all the wrinkles that rendered it practically unstoppable in the years to follow. Of all the successful wishbone teams of the 1970s—Oklahoma, Texas, and UCLA, among others—Alabama was widely considered the most innovative, especially in exploiting the pass.

In 1975, the Crimson Tide won a fifth straight Southeastern Conference title behind quarterback Richard Todd and the nation's number-one defense (6.0 points per game). Todd, a six-two, 204-pound senior from Mobile who was destined to replace Joe Namath as the New York Jets' starter, was the best passer of the wishbone era. After leading 'Bama to a 10–1 season, he won MVP honors in the 13–6 victory over Penn State in the Sugar Bowl that broke the Bear's eight-year bowl jinx and launched a six-year span of postseason victories. His favorite target was a sophomore from Leighton, Alabama, named Ozzie Newsome.

Although the six-two, 209-pound Newsome possessed the speed and talent to go anywhere, he chose Alabama because of the Bear. "I could've gone to a lot of places where I could've caught a lot more passes," he said, "but I wanted to play for him . . . to play for national championships behind the greatest coach."

Graceful, acrobatic, lightning quick, and endowed with terrific hands, the All-America Newsome caught 102 passes from 1974 to 1977 for a school-record 2,070 yards and sixteen touchdowns. The fans in Alabama joyfully referred to him as "the Wizard of Oz" long before the incredible Ozzie Smith won the tag. Although his number of catches pales in comparison to modern-day receivers playing in pass-oriented offenses, he averaged 20.3 yards per reception for his entire career, including 22.3 as a senior, one of the reasons 'Bama fans anointed him the "Player of the Decade" in a special poll. He later became an All-Pro tight end for the Cleveland Browns.

"People always talk about the Wishbone as just a running offense, but it was great for me," Newsome said. "I didn't catch as many balls as I might have a lot of places, but the way the offense was designed, if you ever get one-on-one coverage isolated with a defensive back, boom!—we're going for the home run."

After senior Jack O'Rear suffered a career-ending injury in 1976, junior Jeff Rutledge took over at quarterback and piloted a disappointing season by Alabama standards. The Crimson Tide finished 8–3, failed to win the SEC championship for the first time in six years, and arrived at the Liberty Bowl in Memphis as a rare underdog to UCLA, which had barely missed a trip to the Rose Bowl. But the Alabama defense—led by game MVP Barry Krauss—had a field day as the Tide crushed the Bruins, 36–6. Bryant eschewed his trademark houndstooth hat in favor of a red ski mask to escape the bitter cold. After spending the entire week sweet-talking UCLA in his typical self-deprecating style—"they're just too fast, too talented, too well-coached"—he was asked if he was surprised by the size of the rout. "Hell, yes," he replied. "Weren't you?"

With Rutledge, Newsome, halfback Tony Nathan, and the guts of the defense back, 'Bama rallied from an early-season loss to Nebraska in 1977 to finish 10–1, capture another SEC championship, and earn a showdown with Woody Hayes's Ohio State Buckeyes in the Sugar Bowl. Billed as a titanic matchup of legends, the game featured the sport's two winningest active college coaches, who owned more than four hundred combined victories as well as a similar bulldog mentality. But number-three Alabama outclassed the number-seven Buckeyes, 35–6, in a performance worthy of a national championship.

"Our winning doesn't have anything to do with me being a better football coach than Woody," Bryant said afterward. "Woody is a great football coach . . . and I ain't bad."

After number-five Notre Dame knocked off number-one Texas in the Cotton Bowl, number-six Arkansas upset number-two Oklahoma in the Orange Bowl, and number-thirteen Washington shocked number-four Michigan in the Rose Bowl to complete the strangest New Year's Day since 'Bama leapfrogged to the national title in 1965, the Crimson Tide faced the Fighting Irish once more at the ballot box—and lost. Although

Notre Dame had been upset during the regular season by lowly Ole Miss—a team Alabama trounced, 34–13—the Irish jumped past 'Bama to claim the prize by a skinny margin in both polls. On the field and in the polls, the Bear just couldn't beat Notre Dame.

"I'm disappointed for our players and staff," Bryant said after the results were announced. "But Notre Dame has our congratulations."

Despite Alabama's unparalleled success and Bryant's unmatched marquee value, opposing recruiters were beginning to score points with a line 'Bama coaches found difficult to counter: *The Bear's not going to coach forever.* "There's no telling how many good players we lost with that line," said recruiting coordinator Clem Gryska. "Kids wanted to play for him, but were afraid he would retire while they were playing." The Bear would see about that. He decided to create an elixir for his own old age.

14
The Number

SEVERAL WEEKS AFTER THE 1977 football season ended, Charley Thornton found himself flipping through the voluminous NCAA record book, past a century of college football's fine print, in search of The Number. Bear Bryant's longtime publicity director, an amiable, somewhat stocky man with a round face, reached for a pen and a piece of scratch paper and performed some basic arithmetic. Excited by the results of his scribbling, he asked his secretary to type up the figures, and later on the very same day, he took the paper to his boss, who thanked him and stuffed it in a desk drawer without further comment.

Months later, while driving to a speaking engagement in Birmingham, the coach, sitting in the front passenger seat of his car, looked up from his legal pad with a rather frustrated expression. Billy Varner, his bodyguard, sat behind the wheel and Thornton rode in the backseat as they traversed the northbound lanes of Interstate 59, the surrounding countryside a blur of greenery in their wake. "I haven't got anything to talk about today," Bryant mumbled, turning toward his publicity man. "You remember that deal you brought me about Stagg?"

Amos Alonzo Stagg, born during the Civil War, educated at Yale when the electric lightbulb represented the cutting edge of technology, began his coaching career in 1890, when a touchdown counted five points. Credited with innovations ranging from the huddle to the man in motion, Stagg coached for a staggering fifty-seven seasons at Springfield, Chicago, and Pacific—institutions of higher learning that have long since abandoned any aspirations toward big-time football—and became the winningest coach in college football history by capturing 314 victories against 199 defeats and 35 ties, for a 60.5 winning percentage. A rather stern man with flowing white hair, he coached into his eighty-fourth year and took The Number to his grave, his link to forever as certain as Babe Ruth's magical, unbreakable 714.

Even as Hank Aaron redefined the meaning of forever in baseball, Paul "Bear" Bryant crept closer and closer to Stagg's monumental achievement. On the night in 1971 when he sprang the wishbone on unsuspecting Southern Cal, the Bear notched number 200, snatching it amid the whispers of his own coaching obituary. Only five men before him had won so many. The 23–10 victory over Charley McClendon's LSU Tigers in 1975 that secured an unprecedented fifth straight SEC championship served also to make him only the third man in history to amass 250 wins. Heading into the 1978 season, Bryant owned 273 victories and trailed only Stagg (314) and Glenn "Pop" Warner (313) on the all-time list.

Although Bryant needed just forty-two more victories to become the winningest coach in the history of the game, his age loomed large in any realistic consideration of a run for the record. He would turn sixty-five in September, and the cavernous wrinkles lining his face made him look a decade older at least. His had been a life lived hard, and it showed. Rival recruiters, anxious to seize any advantage during Alabama's unprecedented stampede through the conference, began to use the Bear's age and his "imminent" retirement against him in the early 1970s. With each passing year, an increasing number of talented high-school players bought the perfectly logical assumption: Even the greatest couldn't coach forever.

So, after Thornton told his boss all he could remember about the figures he had assembled several months earlier, Bryant stood up before a group of Birmingham football fans and announced his final, most historic goal: The Bear was gunning for Stagg. He said he was prepared to coach "at least four more years" to become the winningest coach in college football history, which was how long it would take if the Crimson Tide kept averaging 10.6 victories per season. Although he spent much of the impromptu announcement playing down the aspect of personal glory in his familiar self-deprecating way, his verbal swagger seeped through a memorable line: "If anybody's going to break Amos Alonzo Stagg's record, it might as well be me!"

A solitary figure not only in pursuit but in survival, the old man embarked on the final adventure of his coaching career after most of his contemporaries had either retired or died. He later told a reporter, "All I know is, I don't want to stop coaching and I don't want to stop winning, so we're gonna break the record unless I die." The chase gave him new life while his old rivals leisurely traveled the world and polished their golf games.

"The difference between me and Coach Bryant," observed longtime Texas coach Darrell Royal, who retired in 1976 at age fifty-two, "was that I was a guy who coached football and then moved on. I didn't want to [coach] forever. I didn't need that. Coach Bryant was a man on a quest, a quest for immortality."

With figurative immortality in his sights, Bryant, like most men aging into their late sixties, confronted the grim reality of his own creeping mortality. The decades of hard living—punctuated by all the whiskey and cigarettes and pushing and prodding and worrying about getting over that next mountain—exacted a heavy toll, and as he pursued Stagg, he struggled with a variety of ailments. The top of his desk looked like a pharmacy. His walk grew slow and labored, and his arthritis often rendered the simple act of crossing his legs difficult and painful. But he never complained, never stopped working sixteen-hour days during the football season. His mind remained sharp even as his once-strong body withered, and he managed to conceal most of his physical infirmities.

"He got to where he wanted me to walk to practice with him every day," Charley Thornton said. "I'd meet him down at the edge of the tunnel [to the practice field] and we'd stand there and go over various things. It finally dawned on me after we'd done this a few times that he wanted to meet me there because he needed to rest" before walking the rest of the way.

During an off-season visit to Florida with his friend Logan Young, the Bear collapsed in the shower, where he lay unconscious when the paramedics arrived. "God," one of them remarked, momentarily stunned, "that's Bear Bryant!" Some time later, he regained consciousness at the hospital with several cracked ribs, sustained in the fall, prompted by what the doctors diagnosed as heart failure.

"Get me out of here," he demanded. "If I'm gonna die I'm gonna die in Alabama!"

So the university's airplane swooped into Palm Beach, retrieved the legend, and flew him back to Tuscaloosa without word leaking to the press. He returned to work within a few days. Some time later, he suffered a minor stroke during a staff meeting, but was back on the practice field within a week.

The night before former Auburn coach Shug Jordan checked into University Hospital in Birmingham for the final time, in the spring of 1980, the two longtime rivals met for drinks at a Southside bar. Bryant was visibly shaken by the news of Jordan's acute leukemia. "You old sonofabitch, you can't die before me!" he said, his arm draped around Shug's shoulders. "You'll get all the headlines!" They drank to the old times like a couple of aging soldiers; within three months, Jordan was dead.

More introspective as he grew older, Bryant became more conscious of his own foibles, including his tendency to drink to excess. Determined to prove a point, he secretly checked himself into an alcohol rehab clinic in Shelby County, south of Birmingham, in the spring of 1978. "Coach said he wanted to prove to himself that he could go down there for a month and not need a drink of whiskey," recalled Logan Young. "He said he didn't think he had a problem, but he wanted to show himself that he could stop drinking for a month if he wanted to. He didn't stop drinking [afterward], but he said he felt great when he left that place."

Throughout his life, Bryant struggled with his spirituality. He believed fervently in God, often led his team in prayer, encouraged his players to go to church, and counted the Reverend Billy Graham as a personal friend, but he knew some of his hard living through the years conflicted with the pure Christian way of life, the way his blessed mama raised him and the other children back on that patch of dirt in Moro Bottom.

His final years included a deep examination of his spiritual side.

In the late 1970s, when former 'Bama quarterback Steve Sloan was the head coach at Ole Miss, he received a call from his old coach, who asked him to fly to Washington, D.C., to meet him the next day. Sloan didn't ask why; he just caught the earliest flight to Dulles. When he arrived at the coach's hotel suite in the middle of a coaching convention, Bryant ushered everybody out and plopped down in the chair opposite his former pupil. Rather than some emergency, Bryant had asked Sloan to fly from Oxford, Mississippi, to Washington, D.C., so they could spend two or three hours discussing theology.

"Coach had a real problem with the concept of grace, which is a gift," Sloan said, "It really weighed heavily on his mind. It was totally opposite of his philosophy of working hard and earning everything you get in this world. He didn't feel like he measured up. He didn't feel like he'd earned the right to be called a Christian."

On an airplane trip to the West Coast during the early 1980s, Bryant found himself seated next to the televangelist Robert Schuller. Although Schuller failed to recognize Bryant on first glance, the Bear struck up a conversation with the preacher. "You're my wife's favorite preacher," he told the silver-haired Schuller as he introduced himself. The two men spent most of the trip talking about religion, and Schuller finally pulled out his boarding pass and wrote down several tenets of his belief. "If you sign this and really believe it, you'll be saved," Schuller told the Bear. Bryant signed it, and although it's impossible to say whether he really experienced a religious epiphany on the airplane ride, he often spoke with pride about the incident with friends and associates in the final years of his life. Bryant was not a man to make frivolous commitments—especially in writing.

Like many workaholic overachievers, Bryant grew to regret how little time he spent with his children during their formative years. In addition to trying to grow closer to Paul Junior and Mae Martin in his golden years—Paul Junior became his principal financial adviser in the 1970s—he spent more time with his grandchildren when they were young. Marc Tyson, Mae Martin's son, was a teenager while his grandfather was chasing Stagg, and during the off-season they often fished together at Lake Martin. Marc was, in fact, the only person capable of curbing the Bear's three-pack-a-day Chesterfield habit; when he got his first new car, he declared it smoke-free, and his grandpa reluctantly respected his wishes.

With barely six minutes to play in the 1979 Sugar Bowl, Alabama defensive tackle Marty Lyons approached Penn State quarterback Chuck Fusina during a time-out. The Superdome roared with the sound of 78,824 delirious fans who had been treated to a classic defensive struggle between two extremely talented, well-coached teams. The noise echoed around the sparkling sea of blue and crimson like a bone-quivering earthquake that refused to shake itself dead. After three failed stabs from inside the 'Bama one-yard line, the unbeaten, number-one-ranked Nittany Lions trailed the once-beaten, number-two Crimson Tide, 14–7, and faced fourth and goal, fourth and the national championship, fourth and history.

"How far do you have to go?" Lyons asked Fusina.

"About ten inches," Fusina replied.

Lyons flashed a determined look. "You'd better pass."

Ignoring the rival defender's cocky gamesmanship, Fusina lined up his team, took the snap, and handed off to tailback Mike Guman, who ran over right tackle. A wall of crimson rose up to stop him, and just as he tried to leap the pile, All-America linebacker Barry Krauss, a wild man from Pompano Beach, Florida, with long curly hair and a devilish grin, drove through the pile and pushed him back, stopped him cold with help from a swarm of defenders led by cornerback Murray Legg and linebacker Rich Wingo. The Bear owned his fifth national championship, and Alabama fans basked in the glow of a defining moment of their age at the summit of college football.

"We asked ourselves for a gut check," Krauss said afterward, echoing one of his coach's pet phrases. "When you are tired and hurting, that's all you can do. We wanted it badly."

Several months later, limited-edition lithographs of *The Goal-Line Stand* by twenty-two-year-old University of Alabama art graduate Daniel A. Moore began showing up in mansions and house trailers alike across the Heart of Dixie, cementing the transcendence of a moment when 'Bama refused to yield. Like all true works of art, it evokes something deeper than the crucial play; although Alabama has produced many outstanding offensive stars through the years, the reign of the Bear is defined in the consciousness of the Crimson Tide faithful by the rock-ribbed, unbreakable defenses symbolized by *The Goal-Line Stand*. It reflects what 'Bama people believe about the sport, their team, and their legendary coach. To the Alabama fans who were shaped by the Bear Bryant era, football will always be less a game of individual skill than of the steely determination of their eleven versus the other team's eleven in an ugly, bloody, exhausting test of wills. When the Bear's great defensive teams lined up with the game in the balance, Alabama people took comfort in the challenge, because they knew the game meant more to their boys, and they knew that their boys, more often than not, would find a way to win.

After sharing the 1978 national championship with Southern Cal—which handed the Tide a 24–14 defeat, the last time any team would stop 'Bama for more than two full years—the Crimson Tide finished 12–0 and captured both the UPI and AP trophies in 1979, the peak season of the Bryant era. His wishbone, led with skill by the prototypical option quarterback, Steadman Shealy, churned up yards with a methodical nonchalance, averaging a league-best 31.9 points per game. Major Ogilvie was a bigger, faster Johnny Musso, and he became the first back to score touchdowns in four consecutive New Year's Day bowls. The defense, anchored by All-America cornerback Don McNeal, and E. J. Junior, and tackle Byron Braggs, became his fourth and final unit to lead the nation in scoring defense (5.3 points per game) while recording five shutouts. Scholarship restrictions imposed by the NCAA in 1976 were well on their way toward fundamentally altering the game, but 'Bama remained capable of fielding three complete units and smothering lesser teams with its enormous depth.

Although the 24–9 domination of Arkansas in the Sugar Bowl seemed more like a coronation than a battle, the Tide proved its mettle at midseason by rallying from a 17–0 halftime deficit to stun Tennessee, 27–17. 'Bama also came from behind in the fourth quarter to knock off archrival Auburn, 25–18.

The steel in Shealy's spine was reinforced during his junior year of 1978, when he shared playing time with senior Jeff Rutledge. After sustaining a knee injury during the spring, he returned to practice the week of a big game against Missouri, and none of the offensive coaches wanted to play him. They were skeptical of his recovery, doubtful of his ability to return to playing shape in less than four months. Bryant interceded. He recognized Shealy's toughness, and he also realized that the former Dothan high-school star needed to play immediately to surmount the lingering psychological effects of his injury, so he overruled his offensive coaches and inserted him during the first quarter against Missouri. Shealy ran for a first down on his first snap and led the Tide to a field goal in an eventual 38–20 road victory.

"Coach Bryant stood up for me when, in the view of the other coaches, it didn't make a lot of sense," recalled Shealy, who became as close to the boss as any player of the era. "A lot of the coaches had written me off."

Although Bryant mellowed in his later years, he retained a firm grip on every aspect of his team. "When he came out of that tower," noted split end Keith Pugh, "one of two things was about to happen: Either practice was over or somebody was gonna get their butt chewed out." Discipline remained the dominant feature of the program. The trains always ran on time, and his teams continued to excel because they were better prepared, better conditioned, and made fewer mistakes than their opponents. They also won because the old man knew how to suppress all those egos in order to promote a game in which seventy to eighty players routinely saw action.

Jasper's Linnie Patrick was a direct challenge to the Bear Bryant school of football. A perfect physical specimen at six feet and two hundred pounds, he ran the forty-yard dash in 4.3 and arrived in Tuscaloosa as a freshman in 1980 with an incredible pedigree. Widely compared to Herschel Walker, who joined the Georgia team the same season, Patrick was a running back for the ages, with speed, moves, and strength, but he was also full of himself. The product of a poor environment without a stable male influence, he was too much for his mother to handle, and he saw Alabama as little more than a way station between Jasper and the NFL. During the state high-school all-star game in the summer of 1980, he bragged to a reporter, "I'll win three straight Heismans . . . and contend for it my freshman year."

The Bear was not amused. His players didn't win Heismans. They won championships.

"The one thing about Coach Bryant, no matter who you were, sooner or later he was going to gut you," said longtime assistant coach Jack Rutledge. "He was going to find out whether you were prepared to lay it on the line."

During a scrimmage in 1980, Patrick looked like an All-America. "Man, for about ten carriers, he was really rippin'," said offensive lineman Willard Scissum. "Nobody could lay a hand on him, much less tackle him." Then Patrick decided he'd had enough, so he walked away from the huddle and pulled off his helmet.

"I can't run no more," he said.

Bryant bolted from the tower, ran up to Patrick, and shoved the helmet back on his head as the entire team watched. The coach, holding Patrick by the face mask, gave the young man a refresher course on the hierarchy of command. Then he ran him until he couldn't stand up.

Although Patrick would produce moments of glory in an

Alabama uniform, he spent much of his career in the Bear's doghouse with a variety of disciplinary problems. While Herschel Walker won a Heisman Trophy, Patrick never earned so much as All-SEC, although he later played in the United States Football League. Two years after his first gut check, he continued to confound his coach, who lamented to a reporter, "What I would give if I could reach that young man, make him understand the importance of total dedication and discipline."

Seven games into the 1980 season, the Crimson Tide was ranked number one, riding a school-record twenty-eight-game winning streak, and smelling an unprecedented third straight national championship. A 45–0 win over Kentucky gave Bryant three hundred wins for his career, pushing him within striking distance of the record in 1981. But the wishbone started showing fissures; teams were beginning to learn how to defense the offense, and worse, 'Bama started doing the unthinkable: beating itself. Driving for a go-ahead touchdown in the waning moments against Mississippi State, the Tide fumbled within the shadow of the goal line, and the Bulldogs claimed a 6–3 upset—their first victory over 'Bama since 1957, the year before the Bear returned to Tuscaloosa. It was the Tide's first SEC loss in five years, only their fourth in a decade. Two weeks later, another costly turnover set up the winning touchdown in Notre Dame's 7–0 victory, which ran the Fighting Irish's record to 4–0 against the Bear, by margins of one, two, three, and seven points. For only the second time since 1971, 'Bama—which finished 10–2 and ranked sixth—failed to win the Southeastern Conference championship.

In Alabama, the march to 315 in 1981 was hyped like a Super Bowl and a moon shot rolled into one. There were songs devoted to the number; it was painted on faces, houses, T-shirts and, invisibly, across Bryant's scalp. The constant media attention became a distraction to the team and a burden to the coach, who grew weary of the incessant questions about something other than the Tide's annual pursuit of the national championship. "He'd pooh-pooh it in public," noted Bill Battle, who served as his marketing representative during the period, "but those close to him could tell all that attention weighed heavily on him. He just wanted to get it over with."

The Crimson Tide opened the season needing nine victories to place the Bear's name in the history books, but a 24–21 loss to Georgia Tech in week two was like a splash of cold water. The Yellow Jackets didn't win another game the rest of the year, and the upset represented the first time in anyone's memory that a Bryant-coached team had lost to such an inferior opponent. Thanks to a time-out called in error by the 'Bama coaching staff, Southern Miss kicked a late field goal and escaped with a 13–13 tie in October. Like a moon shot, the record attempt was bumped back another week.

Although the Crimson Tide finished unbeaten in conference play and 9–1–1 overall to win a share of its ninth SEC crown in eleven years, the aura of invincibility was quickly fading in Tuscaloosa. Several highly publicized suspensions—and an altercation with halfback Kenny Simon involving a gun—made the Bear's program seem in turmoil. History became a consolation prize, and after drawing even with Stagg with an impressive 31–16 victory over number-five Penn State, the record took center stage in the Iron Bowl, where such an attempt belonged, if it could not be thrown into a postseason showdown for the national championship, something that only happens in the movies.

With ABC's national television crew and several dozen former Bryant players squeezed among the capacity Legion Field crowd of 78,219, Pat Dye's 5–5 Auburn Tigers gave 'Bama a fight befitting the stakes. Dye, a former Bryant assistant, later conceded his ambivalence about attempting to block the master's path to the history books, but his underdog Tigers entered the dressing room with a 7–7 tie at the half. The Tide's wishbone sputtered, its defense fell to several Auburn big plays, and as his walked the floor, the Bear gave his team a tongue-lashing.

"You're acting like you're playing your little brothers, or children, or something," he scolded. "Like you're afraid you're going to get hurt or hurt *them.*"

Fired up, 'Bama took the opening kickoff of the second half, drove inside the Auburn thirty-yard line, and then the Bear went to his book of tricks. Quarterback Ken Coley dropped back and raised his arms as if he were going to pass for the end zone, which baited the Auburn defense. Meanwhile, receiver Jesse Bendross pulled like a guard, and just at the moment he passed behind the center, Coley flicked Bryant's famous "whoopie" pass to the sophomore speedster from Hollywood, Florida, who darted twenty-six yards for a touchdown.

Two fumbles deep in 'Bama territory by punt returner Joey Jones led to an Auburn touchdown by Lionel James and a field goal by Al Del Greco, which staked the Tigers to a 17–14 lead with 12:58 left. Could the record chase be chased to the Cotton Bowl against Texas?

Custom and pride in those days dictated that the Alabama players, whether trailing or in the lead, hold four fingers aloft at the start of the fourth quarter, because the fourth quarter always belonged to 'Bama. And it did once more. After Auburn placed the record in jeopardy, sophomore quarterback Walter Lewis marched the Tide downfield and drilled a thirty-eight-yard strike to Bendross for a 21–17 'Bama lead. Then Linnie Patrick emerged from Bryant's doghouse to add an insurance touchdown that ranked among the prettiest runs in 'Bama history, and the Bear owned the number 315 by a margin of 28–17.

"Coach Bryant tells us to keep the faith and not give up," Bendross said after the victory. "If you don't think you can get beat, you won't."

In the postgame melee inside the custom-designed media trailer pulled up behind the south end zone to accommodate the horde of notebooks and flashbulbs, Bryant humbly accepted the record on behalf of all the players, coaches, managers, alumni, and fans of Maryland, Kentucky, Texas A&M, and Alabama. He aw-shucksed his way through the obligatory congratulatory call from President Reagan, and he talked about how proud he was of his team for coming back, for not giving up.

Some weeks later, after reflection, he told a reporter, "I don't feel like we broke Mr. Stagg's record. He had a small budget and a small staff. We have a big budget and a big staff. I think we set our own record."

Although the records of the two men cannot be fairly compared, Bryant is no more defined by the sum of his victories than Babe Ruth was diminished when Hank Aaron hammered past his home run record. But the 315 provides some powerful clues about the man's life. The number testifies to his remarkable ability to win at a high level in three distinct eras in four diverse situations, and more important, to his unsated hunger to cling to the game when age, health, and perhaps even reason suggested he retire to the beach with a stack of paperbacks. Like those boys of his in that ubiquitous painting, the game meant something powerful to him—and he to the game.

"Bear was one of those rare individuals who was truly never satisfied with what he had achieved," said former Arkansas coach Frank Broyles, who won 149 games over twenty-one years. "Most coaches have a hard time maintaining that kind of desire, but he always managed to get hungrier, even after incredible success. He was the only one who could set that record. He was the only one who wanted it enough to sacrifice all those years."

The following March, prominent figures in sports, politics, business, and other fields gathered in Washington, D.C., to laud the new recordholder in a black-tie affair billed as "America's Tribute to Paul (Bear) Bryant." Emceed by Bob Hope, with special tributes by Alabama's senators and congressmen—even Governor Fob James, an Auburn man, said a few words—the gala attracted more than two hundred former players from the four schools where the legend took root, and everybody had a ball. No one said so out loud, of course, but all of the former players walked into the shadows thinking about how old their coach looked, how very old and worn out. For the first time in

his life, there were no doubters left to prove wrong, no records
to chase except his own.

15

As Long As They Want Me

AFTER REACHING HIS RECORD-SETTING 315th victory, Paul "Bear" Bryant vowed to coach "as long as the university wants me." His 1982 Alabama football team looked loaded and primed for another run at the national championship. Although the sixty-nine-year-old legend's health was much worse than most of his friends and associates realized, his doctors had stopped trying to convince him to retire, although they did keep nagging him about his smoking. The demanding routine of a big-time football coach exacted a heavy toll, but the love of the game helped him forget that every time he walked onto the practice field.

"I'm a tired old man, but I never get tired of football," he told a reporter before the season. "The football, the involvement with the young people . . . that's just my life."

With the distraction of the record chase pushed aside, Bryant seemed more relaxed; there was no one left to chase except himself. After spring practice, he spent several weeks away from the office on the pretense of a vacation to North Africa, where he had been stationed during World War II. In reality, he was recovering from plastic surgery. After two or three years of discussion with Mary Harmon—who feared seeing her husband go under the knife—he finally allowed Birmingham plastic surgeon Gaylon McCollough (the center on his 1964 national championship team) to slice some of the "turkey wattle" from around his neck. He returned to the office looking younger, and eagerly anticipating his thirty-eighth year as a major-college head coach, with a team ranked fourth in the preseason Associated Press poll.

Below the surface, however, the Bryant dynasty was cracking under the weight of his age.

Before the 1981 season, former Alabama assistant coach Pat Dye disregarded his mentor's advice and accepted the head-coaching position at Auburn, rather than wait a few years to have a shot at the Alabama job when the Bear retired. While the Bear genuinely liked and respected Dye and saw him as a possible successor, he desperately did not want to compete against the man who appeared to be, in many ways, a younger version of himself. Twenty-five years Bryant's junior, Dye had learned much from the master, especially how to work. Although his first team struggled to a 5–6 finish, the youthful, energetic coach and recruiter provided a stark contrast to his former boss. Time was on his side, and he was determined to out-Bryant Bryant.

"Coaching is a young man's game," Bryant remarked before the 1982 season. "You never see old men winning championships. We're surrounded. All these people are recruiting better than we are."

Although he often denied rumors of his impending retirement, Bryant could no longer promise high-school recruits in good conscience that he would be their coach for four years. The uncertainty clouded the Crimson Tide's recruiting efforts, and in 1982, for the first time in recent memory, Auburn won the in-state battle for talent.

Most ominous of the losses was McAdory High School running back Vincent "Bo" Jackson, the state's top prospect. In addition to citing the belief that if he signed with Alabama he could not hope to play for the Bear for his entire college career, Jackson and his mother expressed concern about the highly publicized discipline problems experienced by the Alabama program during the 1981 season. Amid all the media scrutiny that accompanied Bryant's pursuit of Stagg, the incidents made the 'Bama program seem out of control.

"My mother doesn't feel right about me going to Alabama," Jackson told the *Birmingham Post-Herald*'s Paul Finebaum before signing day, striking a tremendous public-relations blow to the Tide's recruiting efforts. "They've had so much trouble this past season that she wouldn't rest with me down there."

If the future seemed cloudy, the present wore a crimson glow. After watching his wishbone sputter at times in both 1980 and 1981, Bryant slightly modified his offense to include more I-formation plays and take advantage of the rollout passing skills of junior quarterback Walter Lewis. Early results were impressive, including a 45–7 blistering of Georgia Tech in the opener, a payback for the 1981 upset administered by the Yellow Jackets. After a 42–21 victory over eventual national champion Penn State on October 9, the 5–0 Crimson Tide climbed to second in the wire-service polls. 'Bama fans could smell another title.

But then the world turned upside down. The week after the impressive victory over Penn State, the Crimson Tide was upset by unranked Tennessee, 35–28, in Knoxville. It was the Volunteers' first victory over 'Bama since 1970. After unimpressive wins over Cincinnati and Mississippi State that ran the record to 7–1, the Crimson Tide suffered the most devastating month in the history of the program. November 1982 was a nightmare for 'Bama, a surreal comeuppance for all those years of unrelenting dominance.

No Alabama team under Bryant was ever manhandled the way LSU dominated the Crimson Tide in the first half of the 1982 game in Birmingham. The vaunted wishbone could not manage a single first down in the half. Although 'Bama fought back to make it a game in the second half, the Tigers' 20–10 victory—their first over the Tide since 1970—was a chilling wake-up call. The Bryant era was over. Whether the old man called it a career or not, the era of untrammeled dominance was in the past.

Seven days later, Southern Miss, led by scrambling quarterback Reggie Collier, upset the disintegrating Tide, 39–28, to halt an NCAA-record fifty-seven-game winning streak at Bryant-Denny Stadium. Not since 1963 had a Bryant-coached team been beaten in Tuscaloosa. As he walked off the field, the coach stopped and gazed at the scoreboard in disbelief.

The next day, on the way into a Birmingham television studio to tape the *Bear Bryant Show*, the coach lamented his own lapses to Steadman Shealy, his cohost: "I should've put eight men on the line and made that boy throw! Can't believe I didn't do that."

Although his staff maintains they saw no diminution of his coaching abilities during the 1982 season, the events of November shook Bryant's confidence. When Ed Hinton of *The Atlanta Constitution* stopped by for an interview the Monday after the loss to Southern Miss, he found the man unusually subdued. Instead of motioning the reporter to the couch that had swallowed so many visitors like quicksand, the coach pulled up a chair next to his elevated desk from which he had stared down his questioners. They talked for a while, and finally Bryant said, "I can't coach 'em anymore," and stared off into the distance.

"I just knew it was over," recalled Hinton. "There was a feeling of finality about that interview."

After the loss to LSU, Bryant started dropping hints about retirement. Although most in the state's sports media continued to fawn over him, Don Kausler, Jr., of the *Birmingham News* called for the Bear's retirement, and in reply received several death threats and hate mail by the bag. "I was hired to come in and treat him like any other coach," said the University of Missouri graduate, now executive sports editor of the rival *Birmingham Post-Herald*. "But he means so much to this state, it was difficult for many Alabama people to see him get old."

November's cruelest blow came in the Iron Bowl. At the start of the fourth quarter against Auburn, leading 22–14, the Alabama players held aloft their traditional four fingers. But the magic of the fourth quarter was gone for the Crimson Tide. The game ended in a 23–22 loss to the Auburn Tigers, secured by Bo Jackson's one-yard dive with 2:34 left. 'Bama's first loss in a decade to its archrival capped a disastrous 7–4 regular season, the worst mark for a Bryant-coached team since 1970.

On the recruiting trail and in the year's big game, the pupil had finally surpassed the teacher. Through the years, Bryant took tremendous pride in his forty-six pupils who went on to become head coaches, and he relished the opportunity to compete against his students—as evidenced by his lifetime 43–6 record against them—but none of the previous showdowns carried such a sense of finality. Even in the afterglow of the biggest victory of his head-coaching career, Pat Dye was torn between joy and sadness as he stood before a large gathering of reporters. His voice soft and scratchy, almost whispering, he said, "To tell you the truth, I'd rather beat anybody in the world but Coach Bryant. He's done so much for me there's no way I could repay him. It's kind of sad for me."

As usual, Bryant was gracious in defeat. "First of all, I'd like to congratulate Pat and his team," he said. "He certainly did a fine job today as he has all year."

Two weeks later, Bryant walked into a packed news conference on the University of Alabama campus and announced his retirement as head coach. He planned to stay on as athletic director for a few months. Ray Perkins, the steely-eyed New York Giants head coach who had starred as an All-America receiver on Alabama's championship teams of 1964–66, was introduced as his replacement. Despite the bitterly disappointing season, the news shocked the entire state. There was sadness in Bryant's eyes as he read from a prepared statement.

"There comes a time in every profession when you need to hang it up," he said, "And that time has come for me."

Although Bryant's official involvement in the hiring of Perkins was limited to his submitting a list of possible successors to university president Dr. Joab Thomas, many close to the Alabama athletic program believe he wanted Gene Stallings to take the job. Stallings, one of the Junction boys who had coached for Bryant at Alabama, was then a top aide to Cowboys coach Tom Landry. Stallings thought the job was going to be his.

"There ain't no question what [Bryant] wanted," Stallings said.

After the five-member committee formed by Thomas to make the decision rejected Stallings, Bryant, according to several sources in the athletic department, wanted to name Mal Moore as his successor. Moore believed he was going to get the job, but the wheels were already in motion; Thomas's committee was moving independently of the game's foremost expert on coaching talent.

"Coach Bryant called me on the phone and said to come to his office the next day, Sunday afternoon," said Jack Rutledge, who was then the director of Bryant Hall and handled many of his boss's administrative chores. "He was setting it up where Mal would be the guy, and he told me to get ready to have a meeting. But then when I showed up, he said, 'Forget it. It's all been changed. They took it away from me.' He was hurt. I could tell he was hurt. I think the people [Thomas] selected to handle [the selection process] thought [Bryant] was old or whatever and then just didn't go by his wishes."

An hour before he dropped the bombshell at the news conference, the coach broke the news to his team. The players sat in stunned silence. "I felt like us losing those four ballgames is why Coach Bryant retired," said offensive guard Willard Scissum, a sophomore starter on the 1982 team. "There was a lot of guilt among the players . . . [we believed] that we had let him down."

Instead of riding off into the sunset with a national championship on the line, Bryant took his unranked 7–4 team to the Liberty Bowl in Memphis to face unranked 7–4 Illinois on December 29, 1982. the match of also-rans was set before the coach announced his retirement, and after he declared the Liberty Bowl to be his farewell to coaching, the game became the focus of national attention. The temperature in Memphis dipped into the teens that might, and Bryant walked onto the frigid field wearing a parka and an Alabama baseball cap. He looked tired.

Later, he said, "I told the team before the game that people will always remember them and remember me for this game." That was all he needed to say. After the disappointing season and the pangs of guilt, the 'Bama players were determined to send their coach off a winner.

But the final victory of his remarkable career remained in doubt until the very end. The Crimson Tide surrendered 444 yards of total offense to Illini quarterback Tony Eason and company and turned the ball over five times, but somehow managed to win a historic 21–15 victory. It was a game decided, appropriately, by big plays by the 'Bama defense: Tide cornerback Jeremiah Castille tied a Liberty Bowl record with three interceptions, and with the Illini driving for a winning touchdown in the final minute, defensive end Russ Wood blind-sided Eason for a ten-yard loss, sending him to the sideline for the third time with a case of the dizzies. On the next play, linebacker Eddie Lowe intercepted Eason's replacement to secure the victory.

"Any time we got in a tough situation," said Wood, "we lined up and looked at each other eye-to-eye and said, 'Coach Bryant!' In every tight spot, 'Coach Bryant' was the word."

After being carried off the field by his team, the old man made his way to the interview tent. He praised his opponent, named every one of his assistants and thanked them all for their contributions, and minimized his own contribution to his team's victory.

"We won in spite of me," he said, probably for the 323rd time. "I actually had little to do with what they were doing. I don't recall making a decision all night."

More than a half century after he played in the first football game he ever saw, the mama's boy from rural Arkansas stood on top of a mountain of victories and records unlikely to be equaled at the major college level. In 38 seasons, his teams won 323, lost 85, and tied 17 for a winning percentage of 78. Thirty of his teams finished in the nation's top twenty. Twenty-three placed in the top ten: fourteen were in the top five. Twenty-nine played in bowl games. Fifteen captured conference championships. Six won national championships.

His quarter-century in Tuscaloosa included the best record of both the 1960s and 1970s and a cumulative 232–46–9 mark (82 percent).

Several days after his final game, he returned to his office and dictated a letter to be mailed to all his former players:

> ...As I contemplate my many years as a football coach during the post-retirement period, it is not surprising to me that my former players and my former associates are the first people that come to mind. Since you are one of these

people, I want to personally thank you for the contributions you have made to my happy, rewarding career. . . . Also, I want to tell you how proud I am of you and I want to challenge you to become an even bigger winner in life.

To the Bear, football was life. It pulled him out of poverty, provided for his education, and made him rich, famous, and beloved as he taught other young men to strive in his own rugged mold. Football was, to him, an extension of the old-time values of hard work, sacrifice, and discipline, and although he made a career out of self-deprecation, he believed in the importance of the game as more than a game. His was a life shaped by hard times, and the game as he coached it was a reflection of his philosophy of life. Even as he grew old enough to coach the sons of his former players, he clung ever tighter to the game because he could not imagine doing anything else. Only when he believed it was in the best interests of his old school did he decide to make the difficult decision to walk away. He could see his health sliding from poor to worse.

He once predicted he'd "croak in a week" if he stopped coaching. He was off by less than a month.

Twenty-seven days after the Liberty Bowl, on the evening of January 25, 1983, Bryant was rushed to Tuscaloosa's Druid City Regional Medical Center after complaining of severe chest pains. Doctors kept him overnight for observation and expected to release him later the next day. That morning, he met with several visitors, including Ray Perkins, who stopped by on his way out of town on a recruiting trip. They had a nice visit, and the athletic director chided his newest employee for wasting time visiting an old man with a little heart pain.

Even while confined to the hospital bed, the Bear kept a yellow legal pad at his side, making notes, making plans. Before Perkins left, Bryant asked him if he was going to offer Charles Bradshaw, Jr., a scholarship. The young man's father had played for Bryant at Kentucky and coached for him at

Alabama, and Bryant wanted to make sure he had a way to earn an education. When Perkins said he didn't think the wide receiver from Dothan was good enough to warrent an SEC scholarship, the coach said that was fine, he'd make room for him under the Bryant scholarship program at Alabama. He made a telephone call, and it was done.

"[Mary Harmon] told me about that the next day," recalled Martha Gibbs, Bradshaw's mother. "I was just stunned. That's just the kind of man he was. That he would think of helping my Charles right before . . ."

Less than two hours later, at 12:24 P.M., Paul William Bryant was sitting up in his bed trying to eat lunch when he suffered a sudden cardiopulmonary arrest. Attempts to revive him were unsuccessful, and he was pronounced dead at 1:30 P.M. He was sixty-nine years old.

The health problems Bryant had experienced in the final three years of his life "make his achievements all the more remarkable," according to his personal physician, Dr. William Hill. Only after the Bear's death did Alabamians learn of the stroke, the incident of heart failure, and the various other medical problems that had plagued him as he kept fighting for victories.

"He was a very courageous man," Hill said. "I seriously doubt there are many people who could have overcome what he did the last three years to accomplish so much."

The news spread across the state of Alabama like a fog. It was a dreary, overcast day, and when television and radio stations interrupted regularly scheduled programming to break the news, it was met with a range of reactions: stunned silence, weeping, denial. As with the day John F. Kennedy was assassinated, Alabamians of all races, sexes, and ages would remember where they were and how they felt. One future 'Bama quarterback, all of ten years old, was sitting in his fifth-grade classroom in suburban Birmingham when his teacher ran into the room, crying, and broke the news. Shivers ran down his spine.

"We thought he would never die," said Jay Barker, who would grow up to lead the Crimson Tide to the 1992 national championship.

Steadman Shealy, working toward his degree at the University of Alabama School of Law, was sitting through a lecture in his tax class when someone rushed in with the bombshell. Stunned, the former 'Bama quarterback ran out into the hall and cried like a baby.

Frank Broyles and Darrell Royal were playing the back nine at La Quinta Country Club near Palm Springs. Someone from the clubhouse came out to break the news to the two former football coaches. "We just walked off the course," Royal said. "We really didn't know what to do, but we didn't feel like playing golf anymore."

When word reached the Acapulco theater where Joe Namath was preparing for a performance of *The Rainmaker,* he dropped his head into his hands in disbelief. The director told him he didn't have to go on with the show, but he did. He had a commitment to the audience, and Coach Bryant would have wanted him to fulfill that responsibility, he said.

Someone from Texas A&M reached John David Crow at his daughter's house. "I felt numb . . . like I'd lost my father," he said.

Even the tony *New Yorker* was touched by the passing of the foremost southern icon. "When I heard on the radio that he had died, and I started to cry," wrote a "Talk of the Town" columnist, "I knew I was just part of a big chorus."

The state of Alabama descended into an unofficial two-day period of mourning leading up to the funeral—Governor George Wallace ordered all state flags lowered to half-staff—and condolences and praise for the man poured in from throughout the nation. President Ronald Reagan, who called Mary Harmon the night of Bryant's death, lauded the coach as "a man who always seemed larger than life," who "made legends out of ordinary people."

"He was simply the best there ever was," said former Nebraska coach Bob Devaney.

In a scene befitting a state funeral, Bryant's memorial service was conducted in one Tuscaloosa church and piped into two others via closed-circuit television, but the crowds still spilled over into the streets. Dozens of former players sat and stood alongside various state, local, and national politicians, national sports figures, and members of the news media. Eight members of the 1982 Alabama football team served as pallbearers. Regular programming on television and radio stations throughout the state was preempted to cover the funeral and the burial.

Reverend Joe Elmore, pastor of the First United Methodist Church, praised Bryant for his "long years of influence on young people, challenging them to excellence, discipline, confidence, and hard work."

Woody Hayes, banished from Ohio State University after slugging a Clemson player four years before, stood under a tree and recalled being on the practice field as a player the day Knute Rockne died. "I have the same feeling today," he said. "Rockne was the great coach of his era. Bryant was the great coach of his era. There'll never be another like him."

The greatest testament to Bryant's life, however, was the thousands of ordinary citizens who lined the fifty-five-mile route between the Tuscaloosa churches and Elmwood Cemetery in Birmingham, where he was laid to rest. Their tribute was silent, but it was powerful. Some dressed in black, others in crimson. Some tacked signs onto overpasses. One sign read, "We love you, Coach. Thanks for the memories." As the funeral procession moved up Interstate 59, truckers could be seen standing in front of their rigs on the shoulder of the expressway, their ballcaps pressed against their hearts.

"It was the most amazing sight I've ever seen," recalled former Southern Cal coach John McKay. "Like a presidential funeral procession. No coach in America could've gotten that. No coach but him, but then, he wasn't just a coach. He was *the* coach."

Several weeks after the funeral, Butch Baldone, one of the coach's longtime friends, stopped by to see Mary Harmon. "You know, Butch," she said, suddenly looking very frail as she sat on the side of her bed, "I never thought I'd miss Paul, 'cause he was always gone. But every time he left, he always came back to me. I keep waiting for him to come back to me."

16
Afterwards

TIMING WAS ONE OF PAUL "Bear" Bryant's greatest strengths—even in death. Although his sudden passing robbed him of a well-deserved retirement and left a terrible void in the lives of his family and friends, the circumstances of his demise actually enhanced his mystique. The world never had to watch him grow infirm and irrelevant. He died near the peak of his career as the most imposing presence in the coaching profession, the most dominant figure in the state of Alabama. If his climactic last season undoubtedly assumed a melancholy tone, he was still Bear Bryant to the end—strong, charismatic, proud—and like John Wayne's character in his final film, *The Shootist*, he went out in a blaze of glory, as if on cue.

Nearly a quarter-century later, Bryant still dominates the Alabama football program. You can feel it during the pregame frenzy at Bryant-Denny Stadium, when the crowd goes wild at the site of his craggy face on the giant video screen, which somehow seems too small to contain his overarching presence. You can see it walking through the hall of memories at the Paul W. Bryant Museum, where the procession of fathers and sons often resembles a sacred pilgrimage. You can hear it in the way fans of a certain age speak of the coach, their admiration of him undiminished by the passage of time, their deference toward him unaffected by the onslaught of a more cynical age.

"The people love Coach Bryant and just tolerate the rest of us," Gene Stallings, one of the men who followed him, once remarked.

Because Alabama people love him so much, because his high-achieving era still means so much to them, Bryant remains the context for everything in Tuscaloosa. The residue of the Bear's untrammeled ambition can be connected to all of the success the Alabama program has achieved since his death, including the 1992 national championship, the high-water mark of the post-Bryant era. Even from the grave, he pushes the Crimson Tide to reach. But the zeal to live up to his lofty standards also produced two NCAA probations, leaving the program crippled from severe scholarship reductions at the dawn of the 21st century.

The Bear taught his teams—and by extension, their legion of fans—to strive with eternal vigilance, to set the highest goals, and settle for nothing less than domination. But he never taught them how to compete against the yardstick of the greatest coach of all time, or how to deal with the disappointment of falling short.

In the twenty-two years since his death, the Alabama program has been forced to battle new age powerhouses at Auburn, Florida, and Tennessee while simultaneously shadowboxing the legacy of a legend whose name is invoked at every turn. On talk shows and in living rooms across the state, every decision related to the program he left behind is held up to the light of his well-chronicled, mythologized career. At times, Alabama has dominated. At times, the Crimson Tide has wallowed in mediocrity. But in the world of Alabama football, Bryant is a constant, like hash marks and goal posts.

The struggle to find a flamekeeper has led to a period of unprecedented turmoil and instability in Tuscaloosa. Seven different men have walked his field, desperately trying to make Alabama Alabama again, and all have been defined, one way or another, by their relationship to his enduring shadow.

Ray Perkins, who presided over 'Bama's first losing season in more than a quarter-century, survived a rocky start and appeared to have the program on the right track. But his abrasive style alienated many supporters, and some of his decisions were interpreted as an attempt to distance himself from the Bryant era. He eventually returned to the NFL, accepting a record-setting five-year, $3.7 million deal to coach the Tampa Bay Buccaneers.

"There'll never be another Coach Bryant and I always understood that," Perkins said. "I'm not so sure some of the fans understood. They're always going to want Coach Bryant. Always."

By contrast, Bill Curry, who took over the program in 1987, went out of his way to embrace Bryant's memory. Soon after his controversial hiring, he returned the Bear's tower to the practice field and rehired the longtime radio announcer who had been banished by Perkins.

"I never had the illusion that I was going to fill the shoes of Coach Bryant," said Curry, who compiled a four-year record of 26–10. "But hugging that tradition was a great tool."

Curry talked a good game, but hiring the former Georgia Tech coach, who arrived in Tuscaloosa with a losing record and with no ties to the program, was a huge mistake. He never connected with the 'Bama nation and, after guiding the Tide to a share of the SEC title in 1989, he bolted Tuscaloosa for the lower expectations of conference also-ran Kentucky.

Determined not to make the same mistake twice, the university administration turned to the Alabama family for a savior. Like Curry, 55-year-old Gene Stallings was burdened with a losing record as a head coach. But his connections to Bryant trumped everything. A survivor of the hellish Junction preseason camp at Texas A&M, Stallings also coached under the master and, according to some accounts, had been the man favored by Bryant to succeed him. Hiring Stallings was a leap of faith, a conscious decision to try to secure the future by trusting once more in the past.

When Stallings walked into a packed news conference in January 1990, he was greeted at the door by Paul Bryant, Jr., who embraced him. "This is exactly what Papa would have wanted," he said, loud enough for all to hear.

While the shadow complicated the lives of both Perkins and Curry, it proved to be a plate of armor for Stallings, who desperately needed to give 'Bama folks a reason to believe, especially after losing his first three games to start the 1990 season. It also helped that Stallings looked and talked like an heir to the master.

"I think people know that I'm not trying to be Coach Bryant or compete with Coach Bryant," Stallings said.

When Stallings turned out to be an outstanding coach—leading the Crimson Tide to a 70-16-1 record, the 1992 national title, and four trips to the SEC Championship Game, building teams around dominant defenses and offenses that rarely beat themselves—the effect was not only to venerate Stallings but also to further strengthen the Bryant mystique's grip on the program. Even from the grave, he could still seem infallible in many eyes.

The desire to keep the job in the family once more held powerful sway when Stallings retired after the 1996 season. Mike DuBose, Stallings' defensive coordinator, was elevated to the top job as much for his pedigree as his coaching skills. He was one of Bear's boys. It was that simple. But he proved to be a disaster, producing two losing seasons in four years and a gathering NCAA storm, which led to the hiring of Dennis Franchione, a turnaround artist from Texas Christian with no ties to the program. Franchione beat all expectations and then broke 'Bama's heart. Because the program didn't mean the world to him, he wound up using Tuscaloosa as a stepping stone, and accepted a big deal to coach Texas A&M.

Mike Price, hired away from Washington State, never coached a game. He led the Tide through spring practice in 2003 and then self-destructed. After details of a tawdry, drunken outing at a Florida golf resort hit the media—including a cover story in *Sports Illustrated* that spawned a libel suit—Price was dumped by the Alabama administration with little tolerance for bad publicity. Which led to the appointment of former 'Bama quarterback Mike Shula, who struggled to a 10–15 start amid severe NCAA sanctions and faced a difficult path to success and acceptance with Tide fans hungry for championships and stability.

To those old enough to remember when the old man peered down from his practice field tower like a general surveying his troops, they have all seemed like imposters, like guest hosts waiting for Johnny to come back from vacation. That's not fair. But that's life.

Throughout college football, especially the hypercompetitive SEC, the Bear's hallowed place in the culture of Alabama football is often mocked. The folks who wave the crimson and white shakers and yell, "Roll, Tide, Roll!" with a kind of missionary zeal are frequently ridiculed for living in the past, for allowing a ghost to exert such influence. A message scrawled in shoe polish on the window of an RV parked behind Auburn's Jordan-

Hare Stadium after one Iron Bowl said it all: "The Bear's dead. Get over it!"

Some people just don't understand.

While many insist it would be healthy and productive for Alabama people to once and for all cut the cord, to render their hero to a static place in the history books, he remains a kinetic force, not so much because they consciously refuse to let him go, but because their image of the 'Bama program— and, in a sense, themselves—is inexorably linked to him. Letting go is not an option. The Bryant legend and the Alabama program are indistinguishable. It's impossible to say where one starts and the other stops.

Even as Penn State's Joe Paterno and Florida State's Bobby Bowden surpassed Bryant's record for all-time major college victories, the Bear's legend endured. With each passing year, he seemed less like a flesh and blood contemporary of those men and more like a fossilized monument to an increasingly distant and unrecognizable game.

The record didn't make him Bear Bryant, and in Alabama, three hundred twenty-three was almost beside the point. It was, at the very least, overkill. He was a legend way before he climbed his final mountain.

In Alabama, Bryant remains a giant, not just because of how often he won, but also because of how the sum of all his heroics made Alabama people feel about themselves. Nearly a quarter-century after his death, he remains a big part of every person who cares about Crimson Tide football, and that's why they cannot simply snap a collective finger and render him to the dusty scrapbooks.

Regardless of whether Alabama ever finds a coach to completely live up to his standards, Bryant will forever occupy a sacred place not only in the football program he built, but also in the culture he validated. That space belongs to him, and if the resulting friction is too much for some to take, such is the price of greatness Alabama must bear, until the last memory fades.

He always seemed larger than life, and in death, he seems larger still.

Appendix:
Bryant's Complete Coaching Record

PAUL "BEAR" BRYANT

All-time record: 323-85-17 (.780)
Most all-time major college victories
Six national championships
15 conference championships
29 bowl appearances
Three-time national Coach of the Year
Ten-time SEC Coach of the Year
Member of College Football Hall of Fame
(inducted posthumously in 1986)

YEAR-BY-YEAR RESULTS

Maryland
1945 (6-2-1)

60	Guilford	6
21	Richmond	0
21	Merchant MA	6
13	at Virginia Tech	21
13	at West Virginia	13
14	Wm. & Mary	33
38	VMI	0
19	at Virginia	13
19	South Carolina	13

Kentucky
(8 years, 60-23-5)
1946 (7-3)

20	Mississippi	7
26	at Cincinnati	7
70	Xavier	0
13	at Georgia	28
10	Vanderbilt	7
7	at Alabama	21
39	Michigan State	14
35	at Marquette	0
13	West Virginia	0
0	at Tennessee	7

1947 (8-3)

7	at Mississippi	14
20	Cincinnati	0
20	at Xavier	7
26	Georgia	0
14	at Vanderbilt	0
7	at Michigan State	6
0	Alabama	13
15	at West Virginia	6
36	Evansville	0
6	Tennessee	13
	Great Lakes Bowl	
24	Villanova*	14

* Cleveland, OH

1948 (5-3-2)

48	Xavier	7
7	Mississippi	20
12	at Georgia	35
7	Vanderbilt	26
25	at Marquette	0
28	at Cincinnati	7
13	Villanova	13
34	Florida	15
0	at Tennessee	0
25	at Miami	5

1949 (9-3)

71	Southern Miss.	7
19	at LSU	0
47	at Mississippi	0
25	Georgia	0
44	The Citadel	0
7	at SMU	20
14	Cincinnati	7
21	at Xavier	7
35	at Florida	0
0	Tennessee	6
21	at Miami	6
	Orange Bowl	
13	Santa Clara*	21

* Miami, FL

Final Ranking: 11th AP

1950 (11-1)
SEC Champions

25	North Texas State	0
14	LSU	0
27	Mississippi	0
40	Dayton	0
41	Cincinnati	7
34	at Villanova	7
28	at Georgia Tech	14
40	Florida	6
48	at Mississippi State	21
83	North Dakota U.	0
0	at Tennessee	7
	Sugar Bowl	
13	Oklahoma*	7

* New Orleans, LA

Final Ranking: 7th AP & UPI

1951 (8-4)

72	Tennessee Tech	13
6	at Texas	7
17	at Mississippi	21
7	Georgia Tech	13
27	Mississippi State	0
35	Villanova	13
14	at Florida	6
32	Miami	0
37	at Tulane	0
47	Geo. Washington	13
0	Tennessee	28
	Cotton Bowl	
20	TCU*	7

* Dallas, TX

Final Ranking: 15th AP

1952 (5-4-2)

6	Villanova	25
13	Mississippi	13
10	at Texas A&M	7
7	LSU	34
14	at Mississippi State	27
14	at Cincinnati	6
29	at Miami	0
27	Tulane	6
27	Clemson	14
14	at Tennessee	14
0	at Florida	27

Final Ranking: 17th UPI, 20th AP

1953 (7-2-1)

6	Texas A&M	7
6	at Mississippi	22
26	Florida	13
6	at LSU	6
35	Mississippi State	13
19	Villanova	0
19	at Rice	13
40	at Vanderbilt	14
19	Memphis State	7
27	Tennessee	21

Final Ranking: 15th UPI, 16th AP

Texas A&M
(4 years, 25-14-2)
1954 (1-9)

9	Texas Tech	41
6	Oklahoma State	14
6	at Georgia	0
7	at Houston	10
20	TCU	21
7	at Baylor	20
7	Arkansas	14
3	at SMU	6
19	Rice	29
13	at Texas	22

1955 (7-2-1)

0	at UCLA	21
28	LSU*	0
21	Houston	3
27	at Nebraska	0
19	at TCU	16
19	Baylor	7
7	at Arkansas	7
13	SMU	2
20	at Rice	12
6	Texas	21

* Dallas, TX

Final Ranking: 14th UPI, 17th AP

1956 (9-0-1)
SWC Champions

19	Villanova	0
9	at LSU	6
40	Texas Tech*	7
14	at Houston	14
7	TCU	6
19	at Baylor	13
27	Arkansas	0
33	at SMU	7
21	Rice	7
34	at Texas	21

* Dallas, TX

Final Ranking: 5th AP & UPI

1957 (8-3-0)

21	Maryland*	13
21	at Texas Tech	0
28	Missouri	6
28	Houston	6
7	at TCU	0
14	Baylor	0
7	at Arkansas	6
19	SMU	6
6	at Rice	7
7	Texas	9

	Gator Bowl	
0	Tennessee**	3

* Dallas, TX
** Jacksonville, FL

Final Ranking: 9th AP, 10th UPI

Alabama
(25 years, 232-46-9)
1958 (5-4-1)

3	LSU*	13
0	Vanderbilt**	0
29	Furman	6
7	at Tennessee	14
9	at Mississippi State	7
12	Georgia	0
7	at Tulane	13
17	Georgia Tech	8
14	Memphis State	0
8	Auburn**	14

* Mobile, AL
** Birmingham, AL

1959 (7-2-2)

3	at Georgia	17
3	at Houston	0
7	at Vanderbilt	7
13	Chattanooga	0
7	Tennessee*	7
10	Mississippi State	0
19	Tulane**	7
9	Georgia Tech*	7
14	Memphis State	7
10	Auburn*	0
	Liberty Bowl	
0	Penn State†	7

* Birmingham, AL
** Mobile, AL
† Philadelphia, PA

Final Ranking: 10th AP, 13th UPI

1960 (8-1-2)

21	Georgia*	6
6	at Tulane	6
21	Vanderbilt*	0
7	at Tennessee	20
14	Houston	0
7	at Mississippi State	0
51	Furman	0
16	at Georgia Tech	15
34	Tampa	6
3	Auburn*	0

Bluebonnet Bowl

| 3 | Texas** | 3 |

* Birmingham, AL
** Houston, TX

Final Ranking: 9th AP, 10th UPI

1961 (11-0-0)
National Champions
SEC Champions

32	at Georgia	6
9	Tulane**	0
35	at Vanderbilt	6
26	N.C. State	7
34	Tennessee*	3
17	at Houston	7
24	Mississippi State	0
66	Richmond	0
10	Georgia Tech*	0
34	Auburn*	0

Sugar Bowl

| 10 | Arkansas† | 3 |

* Birmingham, AL
** Mobile, AL
† New Orleans, LA

1962 (10-1)

35	Georgia*	0
44	at Tulane	6
17	Vanderbilt*	7
14	Houston	3
27	at Tennessee	7
35	Tulsa	6
20	at Mississippi State	0
36	Miami	3
6	at Georgia Tech	7
38	Auburn*	0
	Orange Bowl	
17	Oklahoma**	0

* Birmingham, AL
** Miami, FL

Final Ranking: 5th AP & UPI

1963 (9-2-0)

32	at Georgia	7
28	Tulane**	0
21	at Vanderbilt	6
6	Florida	10
35	Tennessee*	0
21	Houston	13
20	Mississippi State	19
27	Georgia Tech*	11
8	Auburn*	10
17	at Miami	12
	Sugar Bowl	
12	Mississippi†	7

* Birmingham, AL
** Mobile, AL
† New Orleans, LA

Final Ranking: 8th AP, 9th UPI

1964 (10-1-0)
National Champions
SEC Champions

31	Georgia	3
36	Tulane**	6
24	Vanderbilt*	0
21	N.C. State	0
19	at Tennessee	8
17	Florida	14
23	Mississippi State†	6
17	LSU*	9
24	at Georgia Tech	7
21	Auburn*	14
	Orange Bowl	
17	Texas‡	21

*Birmingham, AL
** Mobile, AL
† Jackson, MS
‡ Miami, FL

1965 (9-1-1)
National Champions
SEC Champions

17	at Georgia	18
27	Tulane**	0
17	Ole Miss*	16
22	at Vanderbilt	7
7	Tennessee*	7
21	Florida State	0
10	Mississippi State†	0
31	at LSU	7
35	South Carolina	14
30	Auburn*	3
	Orange Bowl	
39	Nebraska‡	28

* Birmingham, AL
** Mobile, AL
† Jackson, MS
‡ Miami, FL

1966 (11-0-0)
SEC Champions

34	La. Tech*	0
17	Mississippi †	7
26	Clemson	0
11	at Tennessee	10
42	Vanderbilt*	6
27	Mississippi State	14
21	LSU*	0
24	South Carolina	0
34	Southern Miss.**	0
34	Auburn*	0
	Sugar Bowl	
34	Nebraska ‡	7

* Birmingham, AL
** Mobile, AL
† Jackson, MS
‡ New Orleans, LA

Final Ranking: 3rd AP & UPI

1967 (8-2-1)

37	Florida State*	37
25	Southern Miss.**	3
21	Mississippi*	7
35	at Vanderbilt	21
13	Tennessee*	24
13	at Clemson	10
13	Mississippi State	0
7	at LSU	6
17	South Carolina	0
7	Auburn*	3
	Cotton Bowl	
16	Texas A&M †	20

* Birmingham, AL
** Mobile, AL
† Dallas, TX

Final ranking: 7th UPI, 8th AP

1968 (8-3-0)

14	Virginia Tech*	7
17	Southern Miss.**	14
8	Mississippi †	10
31	Vanderbilt	7
9	at Tennessee	10
21	Clemson	14
20	Mississippi State	13
16	LSU*	7
14	at Miami	6
24	Auburn*	16
	Gator Bowl	
10	Missouri ‡	35

* Birmingham, AL
** Mobile, AL
† Jackson, MS
‡ Jacksonville, FL

Final Ranking: 12th UPI, 16th AP

1969 (6-5-0)

17	at Virginia Tech	13
63	Southern Miss.	14
33	Mississippi*	32
10	at Vanderbilt	14
14	Tennessee*	41
38	at Clemson	13
23	Mississippi State**	19
15	at LSU	20
42	Miami	6
26	Auburn*	49
	Liberty Bowl	
33	Colorado †	47

* Birmingham, AL
** Jackson, MS
† Memphis, TN

1970 (6-5-1)

21	Southern Cal.*	42
51	Virginia Tech*	18
46	Florida	15
23	Mississippi**	48
35	Vanderbilt	11
0	Tennessee	24
30	Houston	21
35	Mississippi State	6
9	LSU*	14
32	Miami	8
28	Auburn*	33

Astro-Bluebonnet Bowl

24	Oklahoma†	24

* Birmingham, AL
** Jackson, MS
† Houston, Tx

1971 (11-1-0)
SEC Champions

17	at Southern Cal.	10
42	Southern Miss.	6
38	at Florida	0
40	Mississippi*	6
42	at Vanderbilt	0
32	Tennessee*	15
34	Houston	20
41	Mississippi State**	10
14	at LSU	7
31	Miami	3
31	Auburn*	7

Orange Bowl

6	Nebraska†	38

* Birmingham, AL
** Jackson, MS
† Miami, FL

Final Ranking: 2nd UPI, 4th AP

1972 (10-2-0)
SEC Champions

35	Duke*	12
35	Kentucky*	0
48	Vanderbilt	21
25	at Georgia	7
24	Florida	7
17	at Tennessee	10
48	Southern Miss.*	11
58	Mississippi State	14
35	LSU*	21
52	Virginia Tech	13
16	Auburn*	17
	Cotton Bowl	
13	Texas**	17

* Birmingham, AL
** Dallas, TX

Final Ranking: 4th UPI, 7th AP

1973 (11-1)
National Champions
SEC Champions

66	California*	0
28	at Kentucky	14
44	at Vanderbilt	0
28	Georgia	14
35	at Florida	14
42	Tennessee	21
77	Virginia Tech	6
35	Mississippi State**	0
43	Miami	13
21	at LSU	7
35	Auburn*	0
	Sugar Bowl	
23	Notre Dame†	24

* Birmingham, AL
** Jackson, MS
† New Orleans, LA

1974 (11-1)
SEC Champions

21	at Maryland	16
52	Southern Miss.*	0
23	Vanderbilt	10
35	Mississippi**	21
8	Florida State	7
28	at Tennessee	6
41	TCU*	3
35	Mississippi State	0
30	LSU*	0
28	at Miami	7
17	Auburn*	13
	Orange Bowl	
11	Notre Dame†	13

* Birmingham, AL
** Jackson, MS
† Miami, FL

Final Ranking: 2nd UPI, 4th AP

1975 (11-1)
SEC Champions

7	Missouri*	20
56	Clemson	0
40	at Vanderbilt	7
32	Mississippi*	6
52	Washington	0
30	Tennessee*	7
45	TCU*	0
21	Mississippi State**	10
23	at LSU	10
27	Southern Miss.	6
28	Auburn*	0
	Sugar Bowl	
13	Penn State†	6

* Birmingham, AL
** Jackson, MS
† New Orleans, LA

Final Ranking: 3rd AP & UPI

1976 (9-3)

7	Mississippi**	10
56	SMU*	3
42	Vanderbilt	14
0	at Georgia	21
24	Southern Miss.*	8
20	at Tennessee	13
24	Louisville	3
34	Mississippi State	17
28	LSU*	17
18	at Notre Dame	21
38	Auburn*	7

Liberty Bowl

36	UCLA†	6

*Birmingham, AL
** Jackson, MS
† Memphis, TN

Final Ranking: 9th UPI, 11th AP

1977 (11-1)
SEC Champions

34	Mississippi*	13
24	at Nebraska	31
24	at Vanderbilt	12
18	Georgia	10
21	at Southern Cal.	20
24	Tennessee*	10
55	Louisville	6
37	Mississippi State**	7
24	at LSU	3
36	Miami	0
48	Auburn*	21

Sugar Bowl

35	Ohio State†	6

* Birmingham, AL
** Jackson, MS
† New Orleans, LA

Final Ranking: 2nd AP & UPI

1978 (11-1)
National Champions
SEC Champions

20	Nebraska*	3
38	at Missouri	20
14	Southern Cal.*	24
51	Vanderbilt	28
20	at Washington	17
23	Florida	12
30	at Tennessee	17
35	Virginia Tech	0
35	Mississippi State**	14
31	LSU*	10
34	Auburn*	16
	Sugar Bowl	
14	Penn State †	7

* Birmingham, AL
** Jackson, MS
† New Orleans, LA

1979 (12-0)
National Champions
SEC Champions

30	at Georgia Tech	6
45	Baylor*	0
66	at Vanderbilt	3
38	Wichita State	0
40	at Florida	0
27	Tennessee*	17
31	Virginia Tech	7
24	Mississippi State	7
3	at LSU	0
30	Miami	0
25	Auburn*	18
	Sugar Bowl	
24	Arkansas**	9

* Birmingham, AL
** New Orleans, LA

1980 (10-2)

26	Georgia Tech*	3
59	Mississippi**	35
41	Vanderbilt	0
45	Kentucky	0
17	at Rutgers	13
27	at Tennessee	0
42	Southern Miss.	7
3	Mississippi State**	6
28	LSU	7
0	Notre Dame*	7
34	Auburn*	18
	Cotton Bowl	
30	Baylor†	2

* Birmingham, AL
** Jackson, MS
† Dallas, TX

Final Ranking: 6th AP & UPI

1981 (9-2-1)
SEC Champions

24	at LSU	7
21	Georgia Tech*	24
19	at Kentucky	10
28	at Vanderbilt	7
38	Mississippi	7
13	Southern Miss.*	13
38	Tennessee*	19
31	Rutgers	7
13	Mississippi State	10
31	at Penn State	16
28	Auburn*	17
	Cotton Bowl	
12	Texas**	14

* Birmingham, AL
** Dallas, TX

Final Ranking: 6th UPI, 7th AP

1982 (8-4)

45	at Georgia Tech	7
42	Mississippi**	14
24	Vanderbilt	21
34	Arkansas State*	7
42	Penn State*	21
28	at Tennessee	35
21	Cincinnati	3
20	Mississippi State**	12
10	LSU*	20
29	Southern Miss.	38
22	Auburn*	23
	Liberty Bowl	
21	Illinois†	15

* Birmingham, AL
** Jackson, MS
† Memphis, TN

Final Ranking: 17th UPI

Notes

(Unless otherwise indicated, all direct quotes were taken from interviews conducted by the author.)

Chapter One: Fordyce
Page

20 *"I can pass that school now and hear those voices"*: Paul Bryant and John Underwood, *Bear* (New York: Little, Brown, 1974), 21.

21 *"He would teach me a few words"*: Ibid., 22.

24 *"He was meaner than hell growing up"*: *Montgomery Advertiser*, Oct. 7, 1981.

24 *"I would have wrestled King Kong"*: *People*, Oct. 24, 1980, 84.

29 *"If I had been writing"*: Mickey Herskowitz, *The Legend of Bear Bryant* (New York: McGraw-Hill, 1987), 41.

Chapter Two: BMOC
Page

37 *"We all respected him"*: Bryant and Underwood, *Bear*, 44.

37 *"You could win him over just by trying like hell"*: Ibid., 48.

41 *"As far as this season is concerned"*: *The Atlanta Constitution*, Oct. 18, 1935.

Chapter Three: Coach
Page

55 *Dear Grandma:* correspondence archive, Paul Bryant Museum.

59 *"I spent the entire night before throwing up"*: *Huntsville Times*, Sept. 13, 1974.

61 *"I knew I had to quit"*: *Sports Illustrated*, Aug. 22, 1966, 35.

62 *WOULD YOU BE INTERESTED IN POSITION:* correspondence archive, Paul Bryant Museum.

Chapter Four: Kentucky
Page

70 *"I'd rather have a young man quit in practice"*: *Birmingham News*, Sept. 1, 1958.

70 *"If you ask me what makes a young man suck his guts up":* *Sports Illustrated*, Aug. 29, 1966, 28.

75 *"We're about six years behind the other teams":* *Lexington Herald-Leader*, April 26, 1951.

79 *"In his performance, he utilized the combined talents":* Mike Bynum with Jerry Brondfield, *We Believe* (College Station, TX: The We Believe Trust, 1980), 113.

79 *"[Parilli] was the best fake-and-throw passer I have ever seen":* Bryant and Underwood, *Bear*, 98.

84 *"Bud was used to playing against all those children":* Ibid., 102.

89 *"You are still my baby and the sweetest little girl in the world":* correspondence archive, Paul Bryant Museum.

90 *"Shucks, son": Kentucky Kernel*, Oct. 22, 1971.

91 *"I don't know [what I'll be doing next year]":* *Lexington Herald-Leader*, Feb. 7, 1954.

95 *"I didn't know the Aggies then like I know them now":* Bryant and Underwood, *Bear*, 126.

Chapter Five: Junction
Page

104 *"They were usually exhausted and kind of down":* *Dallas Morning News*, Aug. 5, 1990.

105 *"He wanted to come back":* *Dallas Morning News*, Sept. 9, 1954.

106 *"The one thing everyone in that camp seemed to have in common":* Herskowitz, *The Legend of Bear Bryant*, 25.

Chapter Six: Aggie
Page

116 *"You mean to tell me that an alumnus can't give these kids money":* Walter Byers with Charles Hammer, *Unsportsmanlike Conduct* (Ann Arbor: University of Michigan Press, 1995), 121.

116 *"I know now that we should have been put on probation":* *Sports Illustrated*, Aug. 22, 1966, 38.

Chapter Seven: Back to 'Bama
Page

138 *"In a situation such as we accepted here":* *Atlanta Journal*, Aug. 28, 1958.

139 *"The riff-raff are fast eliminating themselves":* *Mobile Press-Register*, Sept. 3, 1958.

139 *"My plan was to bleed 'em and gut 'em":* Bryant and Underwood, *Bear*, 165.

144 *"Before the game we said it'd take a superhuman effort to win":* *Birmingham News*, Nov. 29, 1959.

145 *"The state championship of Alabama means more"*: Sports *Illustrated*, Nov. 21, 1971, 32.

151 *"There are several basic rules by which we expect our quarterbacks to operate"*: Coach & Athlete, Sept. 1960, 12.

152 *"As a quarterback, Pat had no ability"*: Tuscaloosa News, Jan. 11, 1962.

152 *"Pat Trammell was the favorite person of my life"*: Bryant and Underwood, *Bear*, 175.

Chapter Eight: Stormy Days
Page

157 *"Bryant says that his [brand of football] is 'an eye for an eye' "*: Atlanta *Journal*, Aug. 16, 1958.

157 *"Since Bear Bryant came back to Alabama"*: The Saturday Evening Post, Oct. 20, 1962, 47.

158 *"I want players who want to go jaw-to-jaw for sixty minutes"*: Bear Bryant Show archive, Paul Bryant Museum.

161 *"Holt forfeited the right to play college football"*: The Atlanta *Constitution*, Nov. 19, 1961.

161 *"I believe Bryant is encouraging such tactics"*: Atlanta *Journal*, Nov. 22, 1961.

161 *"was no accident"*: The Saturday Evening Post, Oct. 20, 1962, 47.

162 *"There's no doubt Darwin fouled Chick Graning"*: Sports *Illustrated*, Aug. 29, 1966, 28.

165 *"Graning wasn't hit that hard"*: Sports *Illustrated*, Aug. 29, 1966, 35.

167 *Not since the Chicago White Sox threw the 1919 World Series*: The Saturday Evening Post, March 23, 1963, 80.

169 *"We are hitting them where it hurts"*: J. Kirby, *Fumble: Bear Bryant, Wally Butts and the Great College Football Scandal* (San Diego: Harcourt Brace Jovanovich, 1986), 59.

171 *"I have been accused in print of collusion"*: video archive, Paul Bryant Museum.

171 *"Our football team is something sacred to me"*: audio archive, Paul Bryant Museum.

172 *"I used to talk to Coach Woodruff down in Florida"*: Nashville *Banner*, Aug. 17, 1963.

173 *"Absolutely not, and if we did"*: Nashville Banner, Aug. 17, 1963.

175 *"Butts was a symbol"*: Nashville Banner, Aug. 21, 1963.

Chapter Nine: Southern Man
Page

195 *"A football coach really lives football"*: Living Football and Making a Living, audio archive, Paul Bryant Museum.

Chapter Ten: Arms and the Man
Page

207 *"There was no question . . . we had to go for two points"*: *Sports Illustrated*, Nov. 26, 1962, 16.

211 *"When you're that close"*: *Tuscaloosa News*, Jan. 2, 1965.

212 *"I went on a personal campaign to get rid of that rule"*: *Huntsville Times*, Sept. 19, 1982.

215 *"the greatest offensive show I've ever seen"*: *Birmingham News*, Jan. 2, 1966.

218 *"They are better than the score indicates"*: *Tuscaloosa News*, Jan. 2, 1967.

Chapter Eleven: Motivator
Page

227 *"blending inspiration and perspiration"*: *Birmingham News*, April 7, 1982.

228 *"I don't want ordinary people"*: *Coach & Athlete*, Aug. 1972, 15.

233 *"a master at taking average athletes and making them believe they are invincible"*: *Tuscaloosa News*, Dec. 28, 1977.

Chapter Twelve: Integration
Page

250 *"When folks are ignorant you don't condemn them, you teach 'em"*: Bryant and Underwood, *Bear*, 302.

251 *"We strongly oppose our boys playing an integrated team"*: Presidential papers, University of Alabama Archives.

252 *"Dont [sic] you realize the consequences of a most certain repitition [sic]"*: Presidential papers, University of Alabama Archives.

253 *"Alabama. . . . It's a great place to march"*: *Boston Globe*, Nov. 22, 1966.

254 *"We're not recruiting Negro athletes"*: *Look*, Nov. 16, 1965, 108.

256 *"Cunningham did more for integration"*: *Mobile Press-Register*, Nov. 29, 1981.

256 *"The point of the game is not the score"*: *Los Angeles Times*, Sept. 13, 1970.

Chapter Thirteen: Wishbone
Page

273 *"I've been around better teams"*: *Tuscaloosa News*, Sept. 11, 1971.

275 *"We were beaten soundly by a far superior team"*: *Sports Illustrated*, Jan. 10, 1972, 10.

289 *"Our winning doesn't have anything to do with me being a better football coach than Woody"*: *Birmingham News*, Jan. 3, 1977.

290 *"I'm disappointed for our players and staff"*: Tuscaloosa News, Jan. 4, 1977.

Chapter Fourteen: The Number
Page

294 *"If anybody's going to break Amos Alonzo Stagg's record, it might as well be me!"*: Birmingham Post-Herald, June 12, 1978.

295 *"All I know is, I don't want to stop coaching"*: Sports Illustrated, Oct. 27, 1981, 107.

299 *"We asked ourselves for a gut check"*: The Tuscaloosa News, Jan. 2, 1979.

302 *"What I would give if I could reach that young man"*: Birmingham Post-Herald, Aug. 19, 1982.

304 *"Coach Bryant tells us to keep the faith"*: Sports Illustrated, Dec. 7, 1981, 39.

305 *"I don't feel like we broke Mr. Stagg's record"*: Jackson Daily News, Aug. 26, 1982.

Chapter Fifteen: As Long As They Want Me
Page

309 *"I'm a tired old man"*: Birmingham News, April 4, 1982.

310 *"Coaching is a young man's game"*: Jackson Daily News, Aug. 26, 1982.

310 *"My mother doesn't feel right about me going to Alabama"*: Birmingham Post-Herald, Feb. 9, 1982.

313 *"There comes a time in every profession"*: Birmingham Post-Herald, Dec. 29, 1982.

314 *"I told the team before the game"*: Birmingham Post-Herald, Dec. 29, 1982.

315 *"Any time we got in a tough situation"*: Birmingham News, Dec. 29, 1982.

315 *"We won in spite of me"*: Tuscaloosa News, Dec. 29, 1982.

315 *As I contemplate my many years as a football coach*: Time, Feb. 7, 1983, 87.

317 *"He was a very courageous man"*: The New York Times, Jan. 27, 1983.

318 *"When I heard on the radio that he had died"*: The New Yorker, Feb. 14, 1983, 12.

318 *"a man who always seemed larger than life"*: Birmingham Post-Herald, Jan. 27, 1983.

319 *"He was simply the best there ever was"*: Anniston Star, Jan. 27, 1983.

319 *"I have the same feeling today"*: Tuscaloosa News, Jan. 29, 1983.

320 *"Our chief OK'd it to come over"*: Birmingham News, Jan. 29, 1983.

Index